A QUEST FOR HUMANITY:
THE GOOD SOCIETY IN A GLOBAL WORLD

A Quest for Humanity is dedicated to realizing a global 'Good Society,' defined in terms of a world grounded on principles of liberty, social justice, and equal human dignity. In this ambitious work, Menno Boldt analyses the process of globalization in light of complex dynamics involving spheres of power, jurisdictions of authority, and dysfunctional responses by national elect bodies. At the same time, he critically assesses the prevailing Western notion that Western democracy and constitutional human rights are the exemplary and essential governing and social-relational doctrines for global social order.

Boldt advances a new theory of the history of globalization that posits expanding social-relational interdependence as a deterministic process. This process is facilitated by the convergence and sharing of knowledge and understanding that are economically, politically, socially, and psychologically joining diverse peoples around the world. Based on the ideal of universal and equal human dignity as an absolute principle and ethical foundation, *A Quest for Humanity* expounds a model of a global moral social order by which humankind can govern and conduct its collective and individual relations in a way that affirms every person's potential for humanity.

MENNO BOLDT is a professor emeritus in the Department of Sociology at the University of Lethbridge.

MENNO BOLDT

A Quest for Humanity

The Good Society in a Global World

UNIVERSITY OF TORONTO PRESS
Toronto   Buffalo   London

ISBN 978-1-4426-4372-7 (cloth)
ISBN 978-1-4426-1224-2 (paper)

∞

Printed on acid-free, 100% post-consumer recycled paper with vegetable-based inks.

Library and Archives Canada Cataloguing in Publication

Boldt, Menno, 1930–
A quest for humanity : the good society in a global world / Menno Boldt.

Includes bibliographical references and index.
ISBN 978-1-4426-4372-7 (bound).   ISBN 978-1-4426-1224-2 (pbk.)
1. Social interaction.   2. Globalization – Social aspects.   3. Globalization –
Moral and ethical aspects.   I. Title

HM1111.B64 2011   302   C2011-902100-5

This book has been published with the help of a grant from the Canadian
Federation for the Humanities and Social Sciences, through the Aid to
Scholarly Publications Prógram, using funds provided by the Social
Sciences and Humanities Research Council of Canada.

University of Toronto Press acknowledges the financial assistance to its
publishing program of the Canada Council for the Arts and the Ontario
Arts Council.

 Canada Council   Conseil des Arts
for the Arts   du Canada   ONTARIO ARTS COUNCIL
CONSEIL DES ARTS DE L'ONTARIO

University of Toronto Press acknowledges the financial support for its publishing activities of the Government of Canada through the Canada Book
Fund.

To the memory of my parents, Peter and Anna Boldt, for their love,
values, and self-sacrifices
and
To Wendell Bell, for his caring spirit, friendship, and encouragement
along my intellectual journey

Contents

Part Four: Social Order and the Good Society

Part Five: Myths of Reality

Preface

The greater part of my academic career has been spent researching the circumstances of Canada's Aboriginal peoples. In the course of my research I have been continually overwhelmed by personal observations and dismal social statistics that describe ongoing violations of and assaults on their humanity – this, in a country that prides itself on its commitment to democracy and human rights. My experience created an awareness of the need for a new paradigm of social order.

While I am a sociologist by training, I have not designed my thesis to fit into any disciplinary tradition. Instead, I have sought to present my ideas on the Good Society – a world of humane relations among all people – 'from my own mind.' My hope for this book is that it will influence readers to see themselves as their children's hope for the Good Society. This is a topic that deserves our full and continuing attention.

My Bibliography provides selected scholarly publications that have informed my work. To evade incurring the cumbrous obligation of justifying my agreements or disagreements with the positions of other scholars who have addressed cognate themes, I have refrained from positioning my views intellectually; consequently, my indebtedness to scholars who have influenced my thinking, especially those whose views differ sharply from my own, is understated. Also, at many points in the text, a topic invited a discussion of other scholars' ideas. I resisted this temptation because to do so adequately would have required that chapters be expanded into volumes. I chose to keep the narrative focused on the main ideas of my thesis. For the same reason I have, at various places, inserted 'boxes' on thematic issues which I could not develop in the body of the text without digressing from the analysis and lengthening the book accordingly.

The basic thesis for this book was conceived prior to 11 September 2001. I realized during numerous subsequent elaborations and refinements of my thoughts that the terrorist attacks on '9/11' (as the date has come to be known), the subsequent invasions of Iraq and Afghanistan, and the economic crisis that began in 2008 could serve to illustrate some of the essential ideas of my thesis and I decided to incorporate references to these events.

Lastly, I want to forewarn the reader that this book is not organized as a logical linear flow of ideas from a 'beginning' to an 'end.' My thesis comprises discrete ideas, which I have pieced together, like a jigsaw puzzle, to form a picture of the Good Society. This style places a burden of patience on the reader to reserve judgment on the merits of some of the ideas until the picture is complete.

Acknowledgments

My deepest gratitude is to my wife, Anne, who was a patient listener and thoughtful adviser throughout the writing of this book. She has provided me with the love, encouragement, and support needed to complete the task.

I extend a special thank you to Carol Tomomitsu for graciously performing the daunting task of deciphering my handwriting, making sense of a maze of marginal notes, and expertly typing numerous drafts of the manuscript. Her help was indispensable for bringing this book to publication.

I owe much to Patricia Chuchryk, who, as friend, colleague, and chair of the Department of Sociology at the University of Lethbridge, created a congenial and stimulating environment for my work, provided encouragement, and extended every courtesy needed to write this book.

For making the future personally meaningful and important to me and for bringing love and joy into my life, I say a heartfelt thank you to my grandchildren, Jordan, Candace, Kimberly, Joel, Taylor, and Adam.

Wendell Bell first stimulated my interest in the idea of a 'good society' when, as a graduate student at Yale University in 1967, I attended his seminar on future studies. His commitment to the potential of future studies as a tool for creating a global ethic that will improve the well-being of all humankind, including future generations, has served as an inspiration for me. I could not have written this book without the knowledge and understanding I have gained from his writings.

I invoke the customary disclaimer: I alone am accountable for the ideas expressed in this book.

A QUEST FOR HUMANITY:
THE GOOD SOCIETY IN A GLOBAL WORLD

Prologue

The United Nations Food and Agriculture Organization reported in 2009 that 1.02 billion people in the developing world suffer from chronic hunger. It is expected that this number will increase as the population grows and food prices rise. This is happening in a world that can produce more than enough food for every man, woman, and child. The United Nations reported that in 2008 global military expenditures were $1.2 trillion and total global humanitarian expenditures by governments were $10.4 billion. The 1993 Parliament of the World's Religions stated in its Declaration of a Global Ethic: 'The world is in agony. The agony is so pervasive and urgent that we are compelled to name its manifestations so that the depth of this pain may be made clear. Peace eludes us . . . the planet is being destroyed . . . neighbors live in fear . . . women and men are estranged from each other . . . children die. This is abhorrent!'

In the decades since this Declaration, the agony in the world has been greatly magnified by mass atrocities in Burundi, Rwanda, Somalia, Angola, Congo, Zaire, Sudan, Afghanistan, Sierra Leone, Bosnia, Croatia, and Iraq. At the end of 2008, the United Nations High Commissioner for Refugees placed the number of people forced from their homes because of violence and persecution at forty-two million, and rising rapidly.

I believe it is fitting that, in the first decades of this new millennium, we – the Millennial Generations – collectively and individually consider how we might create a better world to leave to our descendants. I call this better world the *Good Society:* a metaphor for a world of liberty, social justice, and equal human dignity for all people. How do we create such a world? The thesis of this book is that we need a global moral social order based on a principle and ideal that upholds as a common good the obligation to acknowledge and honour everyone's humanity equally. This begs a definition of humanity.

Humanity is not a 'virtue of being human,' or of 'possessing a divine soul'; nor is it a natural attribute like instinct or cognition. Humanity is an inherent human potential to liberate self-consciousness and sensibility from the constraints and imperatives of naturalism and biological determinism; this potential is the essence of the exceptionalism of the human species. Every human being is conceived with the potential for humanity; however, although this potential is an individual phenomenon, we cannot realize it within the closed borders of egoism. The realization of humanity requires social relationships that esteem and honour one another's human dignity, that is, a cognitive sense of personal value, worthiness, and respect. To achieve such relationships requires a humane moral social order, one that acknowledges and secures everyone's dignity and humanity through liberty and social justice.

The focus of my thesis is on how the Millennial Generations can originate and actuate such a humane social order and place humankind on the path to the Good Society. Throughout the writing of this book, I found myself struggling to find contemporary examples, even appropriate words, to illustrate such a humane moral vision of the Good Society.

I want the reader to know that I did not start out with the ideas I will be presenting on how to realize the Good Society. We all tend to undertake analyses and develop understandings of our world and ourselves with reference to the fundamental premises of the prevailing social order in which we are born. Moreover, we are influenced by a general expectation that new ideas will fit into the prevailing discourse of our time and place. In Western societies, the entrenched certainty that Western democracy and constitutional human rights are the exemplary doctrines for securing liberty, social justice, and human dignity has had the effect of limiting creative thinking, imagining, and discourse about other ideas of government and social-relational order for the Good Society.

I started my research for this book with the conviction that Western democracy and constitutional human rights were the right doctrines for the Good Society, but that they needed to be refined to acknowledge and honour everyone's equal human dignity and humanity. However, as my research proceeded it raised some profound questions and doubts about these doctrines. I had to work my way out of some intellectual thickets, change my thinking, and open my mind to other ways of securing liberty, social justice, and human dignity for all people. I can assure the reader that researching a theme to which I was initially blind has been a disturbing experience, though also an interesting and revelatory one.

How ought we to govern ourselves and conduct our relations with each other to achieve the Good Society? First, we need to challenge some cherished beliefs. As the reader will see in this book, I conclude that Western democracy and constitutional human rights are fundamentally flawed doctrines for realizing the Good Society. While my thesis is based on serious research and analysis, it describes a visionary possibility for the Good Society in terms of a conceptual framework rather than functional examples or a blueprint. This conceptual approach required me to reach beyond present social-political understandings, experience, and convictions. For this reason, I deliberately do not site my ideas on a socio-political spectrum such as liberal/conservative or secular/sacred. Rather, I present my ideas in non-ideological terms.

In a world of ongoing massive violations of human dignity and crimes against humanity – genocide, ethnic cleansing, coerced flight, chronic malnutrition of billions of people, acts of terrorism, and other acts of brutality – there is an urgent need for us to evaluate our legacy to future generations. Fragmented into distrustful, fearful, and often hostile cultures, religions, and political regimes, humankind needs to commit to a global social order of humane social relations among all people.

Any endeavour to create a conceptual framework for the Good Society requires a reach that exceeds our present understanding and knowledge. I have followed Wendell Bell's instruction that 'the purpose of future studies are to discover or invent, examine and evaluate, and propose possible, probable and preferable futures' (Bell, 1997, vol. 1, 73). The emphasis of my thesis speaks to the future; I endeavour to present ideas in harmony with current knowledge and understanding yet envision a better future than what is happening today. I do not present my ideas as a 'quick fix' or 'shortcut' to the Good Society. Clearly, eliminating the deeply entrenched violation of liberty, social justice, and human dignity that prevails in the customs and practices of all societies will require a multigenerational commitment and concerted endeavour. However, we know from past experience that ideas can be influential and it is my hope that the ideas presented here will raise thoughtful criticisms, inspire alternative visions, and stimulate readers to engage in a serious discourse on how to build a global society in which every person's potential for humanity is equally acknowledged and valued. We, the Millennial Generations, stand at a juncture in history that is decisive for the future of humankind; we have the capability to place humankind on the path to the Good Society.

PART ONE

The Nature of Globalization

1   A Theory of Globalization

In our quest to establish the Good Society – a world of humane social relations among all people – we need to understand the forces that shape our world. Given the present fragmentation of humankind into numerous political-economic-social jurisdictions, my conception of the Good Society requires that I explain the phenomenon of globalization. It also calls for an exposition on the essential principles for a global social order that will effectuate humane relations. I will begin my thesis with a discussion of a theory and the reality of globalization.

Globalization is a process of expanding social-relational interdependence and the convergence and sharing of knowledge and understanding across the spectrum of human endeavour. The reader should keep in mind this meaning of globalization. Globalization dates from the beginning of human history; however, it has not progressed evenly: enmities, wars, isolationism, and other disruptive factors have often impeded its progress. In modern times it was retarded by the Cold War. Today, the development of unbordered high-speed Internet and satellite communications, augmented by the universal language, memory storing, and processing capabilities of the computer, is facilitating an expansion in social-relational interdependence and an exponential convergence and sharing of knowledge and understanding which is psychologically joining diverse peoples across the world.

Until quite recently, globalization evolved 'under the radar' of our awareness but it has developed into the primary force of social change in our time. It is redrawing the geo-political map of the world and directly affecting the economy, politics, and culture of every society. In this chapter I will describe a theory of globalization in terms of power, authority, and history and its relevance to our quest for the Good Society.

Power

Power is a critical aspect of human relationships and has been described in a variety of ways. The great scholars, such as Plato, Machiavelli, Rousseau, Hobbes, de Tocqueville, Hegel, Marx, Weber, Talcott Parsons, Hannah Arendt, Jurgen Habermas, C. Wright Mills, and many others, have deliberated on the nature of power and they have variously character-ized it in terms of influence, force, coercion, persuasion, manipulation, knowledge, overcoming resistance, affecting an intended outcome, and military and economic superiority.

Although there is no scholarly consensus on the nature of power, scholars generally have characterized it in empirical, operational terms. For instance, historians typically interpret past developments and events in terms of alignments, pre-eminence, and confrontations of power. And many describe a society's basic character in terms of the power exercised by its political, economic, military, and religious insti-tutions. My discussion of the phenomenon of power is narrowly lim-ited to its relevance for understanding the dynamics of globalization.

To understand the role of power in the globalization of the world, we must look beyond the idea of it as something tangible; we need to think of it as dynamic energy that comes into existence spontaneously and inevitably whenever two or more individuals enter a relationship of social interdependence. I propose that power has no physical real-ity; it exists as an extra-natural phenomenon between or among, not within, individuals. (I use 'extra-natural' to refer to a phenomenon out-side sensory experience but within human cognition; it carries no con-notation of divinity, apparitions, super- humans, unearthly visitants, or miraculous events.) The phenomenon of power is evident in a variety of social-relational forms, such as the family, tribe, ethnic and religious groups, and national societies. I refer to such social-relational entities as *spheres of power*.

The idea of power as a sphere of dynamic energy is governed by two principles. The first is that the boundary of a sphere of power corre-sponds to the borders of social-relational interdependence and shared knowledge and understanding. These borders, however, tend to be variable and permeable, which facilitates 'cross-border' interaction, and consequently the boundaries of spheres of power tend to be fuzzy. I will use the term *primary sphere* to indicate a people with recognized borders of social-relational interdependence and shared knowledge and understanding. Parenthetically, the measure of power present in a primary spheres varies among spheres and is a function of two over-lapping variables: one is the comprehensiveness of the group's social-relational interdependence as measured by its shared social, political, economic institutions, and other activities and purposes; the other is the integrity and intensity of the group's identity as measured by its commitment to collective ideals, values, goals, and sense of destiny.

When two or more primary spheres of power begin to develop sig-nificant cross-border social-relational interdependence, they initially enter into a dynamic which engenders conflict between the merging social-relational entities. This has led some scholars to the view that power is self-opposing and creates its own resistance in the form of symmetrical proportions of counter power arrangements. I propose that power is not self-opposing: the second principle of my idea of power as a phenomenon of extra-natural energy holds that the process of progressive expansion of social-relational interdependence sets off a *deterministic* dynamic towards 'wholeness' which causes spheres of power to coalesce and achieve a stage at which they merge into a larger unitary primary sphere. The greater the 'cross-border' interaction of primary spheres the greater is their reciprocal affinity to merge into a unitary primary sphere.

In ancient times people were separated into many small, isolated, self-contained groupings such as families, clans, or bands, each con-stituting a primary sphere of power. Over time, through trade, com-munications, mating, cultural exchange, and other forms of interaction, these functional groupings achieved an expansion in social-relational interdependence and a convergence of knowledge and understanding that brought about the progressive merging of their power into ever larger primary spheres such as tribes, confederacies, and nations. At present, the significant primary spheres of powers are usually consti-tuted as sovereign states often involving national, ethnic, linguistic, and religious identities.

Reasoning from my theory of a deterministic dynamic of merg-ing spheres of power, the present 'cross-boundary' growth in social-relational interdependence (signified by expanding international trade, investment, and communications) and convergence of knowledge and understanding prefigures the inevitability that all existing primary spheres of power will progressively merge into a global unitary primary sphere. This ongoing merging of primary spheres is the underlying dynamic of what we call globalization. The merging of power and the progress towards a unified world presents a prospect of great social, political, and economic tumult, possibly even ultimate catastrophe. It also offers an opportunity for creating the global Good Society.

Authority

The next important concept for an understanding of globalization is authority. In Europe, the pre-Enlightenment Roman Catholic Church promoted the doctrine of divine power and authority, and proclaimed itself to be the exclusive agent of this power and authority; the implication was that it alone could exercise God's divine commission to rule. The Enlightenment *philosophes* (a group of eighteenth-century European intellectuals who advocated reason, human self-determination, social justice, and secular systems of government authority) challenged the church's claim to divine power and authority, dispelled the myth of divine rule, and proclaimed government to be a prerogative of human agency. But the *philosophes* did not unravel the mystery of the relationship between power and authority.

Authority derives from the energy of power; however, whereas power is an extra-natural phenomenon, authority has the empirical property of social order. Whenever two or more individuals establish social-relational interdependence in the context of shared knowledge and understanding, they invariably actualize their power as social-order authority to regulate their relations with each other. Even ephemeral social groupings such as those formed by children for communal play spontaneously begin to actualize the power generated by their interdependent social relations and shared knowledge and understanding, in order to create social-order authority in the form of ad hoc rules that regulate their relations with each other. The actualization of power as social-order authority involves a subjective process which occurs in an evolutionary trial-and-error fashion by conscious or subconscious reasoning from self-interest and social-relational experience. Functional social-relational groupings have the capacity to transform their power into any style of authority they choose.

Because of its correlation with power, the jurisdiction of authority is subject to the principle of correspondence with the boundaries of the primary sphere. Any jurisdiction of authority that does not correspond with the boundaries of the primary sphere of power will ultimately be brought into alignment with these boundaries. As primary spheres of power merge, existing jurisdictions of social-order authority are assimilated and realigned to coincide with the boundaries of the new, larger, primary sphere. This principle of authority has been demonstrated throughout history by the assimilation and realignment of smaller jurisdictions of authority, such as the family, to correspond with the spheres of evolving social-relational interdependence and shared knowledge and understanding; the result is ever larger unitary jurisdictions, such as the band, tribe, and nation. In the present phase of globalization, we see this principle demonstrated by the progressive assimilation and realignment of selected national jurisdictions of authority into supranational groupings, such as the European Union (EU), and numerous free-trade associations. For the first time in human history, social-relational interdependence and shared knowledge and understanding are approaching a global scale.

The principle of correspondence between the boundaries of authority and primary spheres of power also applies when authority is extended beyond the boundaries of a primary sphere of power, that is, hegemony. History is filled with examples of powerful tribes and nations extending their authority over weaker peoples. Babylonia, Persia, Macedonia, Rome, Byzantium, Mongolia, Turkey, Spain, Britain, Italy, France, and Russia used superior military, economic, institutional, and bureaucratic resources, and legitimating ideologies such as divine will, general will, capitalism, and socialism, to bring weaker primary spheres of power into their empires. Hegemony, however, violates the principle of correspondence and, despite their superior resources, hegemonists invariably are compelled to withdraw their authority to the boundaries of their primary sphere of power.

The hypothesis of 'power law relationships' has some explanatory value for understanding the realignment of authority to correspond with the boundaries of the primary sphere of power. This hypothesis holds that in all power relationships we can observe a state of variable 'self-organized criticality.' The hypothesis is visually demonstrated by trickling sand on a fixed spot on a tabletop. The sand pile always reaches a point where any additional sand precipitates a slide, resulting in a reconstruction of 'self-organized criticality,' which may occur gradually or precipitously. This analogy approximately illustrates how the merging of power, consequent to the expansion of social-relational interdependence and the progressive growth and convergence of knowledge and understanding, achieves a stage at which, gradually or precipitously, it brings about the realignment of authority into a larger jurisdiction corresponding to the new boundaries of the primary sphere of power.

Globalization is an irresistible force and, inevitably, all hegemonies are destined to fail because they violate the principle of correspondence between the boundaries of power and authority. Globalization also undermines 'internal' hegemony, that is, subjugation of ethnic and religious minorities. The disintegration of the Soviet Union and Yugoslavia are two recent examples: the dismantling of the USSR and the Yugoslav federation of republics freed suppressed peoples within these Communist hegemonies to realign their authority coextensively with the boundaries of their respective primary spheres of power. Ultimately, all hegemonies are destined to fragment along the fault lines of power, freeing social groupings to establish their own jurisdiction of authority coextensively with their primary sphere of power.

The process of realignment of authority coextensively with the boundaries of primary spheres of power can cause the displacement of prevailing systems of government by new systems and give rise to civil feuds and political-social turmoil. This is the case in Africa and the Middle East, where European hegemonists disrupted the natural progression of globalization by creating artificial states. We can also observe this phenomenon in the current internal and external ethnonationalist conflicts involving India, Pakistan, Afghanistan, Georgia, Nicosia, Tibet, and the Kurds. These events indicate the need to reintegrate and restructure authority to bring boundaries of jurisdiction into correspondence with primary spheres of power, to avoid endless civil wars and bloodshed. The reunifications of divided peoples in Germany and Vietnam, and creation of the state of Israel by Zionism-inspired emigration of Jews from the diaspora, signify the natural progression of globalization.

History and the Future

Winston Churchill observed about the study of history that 'the longer you look back, the further you can look forward.' Indeed, we need to understand the past to envision and plot a path to the Good Society. However, to benefit from history we need to study the past for successes and failures in creating humane societies, and apply this knowledge going forward. Unfortunately, most decision makers, if they study history, are motivated by self-serving military, political, and economic agendas, not a quest for a humane world; they misconstrue and misapply history, with tragic and disastrous consequences.

The conventional study of history as a chronicle of events, nations, and leaders neglects the crucial fact that, from the beginning, humankind has been on a journey towards globalization. To revise Karl Marx: the history of all hitherto existing societies is the history of globalization. It is a journey that is marked by the deterministic merging of power into ever larger spheres, and the corresponding assimilation and realignment of authority into ever larger jurisdictions. To benefit from the study of history, we need to study the past as a chronicle of the deterministic forces that incrementally bring all powers, authorities, and peoples into a unitary jurisdiction. This view does not deny the reality that other forces such as demography, technology, religion, ideology, and politics influence and colour human history; however, it insists that these forces exist beside the deterministic forces of globalization.

This theory of history does not imply that the great World Wars and other past conflicts were inevitable corollaries of globalization. The forces of globalization are neither 'good' nor 'bad'; calamitous events of the past were the result of dysfunctional responses to the forces of globalization, not globalization per se. While the globalization of human society is inevitable, we can decide how it will proceed. We have the capability to determine how the integration and restructuring of authority caused by the deterministic forces of globalizing power will be accomplished: whether peacefully and humanely or violently. This assertion is exemplified by two historical realignments of authority: American and Canadian independence from British hegemony. American independence was accomplished by a violent insurgency followed by the War of 1812. Americans celebrate their insurgency as a great revolution for freedom, even though the enslavement of African Americans continued until the end of a bloody civil war in 1865. Canada, which achieved its independence through a gradual process of peaceful negotiations, introduced an act as early as 1793 making it illegal to bring persons into the colony for slavery, and in 1834 it followed Britain's example and abolished slavery – without bloodshed.

More recently, humankind was spared unimaginable suffering and possibly a global conflagration when Mikhail Gorbachev, former chairman of the USSR and commander-in-chief of its massive military forces, chose to step back from the abyss of Armageddon and peaceably concede the hegemonic authority of the Soviet leadership by freeing subject states to establish jurisdictions of authority that correspond more closely to the existing multiethnic primary spheres of power. Gorbachev saw the Soviet Union in a global context; he understood and acknowledged that Soviet hegemony could not prevail against the forces of globalization. His enlightened world view enabled the subsequent peaceful reunification of East and West Germany and created conditions conducive to the emergence of the European Union. However, the recent Western political-economic initiative to bring the freed states into NATO for strategic ends constitutes a dysfunctional response to the forces of globalization.

My theory of history as a seamless arc of deterministic and irreversible globalization provides a general framework that can help us to better understand and manage its forces in our quest for the global Good Society. An insightful and objective look into the past can teach us how to avoid dysfunctional reactions and respond constructively to the inevitable social-political challenges, volatility, and tensions that will result as the expansion of social-relational interdependence and the growth in shared knowledge and understanding blur the lines of existing national and hegemonic authority and jurisdiction and destabilize geo-political borders.

2   The Reality of Globalization

As we have seen, the forces of globalization date from the beginning of human history and have given rise to today's nation-states. Before the advent of modern air travel and satellite and Internet communications, spheres of power and jurisdictions of authority were relatively isolated and distinct by virtue of geography, and globalization progressed slowly. Advances in technology have changed the basic dynamic of these forces, and globalization has accelerated at an unprecedented pace. The effects of the expansion of social-relational interdependence and the growth in shared knowledge and understanding signified by cultural exchanges, global trade, and other forms of interaction are evident in every corner of the world.

We can observe the reality of globalization in the large and growing number of international governmental institutions and organizations such as the United Nations, the World Bank, the International Monetary Fund (IMF), the World Trade Organization (WTO), the Group of Twenty, the Organisation of Economic Co-operation and Development, the World Health Organization, and the International Court of Justice. Additionally, there are hundreds of transnational non-governmental organizations (NGOs), representing legal, scientific, religious, ecological, and other interests and concerns. These organizations administer the growing corpus and jurisdiction of international laws, regulations, and transactions which facilitate the worldwide movement of people, goods, and services.

The reality of globalization is also evident in a shared concern over an increasing number of international problems that include wars, genocides, nuclear proliferation, terrorism, economic crises, ecological degradation, global climate change, depletion and shortages of natural resources, overpopulation, mass starvation, and HIV/AIDS and other pandemics. Because of growing global interdependence, these complex problems affect people the world over as never before. They threaten the well-being of all humankind and intensify the need for concerted international efforts and cooperation.

International Economic Institutions

Prior to the Second World War, nation-states regulated their economic and fiscal affairs primarily as domestic matters; however, in the post-war era we have witnessed a huge expansion and intensification of economic interdependence. As a result, the global economy is acutely vulnerable to disruption by the malfunction of any single nation-state's fiscal-political system; a serious malfunction can trigger a chain reaction known colloquially as the 'domino effect.' Such a disruptive event occurred in 1997 when Thailand, with a relatively small national economy, suffered a financial collapse which touched off sufficient uncertainty among investors that they pulled their money out of neigh-bouring Malaysia, Indonesia, and South Korea. The resulting destabi-lization of these national economies precipitated the 'Asian Economic Crisis' and sparked a global recession. Increasingly, national institutions cannot handle emerging economic, political, and social problems; this has prompted an urgent call for effective international regulatory institutions.

Whenever a destabilizing economic event occurs in a non-Western state, such as in Thailand, Western elect bodies attribute it to the failure of that nation to follow the Western capitalist model. Consistent with this assessment, they insist that the only way to prevent recurrences of such international economic disruptions is to supplant the existing nation-based economic-fiscal regulatory systems with an international system governed by the Western capitalist model. To this end, Western elect bodies (see box below) have joined to create international insti-tutions designed to implement and administer economic agreements based on that model.

Western elect bodies actively promote their capitalist economic order via all of the numerous international organizations. I will elaborate on three international institutions created for this specific purpose: the Multilateral Agreement on Investment (MAI), the World Trade Organization, and the International Monetary Fund. These institutions were created to offset the growing inadequacy of nation-state regulations

Elect Body

I use the term elect body instead of elite class. Both terms imply a society divided into rulers and ruled; both carry the connotation of wealth, influence, and prestige; both involve a presumptive entitlement to a favoured, preferred, and privileged status; and both have a practically seamless continuity between generations. However, elect body, as I use it, comprises a broader spectrum of privileged members of society than the limited group based on birth, wealth, and social class implied by the term elite class; and its boundaries are marginally more permeable. In Western democracies elect bodies tend to be socially and politically varied, comprising political, economic, legal, academic, labour union, media, and other 'influentials.' They function as amorphous, fluid, dynamic, collaborative, sometimes conspiratorial, configurations of overlapping authority structures: e.g., legislative, bureaucratic, judicial, corporate, religious. Generally, elect bodies exercise their authority not with malicious intent but to maintain and enhance their status and privileges and, generally, to secure and promote personal self-interests. The ubiquity of rule by elect bodies in all countries – autocratic and democratic – may indicate that they are indispensable for the functioning of a society. I will elaborate on their role and function throughout the text.

and laws to regulate international transactions, and they are designed to subordinate nation-state authority over investment, trade, and monetary regulations to an international authority. They are best understood as functioning in a reciprocal dynamic with the forces of globalization: on the one hand, the international trade, investment, and monetary initiatives are a result of globalization; on the other, they facilitate globalization by assimilating national economic-fiscal authorities into a larger jurisdiction.

The master principle of the MAI exempts international investors from any domestic laws and regulations that favour indigenous financial institutions or investors. The MAI seeks to remove restrictions on foreign ownership of any nation-state's natural resources, public infrastructure, land, financial institutions, and cultural enterprises. Ostensibly, it stands for equal treatment for investors and corporations regardless of

the nation of origin. However, Western elect bodies benefit disproportionately because they comprise the major international investors and
corporations. Although the various national elect bodies are in general
accord on the MAI's master principle, they differ on specific terms of
agreements. Since the MAI was established, negotiations on the agreements have occurred behind closed doors where delegates representing the various national elect bodies haggle over specific provisions
affecting their particular self-interests, away from the scrutiny of their
citizens.

The WTO signifies an initiative by Western elect bodies to develop
a global authority to regulate international trade. The WTO comprises
some 135 nation-states. The master principle of the WTO is free trade
and its mandate is to create an international constitution that will eliminate all national barriers to the movement of goods and services, ranging from manufactured and agricultural products to communications
and intellectual property. To gain admission into the WTO, nations
must make a commitment to unrestricted international commerce and
subordinate their authority over trade to regulation by the WTO. For
instance, to gain membership in the WTO, the Chinese Communist
Party was required to give up its socialist economic system and adopt
a capitalist model; place its regime and its 1.25 billion citizens under
the obligation to allow up to 40 per cent foreign control in the domestic
financial-services and communications sector; reduce duties on imports;
eliminate export subsidies; limit its prerogative to block imports; and
pledge to protect foreign corporate 'property rights.' The readiness of
China's elect body to concede its authority over these domestic affairs
in order to gain access to global trade, investment, and financial markets is a significant indication of the force of globalization and how far
it has advanced.

The IMF is an international financial institution with 185 member
nations. The professed mandate of the IMF, operating under the slogan
'liberation, progress, prosperity, and opportunity,' is to provide loans
and funding to emerging economies so they can achieve self-sufficiency
and consistent growth. In practice, it functions as an international
regulatory agency seeking to assimilate nation-state authority over
monetary policies into a single global monetary market. To achieve its
purpose, the IMF has decreed that, in order to qualify for a loan from
its coffers, national governments and banks must meet specified structural performance criteria pertaining to privatization, banking regulations, and trade policies, and remove most of the domestic restrictions

on the movement of money in and out of their country. This decree effectively imposes a free currency system, one that is outside the borrowing nation-state's control.

While the defining principles of these three international institutions are well, established, there are intense disagreements among national elect bodies (e.g., Eastern versus Western nations, developed versus developing countries, socialist versus capitalist regimes) over key points in implementing terms and regulations. Some commentators perceive these disagreements as evidence of the end of globalization. In fact, the opposite is true; the disagreements signify that globalization is progressing. Although globalization functions as an integrative force, it destabilizes geo-economic borders, precipitating a backlash by national elect bodies and hegemons against diminution of their authority. However, despite delays and setbacks, the forces of globalization continue to advance. Even as world trade talks falter, the momentum and progress of globalization is evident in the WTO's list of some four hundred bilateral, multilateral, and regional investment and trade agreements, representing a dynamic intermediate phase in globalization.

The Global Free-Market System

The signature purpose of the three international economic initiatives mentioned above is to enhance international investment and trade opportunities and profits by creating a global market system based on the principle of free trade. However, the global free-market system is more than merely an economic concept, and its growth is causing domestic and international political and social tensions and conflict. Even as multinational corporations press for 'open borders,' meaning no import and investment restriction and free access to all national markets, domestic corporations along with labour unions, agribusiness, and other influential domestic entities lobby for protection against the importation of low-priced foreign goods.

The global free-market system is also encountering opposition from ordinary citizens. Since corporate profit is the primary motive that drives the agenda of the elect bodies, many citizens suspect they have a secret plan to insert provisions in the international economic agreements that will diminish multinational corporate obligations to fulfil national labour, manufacturing, and environmental standards. These citizens point to the 'outsourcing' of jobs to countries with cheap labour costs as evidence of such an agenda. To ease and pre-empt popular domestic opposition to the international economic agreements, Western elect bodies make a public show of pressing for the inclusion of stringent provisions in these agreements that will require all nations to conform to Western labour, social, and environmental standards.

Western elect bodies promote the global free-market system by catering to the materialistic interests of their citizens, promising prosperity and a greater variety of consumer goods at lower prices. They also appeal to their humanitarian sensibilities by representing the global free market as the most effective vehicle to fight world poverty and bring emerging economies into the modern world. They selectively cite data purporting to show significant economic-social progress in developing countries which have embraced the free-market premise. The former chairman of the U.S. Federal Reserve, Alan Greenspan, hailed the removal of investment, trade, and monetary barriers as 'probably the best single action' to combat world poverty.

Yet Western elect bodies deliberately place the poorest countries at a crucial disadvantage by insisting on including provisions in the international economic agreements that eliminate tariffs on agricultural imports. The effect of this manoeuvre is that farmers in countries that can't afford to subsidize their agricultural producers must compete with heavily subsidized imports from wealthy Western countries. This places these farmers at a great disadvantage not only in the global marketplace but also in their own domestic market because it requires that they sell goods produced for local consumption at prices established by Western commodity speculators. Western elect bodies compound the harm to these farmers by denying funding to developing countries for agricultural production of crops that compete with those of Western farmers. Agriculture has historically been a major part of the economies of developing nations, and because they cannot compete with the heavily subsidized products imported from the European Union and the United States, millions of rural jobs have been eliminated in these poor countries.

While a genuine free-market system has the potential to 'raise the ship' in all societies, this will happen only if the benefits are distributed equitably. Self-serving Western elect bodies, however, are undercutting such an outcome by blocking any provisions that could give developing countries a competitive advantage by reason of their lower production costs. Although they have the means and opportunity to place the global free-market system in the service of creating a more humane world, they exploit the international economic institutions to extend their economic dominance over developing countries. Western elect

The Battle in Seattle

Western elect bodies exploit domestic opposition to the global free-market system to gain leverage when negotiating the terms of the international economic agreements. They declare that under their 'democratic' regimes they are obliged to heed popular opinion. Then they cite this rationale as a pretext for insisting on provisions that will give them a competitive advantage in the global marketplace. They used this ploy to gain concessions at the bargaining table at the 1999 WTO's Millennial Round of meetings in Seattle.

The event, dubbed 'the Battle in Seattle,' involved a staged protest against the WTO by an assortment of protectionists. It was broadcast 'live' by the American media throughout the world to dramatize the U.S. elect body's message that its citizens would not tolerate giving any meaningful trade advantages to emerging economies. The impact of the ploy was effectively magnified by a well-orchestrated official overreaction to the staged demonstration. In collaboration with the mayor of Seattle, the governor of Washington State deployed steel-helmeted riot police and camouflage-attired National Guard troops armed with tear-gas bombs, rubber bullets, and lethal weapons to confront the protestors, whose most serious acts never rose above the symbolic breaking of a few storefront windows of global corporations like McDonalds. The message was clear: Western elect bodies intended to protect their self-interest at the cost of a truly global free-market system. This tactic has been imitated by other elect bodies when the WTO has held meetings in their venues.

bodies are exacerbating human deprivation and suffering by widening the gap between rich and poor countries.

Most leaders of developing countries are profoundly apprehensive about ceding authority to the international financial institutions. The regulatory requirements of the IMF and other international financial institutions such as the World Bank have required them to privatize and deregulate their economies, cut social programs, and eliminate protective investment and trade barriers in order to qualify for desperately needed loans. Some leaders accuse Western elect bodies of using these organizations to coerce their regimes into political and economic submission; for instance, they cite threats by the World Bank to devalue their nation's currency on trading markets, thereby forcing them into default for scheduled repayment of U.S.-dollar-valued debt. In their dealings with these institutions, some recalcitrant regimes have suffered bankruptcy of their domestic banks and corporations, disastrous levels of national unemployment, and the subversion of popularly elected governments.

Leaders of developing countries who have experienced or witnessed such actions are persuaded that Western elect bodies will exploit the global free-market system to force their destitute and desperate societies to forfeit their national autonomy. This is a particular anxiety for nations of the African continent, which are emerging from the disastrous experience of Western colonialism. All developing countries, however, are confronted with the ultimatum that, if they do not yield to the international economic institutions, they will be disqualified from receiving vital investments and be denied access to the international marketplace. They see their options as either conceding to Western demands or facing a future of even greater deprivation and social-political chaos.

The international economic institutions currently lack the enforcement mechanisms to prevent the dominant Western elect bodies from manipulating the rules of the free-market system to their advantage. However, as the forces of globalization gain strength and momentum, such violations of the philosophical formulation of the free market inevitably will diminish. In due course, the fundamental competitive dynamic of the global free-market system will compel all regimes to conform to free-trade rules. The impressive rise of China, India, and Brazil in the global marketplace signals a shift in global influence. When their economies and domestic consumer markets mature, they will be in a strong position to insist that Western elect bodies abide by the principles of the free-market system or be denied access to the extraordinarily lucrative trade and investment opportunities they have to offer. A globalizing world will require the redesign of prevailing *international* institutions, which are currently dominated and governed by the interests of superpowers, into *global* institutions based on cooperation among equals and which benefit all societies equally.

Globalization and the Nation-State

The primary spheres of power and configurations of authority in the Modern Age (i.e., 1700 to 2000) have been defined by nation-state borders, and under this system authority has been monopolized by national elect bodies. Despite widely varying and even conflicting ideological rationales for their respective social-order authority, such as capitalism/socialism, totalitarianism/democracy, and religion/secularism, it has always served the interests of the various national elect bodies to respect the principle of national sovereignty established by the Peace of Westphalia treaties in 1648 and thereby secure their own domestic authority, status, privilege, and property. They have voluntarily endorsed international conventions and laws legitimating and guaranteeing the territorial integrity and political independence of the nation-state. Although flagrant violations of nation-state sovereignty occurred during the two World Wars and the invasions of Korea, Vietnam, Iraq, the Balkans, and in the ongoing conflicts in the Middle East and Africa, the various national elect bodies continue to endorse the principle of national sovereignty, and have embedded it in the UN Charter.

Yet, as discussed in chapter 1, the dynamism of 'cross-border' social-relational interdependence and shared knowledge and understanding progressively creates ever larger spheres of power. This merging of power and the consequent assimilation and realignment of national authority into larger jurisdictions are gradually undermining the autonomy of the historical sovereign nation-state. As global realities encroach on national autonomy, they pose a looming threat to the authority, status, and privilege of all national elect bodies. To counter this threat, the various national elect bodies are collaboratively creating the international economic institutions to counter this threat. However, they are wrong in their expectation that these institutions will serve to maintain their national authority.

When the authority of the international institutions becomes fully operational, the global free-market system will inevitably diminish national jurisdiction over trade and investment. While this realignment of authority will not necessarily result in the dissolution of the traditional nation-state – essential domestic social and civic programs and a psychological identity may persist – it will significantly reduce the authority of national elect bodies. The movement of goods, services, and capital will be governed by a complex supranational dynamic, beyond their control. The elect bodies of countries with small economies are more immediately vulnerable to a loss of their authority because they need access to larger markets to achieve a viable economic scale. Currently, the elect bodies of the largest nations can still raise barriers to unwelcome free-market rules, but ultimately all nations will be transformed into 'open markets' and, figuratively speaking, fly the flag of the global free-market system above their national flag. National elect bodies will be compelled to yield their authority to the forces of the supranational free market. Their decisions will be subject to the imperatives and regulations of the global free-market system; they will be reduced to the status of domestic housekeepers whose primary function will be to implement and monitor the international regulations of the global market system.

The emergence of the European Union is a real instance of globalization. Countries marked by a long history of patriotic wars, profound animosities and distrust, intensely competitive economies, and chauvinistic differences in languages, cultures, religions, and political systems, some newly freed from Soviet hegemony and all with citizens who are apprehensive about losing their identity, traditions, and voice, are voluntarily ceding significant elements of their autonomy to the EU. A draft constitution, which eliminates national vetoes in areas such as justice and immigration and creates a single currency and a foreign ministry to represent a unified policy on the world stage, has been overwhelmingly endorsed by the European Parliament, comprised of 785 members elected by voters across 27 member states, on behalf of 492 million citizens.

At present the EU faces huge challenges to integrate its political and economic policies; a single currency necessitates a single economic policy and holds profound political implications for national sovereignty. In effect, however, we are witnessing the early stages of assimilation and realignment of national authority into a larger unitary jurisdiction. The various national elect bodies in Europe are striving to overcome deep differences in political philosophies to develop a common constitutional framework of judicial, economic, and social institutions, with the authority to regulate their competing and often conflicting national and international interests.

Currently, the EU is leading the way in the development of a unitary geopolitical-economic jurisdiction. However, the growing number of overlapping bilateral and multilateral investment and trade agreements in all regions of the world provides compelling evidence that the assimilation and realignment of national authority is a global phenomenon. The proliferation of pan-national agreements enables national elect bodies to defend and promote their economic interests outside their own borders. However, under these agreements, significant sovereign authority and decisions regarding many domestic concerns are taken out of the hands of national elect bodies and every nation's economic, political, and social institutions are materially affected by developments outside its national borders.

The preceding account describes globalization primarily as an economic process. However, as I stated in chapter 1, globalization is a phenomenon of social-relational interdependence and shared knowledge and understanding; as such, it can progress in other ways. For instance, many Muslims, although beleaguered by competing national interests and beset with sectarian divisions and conflicts, are now redefining their primary psychological self-identification and allegiance from their nation-state citizenship to pan-Islamism; this example of merging power and assimilation and realignment of authority describes an ideologically driven process of globalization.

The pan-Islamic movement involves a paradox. Its origin was facilitated by the initiatives of some Muslim elect bodies to defend their national authority against the forces of globalization: to solidify their autocratic rule over their citizens, they fostered fundamentalist Islamic revivalism within their states by introducing strict codes of dress, religious observance, and social structure. However, this expedient 'revivalist stratagem' has fostered cross-border affiliations of Muslim peoples, and a growing number of Islamic fundamentalists perceive state borders as an obstacle to Islamic unity. In states with large Muslim populations, national elect bodies are being pressed by their citizens to align their politics and policies with the interests of the pan-Islamic community. In effect, national Muslim spheres of power are merging into a larger theocratic pan-Islamic unity, undermining nation-state authority and incidentally creating conditions conducive to stateless terrorism.

All national elect bodies vigorously resist the assimilation and realignment of their authority into a larger jurisdiction, and Muslim elect bodies are no exception. Currently, there is growing apprehension among neighbouring Muslim elect bodies about the hegemonic designs and nuclear ambitions of the Islamic theocracy in Iran. To stem the assimilating forces of pan-Islamic fundamentalism, some Muslim national elect bodies, belatedly, are adopting a liberal interpretation of Islam, and some seek to introduce secular nationalist principles of government. However, the leadership of the emergent pan-Islamic movement condemns such initiatives as theological heresy and a Western plot to subvert Islam. On the one hand, the pan-Islamic leadership is exploiting religious fundamentalism and anti-Western sentiment to assimilate existing national parochial authorities into a larger pan-

Islamic jurisdiction; and, on the other, it is exploiting religious fundamentalism and anti-Western sentiment to incite Muslims to resist the
assimilation of its new authority into a global jurisdiction.

Several Latin American national elect bodies are forming nationalist-
populist-socialist political alliances and negotiating intraregional free-
trade agreements. Ostensibly, these initiatives are intended to counter
the U.S. elect body's design to extend its hegemony over their countries
via bilateral and multilateral trade and investment agreements. While
their assessment of the U.S. elect body's motives and intentions may
be correct, the eventual loss of their national authority will occur as a
result of assimilation by the forces of globalization, not of U.S. hegemony. As social-relational interdependence and shared knowledge and
understanding expand to global dimensions, the future world will be
defined not by competing hegemonies or nationalisms but by social-
relational integration.

The assimilation and realignment of national authority into a global
jurisdiction is still a distant prospect but we are seeing the beginning of
this process in the emergence of supranational regional organizations
on all continents – even in Africa, with its colonial legacy of artificial
states, poverty, and many rival parochial groups. There can be no halt
to the expansion of social-relational interdependence and growth in
shared knowledge and understanding to global dimensions. Ultimately,
all national elect bodies are destined to surrender their authority to the
deterministic forces of globalization.

Global Free-Market Capitalism

Western elect bodies have employed the American model of corporate
capitalism to grow their corporations into multinational enterprises.
Today, they are seeking to take advantage of the trade and investment
opportunities presented by the emerging global free-market system to
expand the scope and scale of corporate capitalism and their corporate
holdings to global dimensions. However, by creating a world without
borders to the movement of goods, services, labour, and communications, the international economic institutions are giving rise to global
free-market capitalism. This development involves changes in investment and trade patterns so fundamental as to render the traditional
American style of corporate capitalism obsolete. Global free-market
capitalism is creating a situation in which all corporations are becoming effectively 'stateless' entities that operate freely throughout the

world. This complex dynamic presages the end of traditional corporate capitalism, with major implications for the national and multinational corporate interests of Western elect bodies.

Currently, most of the major multinational corporations are domiciled in the West, with a major hub in the United States. This state of affairs is a legacy of four major factors: military superiority, political stability, economic advantage, and corporate-friendly policies. In an era when the security of capital investments was guaranteed by national state-regimes, these four factors, dubbed the 'Western Advantage,' gave investors huge incentives to favour corporations located in Western states. However, the international economic institutions, when they are fully implemented, will establish international laws and regulatory safeguards for commercial investments the world over; under this new economic order, investors will be able to ignore national boundaries in their investment decisions, and the Western Advantage will fade.

We can see the harbingers of global free-market capitalism in the rise of the economies of China, India, and Brazil. In the past, political barriers and serious concerns about investment security limited those countries' appeal. But, with the introduction of the international economic institutions and new regulatory systems, the barriers and risks of such investments (backed by those countries' own investments throughout the world) have greatly diminished. The cheap labour, minimal social programs, lax regulatory standards, and huge consumer populations of China, India, and Brazil are making them attractive venues for investment. Other developing countries aspire to the economic progress of China, India, and Brazil, and, under the auspices of the international institutions, they hold similar potential for lucrative investment returns.

In the present phase of free-market capitalism, global competition still has significant national implications; that is, when a nation's ability to attract private capital investment declines, then advanced research and innovation, access to higher education and training, the standard of living, and the ability to attract global talent also decline. In this regard, global free-market capitalism prefigures a continuing decline of investments in Western-state-domiciled corporations as a proportion of total global investments. Already, there is a measurable shift in direct investments away from Western countries towards geopolitical areas that offer a better financial return. This shift in capital investments causes production and jobs to move to more competitive countries, and, as they do so, they will take consumer purchasing power with them, further diminishing the economic dominance of Western elect bodies.

The transformation of traditional corporate capitalism into border-less, stateless global free-market capitalism involves a fundamental change in the way corporations are being capitalized. Under traditional corporate capitalism, the major corporate investors were wealthy Western individuals and families who exercised quasi-ownership and control over most national and multinational corporations. Under global free-market capitalism, however, the size and scale of required capital investment is increasing to such a level that, in future, multinational corporations increasingly will depend on big investment pools, in particular public trusts such as pension funds, mutual funds, and non-governmental sovereign wealth funds, representing large groups of anonymous stakeholders.

As the economies and middle-class populations of developing nations such as China, India, and Brazil grow and mature, and as they develop Western-style public trusts, the sheer size of these funds will give them investment leverage far greater than that of private corporate capital and, as a result, will achieve significant portions of ownership and control. Thus, global free-market capitalism will have the dual effect of diversifying corporate ownership and control and diminishing the international economic dominance of Western elect bodies.

The transformation of traditional corporate capitalism into global free-market capitalism implies a fundamental change and significant consequences for the concept of gross domestic product (GDP). Under traditional corporate capitalism, national elect bodies had the authority to create economic-fiscal laws, regulations, tax structures, and corporate policies that governed the distribution of the GDP in their respective nations. They determined how much of the GDP they would take as personal income, how much they would reinvest to increase their private wealth, and how much they would allocate to the workers by way of wages, benefits, and social services. Elect bodies flagrantly exploited traditional corporate capitalism to bias the distribution of GDP to their advantage by imposing high taxes on the middle class, ratifying tax structures favourable to corporate profits and capital gains, and providing tax loopholes for the very rich.

In the borderless, stateless world of global free-market capitalism, GDP will gradually change into gross global product (GGP). In this new world, the authority of national elect bodies to determine the distribution of wealth will be significantly diminished. The diversification of corporate equity via public trust funds will serve as a fundamental force in this transformation. Public trust funds are administered by manager-hirelings 'once removed' from corporate governance; their salaries, careers, and tenure depend on maximizing returns to the pension trusts, mutual funds, and sovereign wealth funds which they manage. As trustees of investors' voting proxies, these hireling fund-managers have a measure of influence to impose fiscal discipline and accountability on the governance of the corporations in which the trust funds are invested. However, the mandate of the manager-hirelings does not involve corporate ownership or authority to contrive corporate policies for their personal benefit, as is the case with corporate boards and executives under American-style corporate capitalism.

Under this new order, elect bodies will be effectively demoted from corporate 'owners-commanders' to the status of 'investors-spectators,' implying a resulting loss of authority over the policies that determine distribution of gross product. While the elect bodies will continue to receive a disproportionate share of the GGP, their share will be determined on the same terms as all others – proportionately to their investment holdings.

Global free-market capitalism also has an impact upon the worker-consumer's share of gross product. In Western capitalist democracies, labour unions have served as 'brokers' on behalf of their dues-paying membership, negotiating with employers for wages and benefits in an effort to gain a fair share of the GDP. Union corruption aside, the union is the workers' only dedicated voice. Present trends, however, indicate that the social-political clout of labour unions is on the decline. Their membership, economic-political influence, and bargaining power are being eroded by several factors: the decline of the manufacturing sector caused by importation of lower-priced goods from developing economies; the inflow of cheap migrant labour; outsourcing of work to countries with lower wages; displacement of unionized blue-collar workers by robots; and the shift of jobs from the unionized public sector to the non-unionized private sector. Moreover, global competition is forcing workers to accept the lowest global standard in wages and benefits, thus further depressing the worker-consumers' share of GGP.

In sum, global free-market capitalism signals a significant decrease in the union movement's ability to secure an equitable share of the gross product for the worker-consumer. In this respect, the essential logic of Western capitalism contains a fundamental contradiction. It is dedicated to the maximization of investor profits. To maximize profits, however, requires ever-increasing consumption, which, in turn, calls for ever-increasing consumer purchasing power. As it is currently structured, however, Western capitalism skews the distribution of gross national product in favour of the elect body at the expense of the worker. A poor working class lacks the purchasing power needed to meet the consumption requirements of capitalism.

In the recent past, Western elect bodies drew on foreign loans to artificially increase the purchasing power and consumption of their worker-consumers by extending easy credit instead of higher wages; and they added to their profits by charging exorbitant interest rates. The result is an unprecedented and unsustainable level of consumer indebtedness. It is a supreme paradox that the elect bodies, driven by greed, have impoverished the very worker-consumers on whose spending they depend for their profits.

How will the working class acquire purchasing power in a world where investor greed and global competition are depressing wages and where automation effectively disjoins wages and purchasing power from consumption by rewarding the investor, not the worker? Looking to the future, the diversification of corporate ownership through public trust fund investments has the potential to give workers, as pooled corporate shareholders, a significant voice on corporate boards and an alternative to labour unions as a means of ensuring a more democratic distribution of corporate profits. Subject to the imperative of global free-market competition, they can exploit the growing leverage of their corporate voting proxies to generate humane corporate policies that will enhance their job security, wages, and benefits. The idea of wage earners as significant shareholders in the companies for which they work presents an interesting conflict of interest as to which will secure the better future: raising wages or increasing profits on their investment.

3   Globalization and the United States

All national elect bodies aspire to retain or expand their authority. The U.S. elect body, however, is distinguished from all others by reason of its global political, military, and economic dominance; much more than any other national elect body, its policies and actions are decisive for the destiny of humankind and for our quest for the Good Society. Thus, it merits special consideration in our discussion of globalization. How will it respond to the forces of globalization? I will address four issues in respect to which the U.S. elect body's policies and actions cause concerns about the future of globalization: economic-fiscal policies; military stratagems; nationalism and patriotism; and human sensibility. I will conclude with a discussion of prospects for the future.

Economic-Fiscal Policies

The U.S. elect body is a vigorous and forceful champion of international economic institutions. Applying the logic of traditional corporate capitalism, and based on its international economic pre-eminence, the U.S. elect body reasons that requiring all nation-states to conform their economic systems to the Western capitalist model will advance and enhance the global economic domination of its multinational corporations. To appease national corporations within their borders and mitigate any unfavourable consequences of the international economic institutions on their domestic production and exports, the U.S. elect body has legislated protective tariffs, monetary incentives in the form of direct subsidies, and, as an encouragement to investors, reductions in capital gains, inheritance, and upper-level income taxes. Under the American model of corporate capitalism, such measures have attracted huge inflows of private capital for investments.

However, free trade and investment, the defining principles of global free-market capitalism, are revolutionizing the rules and circumstances of economic competition and success in the global marketplace. Offering monetary subsidies and protective tariffs to encourage domestic production is ultimately counterproductive in a global free-market system because they serve to compensate and breed economic inefficiency. Annual trade-account deficits (the difference between what a country produces and consumes) in excess of $500 billion indicate that the policies and practices of traditional corporate capitalism are causing the U.S. economy to fall behind in global trade and investment competition. Moreover, the diversification of corporate ownership via public trust funds that is occurring under global free-market capitalism is rendering tax havens in the form of reductions in personal capital gains, inheritance, and income taxes for the wealthy increasingly ineffective as an incentive for attracting major investments, although it significantly reduces government revenues.

The United States began the new millennium with a federal government debt of $5.6 trillion, which increased to $13.25 trillion as of July 2010 (estimated at $30,400 per person). This daunting reality is compounded by large and growing state and local government debts. The 'Long-Term Budget Outlook' published by the U.S. Congressional Budget Office in June 2010 projects that in fifteen years the national debt will exceed annual GDP. This massive debt and the ongoing annual deficits (calculated at $1.4 trillion in the fiscal year ending in September 2009, and projected by the Congressional Budget Office to reach $1.5 trillion in 2010), are being financed, in part, by drawing on domestic trust funds such as social security and civil service pensions; by underfunding social benefits such as Medicare, Medicaid, and food stamps; by reducing important expenditures like federal aid to states for infrastructure, education, and health programs; and by printing more dollars. But the principal source of deficit financing (forty cents for every dollar spent) is loans, much of it from foreign countries and mainly from Asian banks; over 40 per cent of U.S. accumulated foreign debt is owed to Asian banks, principally in Japan and China. Three-fourths of new debt is being covered with loans from foreign banks; China is the biggest buyer and holds over $800 billion in U.S. Treasury bonds.

To keep the government in operation and avert a default on U.S. Treasury notes and other federal liabilities, the U.S. elect body routinely increases the legislated debt limit. It covers its annual budget shortfall and the $170 billion in annual interest costs on its accumulated debts by making more loans and printing more dollars. Such a pyramid-Ponzi model of economics is sustainable only as long as other nations continue to finance its debt and ongoing deficit spending. As the U.S. annual budget and trade deficits continue unabated, the country's economic predicament grows more serious with each passing day and portends disaster. The prospect that the U.S. economy will grow out of its plight is greatly complicated by the fact that it is interlocked globally in its indebtedness and in free-market competition for trade and investment capital, which are outside its control.

In the past, private investors were motivated to invest in the United States because the U.S. dollar serves as the international reserve currency and it was the most stable of currencies. However, the stratagem of financing the growing federal government debt by borrowing vast sums in the form of U.S. Treasury bonds and printing its own money is destabilizing the value of the U.S. dollar. Theoretically, devaluation of the dollar helps the U.S. economy by making U.S. goods less expensive and improving the country's export position in the global marketplace. I stipulate 'theoretically' because the manufacturing sector has deteriorated to a level where not enough production takes place in the United States to meaningfully narrow the trade imbalance. In this regard, foreign loans have facilitated the purchase not of American manufactured products but of imported ones, especially from China. Consequently, the United States is becoming increasingly dependent on imports for manufactured goods. This is indicated by the fact that, despite a 25 per cent depreciation of the U.S. dollar against other major currencies since 1990, the U.S. trade-account deficit stands at a new record.

The long-term fundamentals of a devalued dollar are seriously negative for the U.S. and world economies. Already, the prospect of a downward spiral in the worth of the U.S. dollar is generating worldwide anxiety among private investors about their investments in the United States. As the full extent of evolving U.S. economic problems becomes more apparent, private investors, always chasing the most secure and highest return, will step back and look for more promising and stable investment venues. Following one of the basic rules of financial speculation – those 'first out' of a failing business enterprise will lose the least – the deteriorating condition of the U.S. economy warns of investor loss of confidence and a market psychology that could trigger a sudden and huge outflow of investment capital. When this happens, national wealth, which is determined primarily by international stock-market assessments of real and projected earnings, would suffer a precipitous decline. Even a hint that the Chinese elect body is losing confidence in the soundness of the U.S. economy and considering moving some of its U.S. dollar holdings into stronger currencies is enough to provoke serious alarm among all investors in U.S. equities.

Private investors are not the only losers when the U.S. dollar depreciates. The U.S. elect body issues debt in its own currency, primarily in Treasury bonds. Consequently, when the value of the U.S. dollar declines, the foreign governments that have made huge loans to the U.S. suffer significant erosion in the value of their loan portfolios. Unlike private investors, however, foreign governments are subject to a significant constraint against stemming their losses by withdrawing or withholding their loans. If foreign governments should begin to withdraw or even curtail their loans, the U.S. elect body can resort to printing vast sums of its own money to cover the shortfall, thereby triggering a precipitous depreciation of the U.S. dollar and an enormous capital loss to foreign government creditors in the value of their Treasury bond holdings. (As noted above, the U.S. dollar has already depreciated by 25 per cent since 1990.) By this ploy, the elect body can shift a significant portion of U.S. debt to foreign government creditors. Partly as a counter to this tactic, the Chinese elect body is pegging its yuan to the U.S. dollar.

An additional restraint on foreign governments against stemming their losses by withdrawing or withholding their loans arises from the fact that the U.S. dollar serves as the reserve currency used in international trade and finance; any erosion in the U.S. dollar's value affects the currencies of all other nations, and a significant depreciation threatens a catastrophe for the international financial system. This reality is causing deepening concern about the U.S. dollar's status as the reserve currency. Currently, China, Russia, India, and Brazil are joining in a call for a new financial order that would begin to diversify U.S.-dollar-valued currency reserves and assets; they are advocating the creation of a global monetary 'basket' of reserve currencies which would include dollars, Euros, pounds, rubles, and yuan. Already, some intraregional trading partners are sidestepping the U.S. dollar by signing currency-exchange agreements that require the central banks of the partnered countries to carry sufficient deposits of each other's currencies to cover deals between each other. Erosion in the U.S. dollar's status as the reserve currency will seriously affect the ability of the United States to sell Treasury notes in the amounts needed to finance its huge annual budget deficits and its accumulating national debt.

Another significant constraint on foreign governments against withdrawing or withholding loans arises from their dependence on exports to the United States. The principal government lenders, China and Japan, are selling far more goods to the United States than they are buying and their low-interest loans give the U.S. consumer the financial means to purchase the goods they export. Foreign government lenders whose economies are dependent on exports to the United States would like to insulate themselves from the impending financial crisis by forming other economic alliances, but they find themselves in the 'banker's dilemma' – their client owes them so much that a U.S. default on its debt would bring down their economies. Immediate expediency obliges foreign governments to provide the United States with bankruptcy protection by sustaining an economy that may be sinking in quicksand.

The U.S. elect body fully understands that an economy cannot survive on escalating loans and mounting debts, and that to avert a domestic economic crisis it must urgently reduce its massive military expenditures and initiate fundamental structural economic reforms. Yet, within the U.S. elect body, the primary economic concern and debate is over how the huge borrowings in the next deficit budget will be apportioned among their competing factional interests. If this delinquency does not signify ignorance, then what is the explanation for the reckless disregard of the impending economic calamity? The answer is that the U.S. elect body has a significant incentive to maintain its existing economic structures and policies. This becomes clear when we consider that the U.S. economic system is divided into two separate accounts: the government or public-sector account; and the corporate or private-sector account. Under this dual accounting system, the U.S. government's accumulated debt and annual borrowings constitute a *public* liability for which all citizens are responsible; corporate investments and profits constitute a *private* asset of the elect body, not directly liable for the growing national debt and annual deficits.

This dual accounting system obscures an ongoing mammoth fraud that is being perpetrated on U.S. citizens by their elect body. Foreign borrowings by government that accrue as a public liability are not being allocated to benefit ordinary citizens. That is, they are not being used to ease the tax burden of workers negatively affected by global competition, or for domestic social programs like medical insurance, or for job creation or to fix a seriously deteriorating infrastructure. Instead, they are being spent in ways that serve to swell the corporate and privately held assets of the elect body. Billions of the government's borrowed dollars have been spent on lowering corporate and personal income taxes of the wealthiest citizens. Further, hundreds of billions of borrowed dollars are diverted to military and other government expenditures that translate into corporate profits and private wealth which accrue disproportionately to the elect body.

The U.S. elect body severely censures socialist governments for violations of corporate-capitalist principles when, in the name of the 'public good,' they transfer ownership of profitable privately owned corporations to the public sector. However, when the U.S. private sector experiences financial exigency, the elect body abandons corporate-capitalist principles and, under the pretext of doing the 'public good,' 'averting chaos,' and 'saving the economy,' legislates 'bailouts' by committing vast sums of present and future taxpayers' money to cover the losses and debts of privately owned corporations. In effect, the U.S. elect body is using privately owned banking, financial, and insurance companies as fronts and conduits to perpetrate an enormous legalized money-laundering scheme. Meeting in government and corporate backrooms, it exploits the dual accounting system to transform private debt into public debt; as well, it makes huge transfers of borrowed and 'digital dollars' from public accounts to private-sector accounts. By these artifices it places the future of the public sector in grave jeopardy.

The U.S. elect body's dysfunctional response to the forces of globalization extends to the international arena. Driven by its ambition to take advantage of the lucrative investment opportunities offered by China's cheap labour force and 1.3 billion consumers, the U.S. elect body initially advocated and helped China's entry into the global free-market capitalist system. The Chinese elect body, eager to exploit the lucrative export potential presented by the extravagant lifestyle of 300 million American consumers, assertively courted the U.S. elect body by offering huge loans at low interest rates to cover budget and trade-account deficits. In effect, the two elect bodies, both acting exclusively in their own self-interest, are locked in an embrace of reciprocal exploitation that portends a confrontation which jeopardizes the security of all nations.

The two elect bodies have the opportunity to respond constructively to the forces of globalization: they could collaboratively develop a relationship of interdependence that would benefit their own and the world's poorest citizens; they could work cooperatively on pressing issues such as halting ecological devastation and resource depletion. Instead, they are engaging in a rivalry for scarce resources and a confrontation over Taiwan that raises the spectre of a military conflict. Although China does not present a military threat in the foreseeable future, the U.S. elect body is portraying China as a significant menace to its national security and has begun to forge a 'containment' policy involving strengthened relationships and alliances with states surrounding China, in particular India, Japan, Pakistan, South Korea, Singapore, Indonesia, and, ironically, Vietnam, to maintain its political-military dominance in Southeast Asia.

Although the U.S. economic decline is self-inflicted, the U.S. elect body is blaming the U.S. trade deficit on an undervalued yuan and charging the Chinese elect body with manipulating the exchange rate on its currency. Under the specious pretext of 'rebalancing' the global economy, the U.S. elect body is threatening protectionist action unless the yuan is revalued at a higher rate. Curiously, prior to its economic decline, during its century of global superiority, the U.S. elect body expressed no interest in a balanced global economy, and it expresses no interest in a balanced global military arrangement.

China

With a billion-plus consumers, a swelling middle class, and a huge domestic market potential, China is on a path that will diminish its dependence on the U.S. market. Its rapidly expanding manufacturing capacity, diversified exports to all regions of the globe, and immense savings accumulated in the form of foreign reserves place China on a trajectory to displace the United States as global economic leader in the foreseeable future. The extent of its U.S. debt holding is a political asset in its dealings with the U.S. elect body. It can exploit the desperate need for financial liquidity as a political lever to gain U.S. government approval for the purchase of significant portions of U.S. private assets such as banking, real estate, corporate stocks, and high-tech companies. And, if the U.S. economy fails, it can acquire them at bargain prices.

Both economies function to earn money for their respective elect bodies; however, China's mix of state and free-market corporate capitalism is better structured than is U.S. corporate capitalism to adapt to the free-market system's principle of unfettered trade and competition. Already China is overtaking the United States as the preferred venue for new capital investment. Also in favour of

China's economic prospects is the fact that it emphasizes a mercantilist policy in its relationship with other nations; thus, many countries perceive it as less threatening, militarily and ideologically, than the United States. The Chinese elect body does not mix commerce with political ideology; it pursues its economic ambitions and secures its essential supplies of oil and raw materials from other countries through mutually beneficial commercial arrangements. By contrast, the economic ambitions of the U.S. elect body involve military, ideological, political, and cultural facets that are perceived by leaders of developing countries as a threat to their national authority.

To appreciate fully the implications of China's impressive progress towards global economic leadership, we need to look beyond international economic parameters and evaluate the Chinese elect body's domestic policies in the context of a globalizing world. Its practice of underpaying its workers and its lack of transparency, accountability, and responsiveness to the grievances and aspirations of its citizens pose a serious threat of domestic social unrest; as well, the absence of a rational system for resolving rivalry for dominance in the state dictatorship threatens political instability. Both of these domestic circumstances portend dysfunctional consequences for the future of globalization and the security of the rest of the world. To play a constructive role in the process of globalization, the Chinese elect body must begin to diffuse its domestic authority, moderate its economic ambitions, and formulate a cooperative economic-political accommodation with the international community.

The dysfunctional implications of the U.S. elect body's economic policies and actions for the future of globalization came into sharp focus in 2008 when a meltdown in U.S. subprime mortgages was exported to the rest of the world, triggering a crisis in the world's financial markets. The U.S. elect body obscured its own responsibility for originating the global crisis by rendering it as a complex conundrum of corporate-executive miscalculations, by expressing surprise, concern, and dismay, and by launching investigations. Put simply, however, the subprime-mortgage debacle that precipitated the global economic crisis was caused by a corporate-capitalist model and U.S. government policies which not only allowed but encouraged – as something both rational and audacious – unrestrained predatory profiteering by banks, investment institutions, credit-rating agencies, and insurers of mortgage-backed securities. Following is a very brief description of how the crisis came to be.

Under the corporate-capitalist model and U.S. government policies, banks were allowed to sell their mortgage-based assets to investment institutions. This arrangement gave the banks more money for mortgage loans and relieved them of liability for mortgage delinquencies. Greedy bankers granted mortgage loans to subprime borrowers and, ultimately, to people with no income, no assets, and no reasonable prospect of repayment.

The U.S. investment institutions that purchased the dubious mortgages from the banks bundled large numbers of them together with other income-producing assets and converted them into securities for sale to investors at home and abroad. The investment institutions' money managers were paid huge bonuses based on the dollar volume of their trades in securities, with no accountability for losses generated by the securities they traded. This system of compensation played a significant part in swelling the sale of subprime-mortgage-backed securities and the growth of subprime lending.

U.S. credit-rating agencies are paid fees by the companies whose securities they are evaluating. Competition among rating agencies for service fees gives them a strong incentive to enhance the ratings they assign to clients' securities. By understating the underlying risk of default of subprime-mortgage-backed securities, they significantly fuelled the worldwide sale of these securities.

U.S. insurance companies sell coverage for potential losses on securities. To maximize their profits, they sold more risk coverage than they had in capital reserves to cover the insured losses resulting from subprime-mortgage defaults. To avert a torrent of bankruptcies, the U.S. government was compelled to cover $180 billion of the American International Group's insurance liabilities.

By its failure to regulate and control the greed-driven speculation, deceit, and fraud endemic to the corporate-capitalist model, the U.S. elect body not only crippled an already deteriorating domestic economy, it precipitated a global economic calamity: the defaults on repayment of U.S. subprime mortgages created havoc in financial institutions and equity markets the world over, and the resulting collapse of the U.S. consumer market caused major disruptions in global trade and investment. The government saved the U.S. economy from an immediate collapse by printing new dollars and with foreign borrowing (principally from China), but with as yet unknown future consequences for domestic and global financial equilibrium.

Foreign investors concerned for the security of their economic future point to this compelling demonstration of global economic interconnectedness as cogent evidence for the need of effective regulation over cross-border banking, securities, and capital transactions. Led by France and Germany, they insist that a restoration of international trust and confidence will require the creation of a global super-agency with authority to monitor national financial institutions. They call for a 'global financial architecture' and a 'global regulator' with authority to enforce stringent new regulations on international financial corporations, tax havens, and hedge funds. However, even in the face of a global economic crisis and a serious threat to its own national security caused by the failure of its corporate-capitalist model and economic-fiscal policies, the U.S. elect body adamantly refuses to acknowledge the need for a constructive response to the forces of globalization, and insists on exempting itself from any and all external regulation of financial institutions that would intrude on U.S. sovereignty.

The impending crisis in the U.S. economy will affect all of its citizens; however, it will be the ordinary citizens who eventually will pay the price for massive debt, embezzled public trust accounts, bankrupt social programs, and dilapidated infrastructure. In the borderless world of global commerce, the U.S. elect body can insulate itself from the effects of the domestic economic collapse that its greed has caused. Anticipating the contingency in which foreign loans and investments are cut off and the U.S. economy melts down, it is already betraying the national interest and security by 'off-shoring' its investments. Significant sums of the morally illicit proceeds the elect body has derived from its money-laundering scam are being invested in foreign corporations for personal gain, and multinational U.S. corporations are moving major operations together with production and jobs to more auspicious venues. Grotesquely, the U.S. elect body stands to gain from the domestic economic collapse it has brought about: as the U.S. dollar value declines, it can convert its annual returns from foreign investments (valued in more favourable foreign currency) into extra U.S. dollars. Thus, the U.S. elect body, the perpetrator of the economic disaster, gets richer even as the public sector and ordinary citizens become insolvent.

Military Stratagems

Historically, hegemony, meaning the extension of authority beyond the boundaries of primary spheres of power, was accomplished mainly by military occupation and control; that is, it was *territorial* hegemony. As pointed out earlier, such enterprises invariably succumbed to indigenous opposition and the hegemons were forced to withdraw their authority to the boundaries of their primary spheres of power. Owing in part to its history as a colony, the U.S. elect body has infrequently followed the course of territorial hegemony to maintain control over another nation. More often, it has followed the less aggressive and intrusive course of *strategic* hegemony. That is, instead of enforcing its authority by continuing military occupation, the U.S. elect body extends its hegemony in various regions of the world by installing, supporting, and guaranteeing the geopolitical security of compliant indigenous regimes; not incidentally, this also discourages them from developing advanced weaponry for their own defence. In return, these regimes serve as 'client states' and proxies for U.S. strategic interests. The U.S. empire has endured, in part, because strategic hegemony has been less disruptive to the social-political order of its client states than were the territorial hegemonies of colonial Britain, France, and, more recently, the USSR.

Since the end of the Second World War, the U.S. elect body has established client states for purposes of strategic hegemony in every region of the world. It has employed a variety of stratagems in this endeavour, including clandestine operations planned and funded by the Central Intelligence Agency (CIA) that involve powerful propaganda campaigns to overthrow unfriendly governments and replace them with compliant regimes; inciting and financing assassinations, insurrections, and coups against defiant leaders, even if popularly elected; bribing corrupt leaders and officials to endorse U.S. policies; and intimidating vulnerable state regimes by imposing or threatening trade embargos and other punitive economic-political actions.

In developing countries with fledgling democratic governments, the authority of military leaders is institutionally better established and more stable than civilian authority. The U.S. elect body has exploited this situation by channelling billions of dollars, weapons, training, and planning aid through the Pentagon and the CIA to indigenous military leaders. By indenturing the military command structure in this way, it acquires the capacity to persuade a popularly elected government to submit to its will or risk a coup by the indigenous armed forces.

Although generally the U.S. elect body has adopted the less aggressive and intrusive course of strategic hegemony, it is dedicated to the stratagem of using military intimidation as necessary to bully client states into acquiescence with its objectives. To this end, it has developed an overwhelming global military pre-eminence. Using the pretext of national security, it has established huge military bases in every region of the world to discourage any challengers to its strategic interests; and it has developed and stockpiled an enormous cache of sophisticated weapons of mass destruction, including nuclear, chemical, and biological devices with vehicles for delivering them swiftly over great distances to selected human targets.

The terrorist attack of 11 September 2001, the insurgencies in Iraq and Afghanistan, and the increase in terrorist-training camps and operations in several Muslim countries have revealed that military bases and stockpiles of lethal weapons are ineffectual deterrents against terrorism in the emerging borderless world. Yet military stratagems have become the U.S. elect body's new norm of strategic hegemony, and it is using the 'War on Terror' as a pretext and rallying cry to win citizen support for allocating additional huge sums of borrowed and taxpayers' money to maintain its strategic hegemony by military means.

Even as the U.S. elect body advocated harsh international political and economic sanctions against regimes with nuclear ambitions, its military stratagem called for modernizing the long-range nuclear missiles permitted by the Strategic Arms Reduction Treaty (START) signed by George H.W. Bush and Mikhail Gorbachev in 1991. For a number of years, the U.S. Department of Defense has been conducting research into nuclear devices that will change its arsenal's primary purpose from 'last resort' response to nuclear attack to pre-emptive 'first strike' against potential aggressors. Recently, the Department of Defense announced plans to spend an estimated $100 billion on creating a new generation of nuclear weapons and the development of a space-based missile capability. It has applied for and been granted approval of funding by the U.S. Congress to build prototype nuclear devices ranging from miniaturized field weapons to earth-penetrating 'bunker busters.' These initiatives contravene several international treaties.

The U.S. elect body refuses to ratify the Comprehensive Nuclear Test Ban Treaty, and it stands alone in its opposition to the United Nation's call for keeping weapons out of space. In May 2005 a month-long UN conference to affirm the international Nuclear Non-Proliferation Treaty ended in failure, with non-nuclear states aligned against the United States because it refused to offer the assurance that it would not use its nuclear weapons against them. Four months later, the U.S. Department of Defense released a draft paper titled 'Doctrine for Joint Nuclear Operations' which would allow presidential approval of regional military commanders' requests for nuclear strikes to protect U.S. strategic interests.

The U.S. elect body's stratagem to assert its hegemony by military means is currently in deep trouble in the Middle East. By way of background, the U.S. elect body first established a significant level of strategic hegemony in the Gulf region in 1953 when, with support from the British elect body, it overthrew the democratically elected socialist government in Iran headed by the assertively independent Mohammed Mosaddegh. It then installed and armed the amenable despot Mohammed Reza Shah Pahlavi as proxy for its hegemony in the region. This contemptible arrangement triggered the Islamic Revolution and came to an abrupt end when the Iranian people routed the shah and established an Islamic theocracy in Iran under the leadership of Ayatollah Ruhollah Khomeini. The rise of the Khomeini regime on a wave of popular resentment against U.S. hegemony left the U.S. elect body bereft of a client state to protect its vital strategic interests in the Gulf region at a critical time during the Cold War with the USSR. Unable to enlist the support of a Muslim regime, the U.S. elect body forged a partnership with Israel to buttress its strategic interests in the region.

It is noteworthy that the partnership between the U.S. and Israeli elect bodies was founded on a shared expedient, not on a durable shared agenda. The shared expedient was to cooperate in deterring any troublesome ambitions by the Iraqi, Iranian, Syrian, and Saudi regimes in the Middle East. However, the two elect bodies pursue widely disparate long-term goals. The Israeli goal is to secure its biblical homeland and establish a refuge from another Holocaust; the U.S. elect body's primary concern is to secure and control distribution of the supply of oil from the Gulf region. The limitations of their expedient partnership became evident during the invasion of Iraq: Israel, with military superiority in the region, provided no military assistance and no security for U.S. oil supplies against disruption by surrounding Muslim state regimes or Islamic radicals.

Confronted with the rising threat to its vital interests posed by Islamic extremism, the U.S. elect body desperately needed a client state to serve as its proxy in the Middle East. Ideally, it would have liked the Saudis to perform this role: they are the primary supplier of U.S. oil from the region; the Pentagon has been arming and protecting Saudi rulers in exchange for first call on secure and cheap oil; and the ruling Saudi royal family has friendly ties with the U.S. elect body. However, the upsurge of pan-Islamism and the pervasive Arab Muslim perception that the United States is a co-conspirator with Israel in the Palestinians' calamity is fuelling popular hostility in Saudi Arabia towards the United States. A large segment of Saudi society views the prospect of U.S. bases on their territory primarily as hegemony, not as geo-political protection. Recognizing this political reality, the Saudi elect body eschews the label of U.S. ally and opposes a U.S. military presence on its soil, except for its own protection. This circumstance precludes the possibility of Saudi Arabia acting as a client state and proxy for U.S. strategic hegemony in the region.

With no other regime in the Middle East willing and able to protect its interests, the U.S. elect body decided to establish its hegemony in the region by making Iraq into a client state. To accomplish this purpose required a regime change and in 2003 it swiftly dispatched a quarter-million troops to the region to invade Iraq. A related purpose was to send an intimidating message to all Muslim regimes, notably Iran and Syria, that any 'host' or 'sponsor' of terrorism against U.S. strategic interests in the region could expect decisive U.S. military retaliation.

The U.S. elect body had several pragmatic reasons for choosing Iraq as a prospective client state and proxy for its strategic interests in the region: Iraq has huge oil-producing potential; it was functioning as a secular state; its military capability had been decimated by Desert Storm in 1991 and subsequently held in check by continuous U.S. and U.K. air force surveillance and harassment; its citizens were ravaged and demoralized by a decade-long international embargo on the importation of basic necessities; its segmentation into antagonistic Sunni, Shiite, and Kurd communities weakened Iraqi nationalism and patriotism; and, importantly, the ruling Baathist regime, controlled by Saddam Hussein, was distrusted and feared by its neighbours and loathed and reviled by the world at large.

There was, however, a complicating aspect to the U.S. military stratagem. Article 2(4) of the UN Charter expressly prohibits the violation of any state's national sovereignty unless authorized for humanitarian reasons by the Security Council. In response to widespread and intense international demands, the U.S. elect body, pro forma, sought the Security Council's approval for its premeditated and imminent invasion of Iraq. Its professed grounds were that a pre-emptive military strike was justified because Saddam Hussein was in possession of weapons of mass destruction which posed a serious and looming threat to the U.S. homeland and its national security.

In the era since the Second World War, especially during the Cold War, Western states singly and in various alliances, such as the North Atlantic Treaty Organization (NATO), have always refrained from interfering with (and sometimes have cooperated in) the U.S. elect body's ventures to eliminate unfriendly regimes and establish its strategic hegemony; a case in point is the current war against the Taliban in Afghanistan, under the flag of NATO. In the instance of Iraq, however, some key U.S. allies, in particular France and Germany, perceived the huge unilateral deployment of U.S. troops to the region not as a response to a threat to U.S. security but as a design by the U.S. elect body to gain control over the distribution of oil from that region.

In the context of limited and declining global oil reserves, and the rapidly escalating needs of China, India, and Japan for adequate and secure energy supplies, France and Germany deemed the implied relegation of their own significant dependence on oil from the region as unacceptable. They challenged the evidence tendered by the U.S. elect body, that Iraq had contravened international law by developing weapons of mass destruction, as dubious and insufficient to justify violation of Iraqi sovereignty. Joined by Russia, France used its seat on the Security Council to deny UN approval for U.S. invasion plans. It is appropriate to emphasize that this action by Russia and France was motivated by their strategic interests in the Middle East, not by humanitarian considerations.

To justify their predetermined and prearranged invasion of Iraq, the U.S. president, the Pentagon, the Department of Defense, and the CIA collaboratively engaged in an intensive and extensive domestic and international disinformation campaign portraying Iraq as an imminent threat to U.S. national security. They proceeded deliberately and systematically to fabricate, select, tailor, misrepresent, and misinterpret intelligence data by linking Saddam Hussein's Baathist regime to al-Qaeda and the 9/11 act of terrorism. They also purported to have unimpeachable proof that Hussein was developing a nuclear bomb. These concocted data were publicized and repeated many times by the highest-ranking officials of the government as 'truth.' Contrary evidence reported by the International Atomic Energy Agency and the UN, which had extensive on-the-ground access and knowledge about the Iraqi weapons programs and capabilities, was deliberately ignored or arbitrarily rejected by the U.S. administration; only confirming 'facts,' no matter how baseless, were credited. When the great deception subsequently came to light, the U.S. administration blamed it on an

intelligence fiasco and guilefully gave the bizarre alibi that it had committed an 'honest mistake – an 'honest mistake' that caused the gratu-
itous deaths of hundreds of thousands of Iraqi citizens and traumatized
millions of innocent and defenceless civilians.

The 'Coalition of the Willing'

In the absence of UN approval for its violation of Iraqi sovereignty, the U.S. elect body disingenuously gave its invasion of
Iraq the semblance of a multinational enterprise by hastily bribing
or bullying an assortment of governments to join what it spuri-
ously called the 'Coalition of the Willing.' Allegedly, the coalition
comprised thirty countries but only four beside the United States
(United Kingdom, Australia, Poland, and Denmark) contributed
fighting troops to the invasion force; some others offered tem-
porary post- invasion support. Excluding the United Kingdom,
other countries contributed a combined token 5 per cent of the
total troop deployment. Acting against the wishes of a majority of
its citizens, the British government contributed 15 per cent of the
coalition troops, and its prime minister, Tony Blair, dutifully par-
roted President Bush's specious rationale for the invasion. When
the invasion of Iraq subsequently evolved into a military occupation, U.K. participation was initially reduced to a token 8,500
troops, followed by a complete withdrawal in 2009.

In regard to the British elect body, it is worth noting that its strategic interest in the oil-rich Gulf region has been joined with that of
the U.S. elect body ever since their conspiracy to subvert the democratically elected government of Mosaddegh. Their collaboration
continued during Operation Desert Storm as well as during the
interval between Desert Storm and the invasion of Iraq. In these
hegemonic ventures, the British elect body has taken the position
that its interests in the Gulf region are better served if it acts as a
supporting junior partner of the U.S. elect body rather than working in cooperation with its European colleagues.

The U.S. elect body envisioned that following its invasion of Iraq it
would displace Hussein's autocratic regime with a Western-style democracy and promptly transform Iraq into a client state and proxy for its

strategic hegemony in the Gulf region. This vision indicates a profound lack of understanding of the social-political dynamic of globalization. My theory of globalization maintains that for social-political stability the boundaries of power and authority must coincide. Although Iraq was defined by internationally recognized geopolitical borders, it functioned as an internal hegemony, comprising three distinct primary spheres of power: Shiite, Sunni, and Kurd ethnic-religious communities, with deep historical roots. 'Cross-border' social-relational interdependence and shared knowledge and understanding among the three societies have not yet evolved to the extent of merging the three communities into a single sphere of power and social-order authority.

Before the U.S. invasion, Saddam Hussein held the three distinct ethnic-religious communities together by military, economic, and institutional coercion and brutal intimidation. His defeat by U.S. forces freed the three communities from internal hegemony and presented them with the opportunity to realign authority to correspond with the boundaries of their primary spheres of power. History shows that, when freed from hegemony, ethnic-religious communities initially tend towards nationalism, and current events in Iraq show that the Sunni, Shiite, and Kurd communities, respectively, aspire to self-government; moreover, their elect bodies are not above resorting to violence to establish their respective jurisdictions of authority.

My theory of globalization also holds that ultimately the power of the three ethnic-religious communities will merge into a larger primary sphere of power and that their authority will similarly be assimilated and realigned into a larger jurisdiction; however, the timing and the precise path of this process are unpredictable. Given the right leadership, it is possible that the three ethnic-religious communities could forge a federation. Federalism, if it is voluntary, can be a constructive design for facilitating the merging of distinct spheres of power and the assimilation and realignment of authority into a single jurisdiction. Over time, the three ethnic-religious communities could develop the social-relational interdependence and shared knowledge and understanding that would merge their respective spheres of power into a larger primary sphere, and assimilate and realign their authority into a functional national unity and Iraqi identity. Currently, however, the observable and emerging social-political patterns indicate that Iraqi Shiites may join their power and authority with their Iranian-Shia confederates; the Sunnis with their Arab-Muslim confederates; and the Kurds with their regional ethnic-Muslim confederates.

Going into Iraq, the U.S. elect body knew that a Western-style election would yield a state weakened by ethnic-religious divisions. Moreover, it calculatingly destabilized civil authority by disbanding the existing Baathist bureaucratic organizational structure to create a condition of total dependence on the U.S. military for domestic order. From the U.S. elect body's perspective, this seemed a favourable prospect because a weak and factionalized central government could be more readily manipulated than a unified one to perform as a compliant client state and proxy for U.S. strategic hegemony in the Gulf region. However, domestic sectarian distrust, animosity, and strife, exacerbated by the brutality of U.S. occupation forces, have practically precluded the development of an effective unified civil authority within a democratic structure. This poses the possibility of social chaos, civil war, and disintegration of the country along sectarian lines: a nation destroyed.

In such an event, the Shiites, who are positioned to control Iraq's largest oil fields, may establish an Islamic theocratic state with strong ties to Iran and the pan-Islamic movement. This would place the vital U.S. oil supply from the Gulf region in serious jeopardy. To prevent such an outcome, maintain internal order, and provide protection against neighbouring states, the U.S. elect body may be compelled to continue its military presence in Iraq. In any case, President Bush's boastful speech of victory, broadcast from the deck of the U.S.S. *Abraham Lincoln* under the banner 'Mission Accomplished,' revealed a tragic misunderstanding of globalization and the history of hegemony, with disastrous consequences for Iraqi citizens, Americans, and the world at large.

In the long term, U.S. military hegemony over the three antagonistic sectarian communities is economically unsustainable and politically and socially untenable. Confronted with this reality, the U.S. elect body will be pressed to find a diplomatic accommodation with Islam to achieve security for its oil supply. To reach such an accommodation, U.S. elect body must first overcome the widespread and profound feelings of anti-Americanism that prevail in Muslim communities the world over. The extent of Muslim anti-American sentiment can be inferred from the fact that, when free elections are held in Muslim countries, public U.S. endorsement of a political party is a liability not an asset. The depth of Muslim anti-American sentiment was revealed by the popular reaction to the 9/11 act of terrorism. While most Muslim leaders publicly deplored its barbarity, some considered the U.S. elect body to be an accessory to the crime, and many Muslim communities erupted into spontaneous and emotional celebration; nearly all empathized with the grievances that incited the act.

Osama bin Laden conceived the 9/11 terrorist attack as a message to the U.S. elect body to end its hegemony in the Arabian peninsula. However, the invasions of Iraq and Afghanistan, the high toll of Muslim civilian casualties, and the torture of Islamic detainees have contributed to the rise of an Islamic fundamentalism with much broader objectives. These developments, before bin Laden's death at the hands of U.S. forces in May 2011, elevated him to worldwide prominence and boosted his fund-raising appeal. More fundamentally, they have intensified anti-American sentiment in the Muslim world to an unprecedented level, spurred the recruitment of Islamic extremists, and abetted the extension of al-Qaeda from a relatively small and obscure Arab-Muslim organization to a borderless, grassroots religious crusade and network dedicated to committing acts of terrorism against Western societies. The U.S. elect body's military stratagems in the Middle East and Afghanistan are inclining even moderate Muslim regimes to endorse Islamic fundamentalism to legitimate and bolster their national authority, thereby setting back promising indigenous reform movements with a secular outlook.

What sort of policies can the U.S. elect body devise to achieve genuine rapprochement with the Islamic world? This task is complicated by the fact that, although Muslims are socially, ethnically, and theologically diverse and beset by deep and historic national and sectarian divisions, they feel pride in and identify with pan-Islamism. Pan-Islamism has become a unifying force; it is evolving the social-relational interdependence, shared knowledge, and understanding necessary to constitute a larger primary sphere of power and jurisdiction of authority. This social-political transformation has progressed far enough that meaningful U.S. rapprochement with the Islamic world will require more than negotiating a series of bilateral accords with individual Muslim states. Moreover, Islamic anti-Americanism is a complex phenomenon involving diverse grievances. These grievances include past and present U.S. wars against Muslim societies, past and present neo-colonial political-economic exploitation of oil resources, and perceived ongoing cultural imperialism. In the minds of Islamic fundamentalists, these grievances have become fused into a moral image of the U.S. as the 'Great Satan.'

There is, however, one particular issue that, more than any other, incites anti-American passions and on which virtually all Muslims are united: that is the U.S. partnership and support for Israel in the conflict with the Palestinian people. Although Palestinians are ethnically Arab, they are connected by religion to 1.4 billion Muslims and the pan-Islamic movement. Support for the Palestinians' cause extends beyond Arab borders to all states in which Islam dominates politically. It should be noted that Muslims do not consider Israel as a U.S. client state; to the contrary, they perceive the U.S. elect body as a proxy for an Israeli plot to demoralize the Muslim world and make it submissive. For them, U.S. support for the Israelis in the conflict with the Palestinians has become a potent symbol of contempt towards Islam. Evidence that this sentiment resonates throughout the Islamic world is indicated by the unanimous support for the Palestinian cause declared by the fifty-six member-states of the Organization of the Islamic Conference.

Although Muslim anti-Americanism involves a number of grievances, a shift of support by the U.S. elect body from Israel to the Palestinians would lance a huge boil of Muslim antagonism. In the immediate term, such a shift in U.S. policy would be viewed by the Muslim world as a meaningful concession to its sensibilities and would moderate the passions that breed Islamic radicalism and terrorist threats to the U.S. homeland. This would facilitate a U.S.-Islamic rapprochement to secure U.S. oil supplies from the Gulf and might provide a diplomatic way out of the open-ended military quagmire in Iraq. Yet, even as the U.S. need for rapprochement with the Islamic world is growing, popular anti-Islam sentiment in the United States and anti-American sentiment in Muslim countries are on the rise.

While the U.S. elect body's political commitment to the U.S.-Israeli partnership is currently overtly robust, it has never been severely tested. Contingent on how events evolve in the Middle East, there is a looming prospect that the Israelis' goal to secure their biblical homeland could clash with the U.S. elect body's primary concern to secure its supply of oil from the Gulf region. This possibility involves a complex dynamic and is coming into sharp focus in the context of the Iranian elect body's ambition to develop surreptitiously a military nuclear capability. A nuclear-armed Iran poses a potential threat to both the U.S. oil supply and to Israel's homeland; however, although the two countries' interests align on averting this threat, their respective options for dealing with it could ultimately come into direct opposition.

For the people of Israel, the idea of a nuclear stand-off with a regime that threatens their existence and has declared its determination to wipe them from the face of the earth is, understandably, reprehensible and intolerable; and, to avert such a possibility, Israeli leadership is seriously contemplating launching a pre-emptive air strike against Iran. Such an act of aggression could unify the Muslim world and provoke a regional war that would cause severe oil shortages and precipitate a global economic collapse. To pre-empt this contingency, the U.S. elect body is urgently pushing Israeli-Palestinian negotiations in the fervent hope that an agreement will sufficiently moderate the passions that breed Islamic radicalism as to isolate the fundamentalist Islamic theocracy in Iran from its Muslim neighbours. It believes that, in conjunction with comprehensive and severe multinational economic-political sanctions imposed through the UN Security Council, an isolated Iranian elect body can be deterred from developing a nuclear military capability.

However, perfidy often goes hand in hand with hegemonic ambitions and there is a prospect that, if its present stratagem fails and its essential oil supplies from the Gulf region are seriously threatened, the U.S. elect body, daunted by its disastrous conflicts in Iraq and Afghanistan, will devise a rapprochement with Islam and forge an expedient diplomatic alliance with the Iranian theocracy, as it did with the odious Pakistani General Pervez Musharraf. The possibility that the U.S. elect body might renounce its partnership with Israel to appease Islam can be inferred from oft-repeated ambiguous statements by the highest-ranking spokespersons of the U.S. elect body (e.g., past and present presidents, congressmen, and military leaders) calling for a 'new solution' to the Israeli-Palestinian conflict. On the Israeli side, there is a growing distrust of U.S. intentions. But, should the U.S. elect body renounce its alliance with Israel, a likely outcome is a confrontation between Israel and Islam that could quickly escalate into a war that would draw in most of the countries in the Middle East and affect the entire world.

To grasp the full significance of the U.S. elect body's military stratagem in the Middle East, we must view the invasion of Iraq not merely as a disastrous current event but as a dysfunctional response to the forces of globalization that will have disruptive consequences for humankind long after U.S. troops have departed the region. The U.S. elect body had the opportunity for a positive response by applying its influence, resources, and leadership in resolute support of strong and concerted negotiations for a comprehensive peace agreement between Israel and the Palestinians. Instead, by pursuing its hegemonic ambitions in the region, it is contributing to a global ethos of contempt for international laws and treaties. This ethos exacerbates international political instability and serves to extenuate other hegemonic offences, such as that of China against Tibet and Russia against Chechnya. Realizing the Good Society requires that the U.S. elect body acknowledge and respond constructively to the forces of globalization.

Nationalism and Patriotism

Protected on the east and west by moats of vast oceans and bordered on the north and south by the benign countries of Canada and Mexico, U.S. sovereignty has never been challenged or threatened. Yet, under the pretext of protecting U.S. sovereignty, the U.S. elect body demonstrates an extreme preoccupation with guarding its national authority, internationally and domestically. In the international context, the U.S. elect body shields its national authority by ranking its own laws above international laws. Citing the pretext that submission to international law would compromise U.S. sovereignty, the U.S. elect body routinely exempts its authority from international laws and agreements that are intended to diminish danger to humankind.

For instance, the United States has exempted itself from the authority of the UN Charter, the UN Human Rights Covenant, and the UN International Court of Justice; the Chemical and Biological Weapons Convention prohibiting the production and stockpiling of chemical- and biological-warfare agents; the Kyoto Protocol agreement to reduce the atmospheric pollution that causes global climate change; the Convention on the Law of the Sea; and the international Anti-Ballistic Missile Treaty. Also, it has effectively immunized itself and its military from prosecution for war crimes by refusing to join the International Criminal Court (ICC) and threatening to withhold promised economic aid and programs from countries that refuse to exempt U.S. soldiers from the jurisdiction of the ICC.

How do we reconcile this unyielding ultra-nationalism with the fact that the U.S. elect body champions the international investment, trade, and monetary institutions? Clearly, these institutions are a design for the progressive erosion of national sovereignty and for assimilating and realigning significant domestic authority into a unitary global jurisdiction. A credible explanation for this apparent inconsistency can be inferred from the U.S. elect body's past practice of championing self-serving international treaties and laws but asserting the right of self-exemption when compliance is disadvantageous. Presuming on its global military, political, and economic dominance, the U.S. elect body does not consider the international economic agreements a threat to its national authority.

In the domestic context, the U.S. elect body secures its authority and buttresses a fragile unity by means of systematic and intensive indoctrination of its citizens into an ultra-nationalistic, zealous, virtually reflexive patriotism. American patriotism promotes a sense of exceptionalism involving political-economic-military supremacy and moral superiority, which, as noted above, extends to self-exemption from international law. It is sustained and heightened by a deliberately generated paranoia about potential perils posed by foreign enemies that are represented as real and imminent threats to national security. Patriotism is equated with unquestioning acceptance of the elect body's stipulated definitions of national security; accordingly, being a patriotic American, in its political-moral sense, means yielding heart, mind, and soul to the elect body's authority whenever it declares a threat to national security.

Akin to religious fundamentalism, U.S. patriotism fosters a mentality of 'us versus them' and induces an endemic predisposition to paranoia that functions as a quiet tyranny on American citizens, discouraging objective evaluations of their elect body's motives. Most Americans are so convinced of the moral righteousness of their elect body's motives that they are content to place its authority above international law even when it commits war crimes and other egregious violations of human dignity and humanity. Any telling criticisms or censure of its policies and actions are generally dismissed as false, malicious, ignorant, or perverse, or motivated by jealousy and hatred. American citizens with this mindset divide the nations of the world into 'friends' and 'enemies'; neutral nations that do not fall into line with the designs of their elect body are distrusted and contemned. Even learned pundits writing in the country's foremost editorial pages and periodicals express views that are intellectually isolated from objective and cosmopolitan analyses of foreign affairs. They evaluate world developments from the U.S. elect body's narrow viewpoint and foreign policy that what is good for America is good and what is bad for America is bad.

Patriotism and the paranoia it engenders render U.S. citizens susceptible to manipulation by their elect body. This susceptibility was alarmingly revealed by events preceding, during, and following the invasion of Iraq. U.S. citizens had learned from what happened during the war with Vietnam that the invasion of Iraq would orphan and maim tens of thousands of children, destroy the homes and means of subsistence of millions of civilians, and devastate an already destitute society's infrastructure. They also knew that the invasion constituted a clear violation of the UN Charter and international law. However, playing on the patriotism of its citizens, the U.S. elect body had little difficulty perpetrating a great deception and persuading a large majority of Americans to ardently support the immoral and illegal invasion of Iraq.

Then, having ordered their soldiers onto the battlefield, the U.S. elect body manipulated its citizens' patriotism to silence all criticism of the war. Citizens opposed to the invasion and occupation were frightened and bullied into silence by the explicit declaration that criticism of the war constituted a 'betrayal of the troops on the ground,' an act deserving of the worst of all epithets: 'un-American.'

Even after the pretext for the invasion was exposed as a deliberate deception, a significant number of American citizens, motivated by patriotism, persisted in defending their elect body's decision to invade Iraq as essential in the 'fight against terrorism.' Arguably, deception is part of every elect body's political stock-in-trade; however, in this instance, patriotism blinded Americans to a mass deception that resulted in hundreds of thousand casualties and traumatized millions of innocent and defenceless civilians.

Another prominent feature of U.S. citizens' patriotism is susceptibility to their elect body's charade as a humanitarian crusader dedicated to ending tyranny and promoting freedom, democracy, and human rights the world over. This lie has been repeated often enough that it has become part of American citizens' self-image, and it renders them gullible to any humanitarian pretext concocted by their elect body. The U.S. elect body cunningly exploits this self-image and gullibility by representing all of its hegemonic ventures as humanitarian 'missions.' It used the pretext of bringing democracy and human rights to the Iraqi people to gain U.S. citizens' support for the invasion of Iraq. In this instance, Hussein's history of domestic tyranny and war crimes gave credence to the humanitarian pretext of delivering the Iraqi people from oppression. However, if Hussein had not already existed, the U.S. elect body would have invented someone like him to satisfy the ideals of American patriotism.

The hypocrisy of the U.S. elect body's posturing and self-promotion as righteous humanitarian crusader is demonstrated by various past international initiatives. For instance, to keep Iraqi oil flowing, the CIA facilitated Saddam Hussein's worst war crimes – namely, the Anfal campaign against the Kurds, the genocidal assault against the Marsh Arabs, and the use of poison gas against Iranian troops – by providing him with arms, money, helicopters, chemicals, and intelligence.

The U.S. elect body also authorized the CIA to give financial assistance, intelligence, and aid in the training of Taliban and al Qaeda fighters in Afghanistan in their jihad against the Soviet army. The hypocrisy of the U.S. elect body's self-promotion as righteous humanitarian crusader is evident as well in the billions of dollars of aid and advanced weaponry it gave to Pakistani General Pervez Musharraf, a corrupt and repressive villain with nuclear weapons. If the reason for invading Iraq was humanitarian intervention, then Pakistan deserved equal consideration. The U.S. elect body adopts a moralist attitude in judging the behaviour of other nations but takes an amoral 'realist' position in respect to its own strategic interests.

The U.S. elect body's manipulation of its citizens' patriotism is facilitated by a complicit corporate media. During the invasion of Iraq, hundreds of reporters travelled with the various military units, sending daily dispatches on the rapid advance of US armed forces. Closely monitored by military authorities, these 'embedded' reporters acted as virtual public-relations agents for the invading U.S. troops. Appealing to the worst tendencies of American patriotism, the U.S. media portrayed the death and destruction being inflicted on Iraqi society as a humanitarian crusade for democracy and human rights, thus making a virtue out of an unprovoked assault on defenceless civilians. At prime-time press conferences, they lionized the secretary of defense, Donald Rumsfeld, as he gleefully and arrogantly rehearsed the daily military carnage under the callous boast of 'shock and awe.'

Exercising self-censorship, the U.S. media kept the devastation inflicted on Iraqi children, women, and other civilians virtually out of the awareness of most American citizens. It should be noted that the media applied the same self-censorship during its reporting on the Vietnam War: concealing from U.S. citizens the horror of millions of civilian deaths caused by the U.S. military campaign, and the anguish and agony of injured and bereaved survivors. Atrocities like the contamination of large areas of the country with the long-lasting toxic defoliant Agent Orange are reported as abstract events, as if they were 'acts of God,' for which no one bears responsibility. More than a quarter of a century later, this herbicidal contaminant still claims victims, causing birth defects, cancers, and other deadly illnesses in the third generation of Vietnamese children. The U.S. elect body, however, denies all responsibility and refuses to pay for this crime of war, either as reparation or as a humanitarian gesture.

Likewise, following the destruction of Hiroshima and Nagasaki, the U.S. media refused to publish pictorial images of charred corpses of children, women, and other Japanese civilian victims, and they downplayed stories of the survivors' agony from direct and residual radiation burns. This was done not only to hide the monstrous atrocity but also because the U.S. elect body feared that such reports would incite public opinion against testing and building an arsenal of nuclear weapons.

The U.S. corporate media defends keeping the truth from its citizens under the patriotic pretext of 'serving the national interest.' But, if U.S. citizens are to perceive the wars of choice perpetrated by their elect body as war crimes, they require an honest and full accounting of the hundreds of thousands of children, women, and other innocent civilians wounded or killed by the U.S. military; and they need to see the maimed bodies and hear the cries of anguish and agony felt by surviving loved ones. If these atrocities aren't seen or fully reported, then, from U.S. citizens' perception, they haven't happened. Until they know the full truth of the atrocities committed by their elect body under the false banner of humanitarianism, they will not act to stop their elect body from repeating its war crimes. In this regard, the UN can perform an important humanitarian function in the aftermath of every war by mandating a systematic, comprehensive, detailed, and factual accounting of civilian casualties, and officially identifying the perpetrating nations and responsible officials. It should also proclaim a global annual day on which every country commemorates and grieves the horror of children, women, and other innocent victims maimed and killed in past wars.

As part of their systematic and intensive indoctrination into an ultra-nationalistic consciousness and patriotism, American citizens are conditioned to favour an arrogance of power by their leaders. They show a consistent preference for hawkish leaders, who confront their rivals with ultimatums and intimidation, over peacemakers; negotiation and compromise are regarded as weakness and capitulation. Mainstream Americans take personal pride in the projection of U.S. military power around the world; their nation's global military pre-eminence feeds their sense of exceptionalism. This circumstance gives immediacy to the question: Are U.S. citizens to be trusted to control the militaristic tendencies and ambitions of their elect body? Anxiety over the answer to this crucial question is exacerbated by the fact that Americans never renounce their support for hegemonic military aggressions by their elect body when they succeed. They do so only when they fail, and then they focus their criticism primarily on political and military incompetence, and on issues that adversely affect their own interests such as U.S. military casualties, financial costs, and damage to national prestige. They virtually ignore the unconscionable human tragedy inflicted on the innocent victims of these aggressions.

Human Sensibility

A full appreciation of how great a peril the U.S. elect body's dysfunctional responses to globalization pose for the future of humankind calls for a candid evaluation of its capacity for human sensibility. Human sensibility here refers to a respect for humanity that rises above self-interest. The issue of human sensibility is given particular imme- diacy by the U.S. elect body's massive arsenal, which gives it the mili- tary capability to destroy human civilization. Possibly, all that stands between humankind and a doomsday scenario is the U.S. elect body's human sensibility. Is it sufficient to inhibit deployment of its weapons of mass destruction as a last resort when, inevitably, its national and hegemonic authority are seriously threatened by the forces of global- ization? Its past conduct raises some serious concerns about the answer to this question.

On 9 and 10 March 1945, the United States dispatched more than three hundred bombers to Tokyo and, at an altitude immune from defenders, dropped nearly a half-million incendiary bombs on wooden homes. Sixteen square miles of densely populated urban neighbourhood were completely incinerated; the fires and superheated air killed approxi- mately 100,000 residents. In August 1945, in the span of seventy-two hours, the United States ordered the deployment of atomic bombs on the cities of Hiroshima and Nagasaki, killing an estimated 215,000 peo- ple and grievously maiming a million more. The U.S. elect body perpe- trated both of these massacres knowing full well that most fighting-age males were at the war front and that the victims would be mostly chil- dren, women, and older male civilians. These horrific atrocities against a civilian population crossed the moral line of generic crimes of war; they must be seen and condemned as crimes against humanity.

Crimes against Humanity

All violations of human dignity constitute assaults on humanity. Taking this meaning, assaults against humanity can be ranked on a scale beginning with sheer neglect, such as condoning ongoing poverty, hunger, and malnutrition in the midst of plenty; rising to state torture, executions, and terrorist attacks; expanding to the ideologically driven mass exterminations perpetrated by Stalin, Mao, and Pol Pot; and cresting with the genocide of Jews carried out by Hitler. When does an assault on humanity rise to a crime against humanity? This determination comes down to a subjective judgment. The International Criminal Court's legal definition of a crime against humanity is referenced to a threshold of widespread and systematic physical attack against a defenceless civilian population. My meaning of a crime against humanity is broader: I use the term to refer to any deliberate, brutal violation of human dignity, without reference to scale.

The Holocaust is different from all other crimes against humanity and unlike other genocides. The evil and horror of the Holocaust is beyond words, beyond pictures, beyond imagination, and beyond comprehension. It represents much more than sheer numbers and the depravity and butchery of Hitler and his Nazi madmen. First and foremost, Hitler's 'Final Solution' is a very personal tragedy for Jews; and only Jews can truly know, understand, and fully feel the pain, anguish, grief, and menace of this gruesome crime against humanity. However, it holds crucial significance for all of humankind and for posterity. While it was rooted in anti-Semitism, the Holocaust signifies more than anti-Semitism. It was an explicit denial of the humanity of Jews; and, by denying the humanity of Jews, it denied humanity as an intrinsic essence of all humankind. It stands as a crime against everyone's humanity. For this reason, the message of the memorials to the Holocaust goes beyond the need to mourn the greatest evil and tragedy in human history; the oneness of humanity demands that all of humankind declare 'never again.'

Crimes against humanity are generally attributed to morally pathological political and military leaders (e.g., Stalin, Mao, Pol Pot, and Hitler) and to totalitarian political systems. Such explanations are deficient because they neglect the fact that so-called democratic governments also have perpetrated crimes against humanity. To understand crimes against humanity, we need to go beyond leadership and political systems. The authority of leaders is derived from the power of the people, and, in nearly every case, the leaders who mandated crimes against humanity had the explicit support or silent compliance, if not acquiescence, of a significant part of their citizenry, without which they could not have perpetrated their atrocities. This indicates not just a morally pathological political and military leadership but a critical moral deficiency of the citizenry in general. In the absence of a humane moral social order, there can be no humane conscience and the people are vulnerable to ideologies that legitimate crimes against humanity.

Unless we create a global moral social order that acknowledges, values, and honours humanity as our ultimate shared essence, people will go on empowering evil leaders and remain silent in the face of monstrous crimes against humanity.

A pessimistic assessment of the U.S. elect body's human sensibility is confirmed and underscored by the fact that, after the end of the Second World War, it ordered no less than 230 more nuclear tests to 'perfect' its lethal bomb. Over the past six decades it spent many billions of dollars more on developing sophisticated vehicles for delivering its weapon of mass and indiscriminate destruction to any human target on earth. Today, it continues to spend huge sums of money updating its nuclear arsenal and developing new tactical nuclear weapons. To ease moral revulsion against deploying this horrific weapon, it is building 'user-friendly' miniaturized bombs, allegedly for 'limited use.'

Additional evidence for the U.S. elect body's deficient human sensibility is readily inferable from its war against Vietnam. Running for fifteen years, from 1961 to 1976, this war of choice spanned the rule of four U.S. presidents. Vietnam was spared from nuclear attack not out of human sensibility (witness its use of Agent Orange, massive bombings of civilian populations, and other atrocities) but because the U.S. elect body feared a retaliatory response by the USSR. Even so, this unprovoked war caused the deaths of over two million Vietnamese and 1.5 million Laotians and Cambodians; countless more suffered serious injuries. The victims included many civilian non-combatants including children and women. The U.S. elect body poses as a moral champion of prosecution and punishment of individuals who have perpetrated war crimes; however, its own atrocities against various innocent and defenceless civilian populations have always gone unpunished.

More recently, the U.S. elect body demonstrated a tragically deficient human sensibility by its decision to invade Iraq. Seven years after the beginning of the invasion, no one knows precisely how many Iraqi civilians have died as a consequence of this illegal aggression. The U.S. military has kept a meticulous count of its own dead but has deliberately hindered all efforts to gather valid and reliable statistics on Iraqi civilian deaths resulting from its invasion and occupation of Iraq, making it difficult to establish an accurate number. For purposes of public propaganda, the U.S. elect body fabricates and disseminates implausibly low estimates of civilian casualties (e.g., in December 2005 President Bush, without citing a source, off-handedly stated that 30,000 Iraqis had died in the war), and, without regard for authenticity, it quotes from reports that record the lowest numbers of civilian deaths. This manipulation of numbers makes all U.S. government statements regarding civilian casualties suspect.

Various studies of the numbers of Iraqi civilians who have died as a consequence of the U.S.-led invasion and occupation of Iraq have yielded widely divergent estimates. The reliability of the different figures is a subject of fierce debates. The following review briefly summarizes the methods and findings of three studies of Iraqi casualties which have received the greatest public attention. These surveys were conducted at different points in the conflict and with different methodologies.

A team of epidemiologists at the Centre for Refugee and Disaster Response at John Hopkins University's School of Public Health conducted a study between 20 May and 10 July 2006 designed to measure 'excess mortality,' that is the *additional* deaths incurred by the U.S.-led invasion and occupation of Iraq. The findings were published in October 2006 in *The Lancet*, one of the world's best-known, oldest, and most respected peer-reviewed medical journals. The study used a tested scientific sampling technique comprising a random selection of 47 household clusters and a sample of 1,849 households. The interviewers asked one adult person in each household about the date, cause, and circumstance of any deaths in the family during the 14.6 months before the invasion and the deaths that occurred in the 17.8 months after the start of the invasion. With the survey results extrapolated to the general population, the study's findings indicated that between March 2003 and June 2006 an estimated *additional* 654,965 Iraqis died as a consequence of the invasion and occupation. Of these excess deaths, an estimated 601,027 were a direct result of the violence, and the remainder were due to collateral factors such as increased lawlessness, degraded infrastructure, and poorer health care.

The Iraq Body Count (IBC) is an independent U.K.-based research group which compiles, maintains, and updates documented violent Iraqi civilian deaths incurred by U.S.-led military forces, insurgent action, sectarian violence, and increased criminal violence during and since the 2003 invasion of Iraq. The IBC's death counts are compiled from cross-checked media fatality reports of civilian deaths or of bodies found, supplemented by NGO, hospital, morgue, and other official sources. For the period from March 2003 to October 2010, this method (called 'passive surveillance') yielded counts in the range of 98,876 to 107,938 civilian deaths, and a total of 150,726 when combatant deaths are included. The accuracy of the IBC's passive surveillance count of reported civilian deaths in Iraq is compromised by several factors. The methodology relies heavily on information gathered by media, which report deaths almost exclusively in the big cities. Another primary source used in the IBC's death counts, Iraqi morgues, are notorious for inconsistent or non-reporting, and the victims of U.S. and terrorist bombings and sectarian killings are rarely taken to morgues, resulting in substantial undercounting of civilian deaths. Moreover, the Islamic requirement that bodies be buried within twenty-four hours of death has resulted in civilians being buried without official records; many deaths go unreported as families often bury their dead without notifying authorities; many more unknown and unrecorded victims of violence lie in mass graves, known only by relatives and friends. The Health Ministry of the Iraqi government has acknowledged official underreporting of the actual number of deaths by countless thousands.

Opinion Research Business (ORB), a prestigious British polling agency, commissioned the Independent Institute for Administration and Civil Society Studies (IIACSS), a polling/research company in Iraq which has a network of interviewers covering all regions of the country, to conduct a survey between 12 August and 19 August 2007. The IIACSS conducted face-to-face interviews with 1,499 of 1,720 randomly selected urban Iraqi adults, aged eighteen and over, in fifteen of the eighteen governorates within Iraq (two governorates were excluded because they were too dangerous to risk entering and one was declared off-limits by official authority). All subjects were asked if they had lost a family member by violence since 2003. Subsequently, between 20 September and 24 September 2007, some 600 additional interviews were conducted with randomly selected adults in rural areas of Iraq. Based on the combined surveys, the ORB, on 28 January 2008, published estimates of war deaths totalling 1,033,000 since the beginning of the 2003 invasion. The results are based on a nationally representative sample with a standard margin of error of +/–2.5 per cent. (It is worth noting that the larger ORB numbers lend a measure of credence to the findings of the Lancet Study inasmuch as they report deaths up to 24 September 2007, whereas the Lancet Study count ended on 10 July 2006.)

Four and a half years after the beginning of the invasion of Iraq, Oxfam International and a consortium of non-governmental relief agencies working in Iraq issued a report detailing the legacy of the U.S. elect body's hegemonic enterprise: it described a population devastated by chronic malnutrition, untreated illness, shattered psyches, lack of access to water and basic services, and the destruction of homes, vital facilities, and infrastructure. The report declared Iraq to be the fastest-growing refugee crisis in the world, with almost three million Iraqi citizens, mostly children (Iraqi government statistics report hundreds of thousands are orphaned), displaced by the invasion and occupation. Moreover, the invasion has left a legacy of ongoing sectarian violence and civilian casualties as part of daily life. The catastrophic aftermath of the U.S.-led invasion and occupation of Iraq has been virtually blacked out by the corporate media; they have no reporters 'embedded' in war-devastated neighborhoods to send daily reports and photographs showing and telling the story of ongoing destitution and the personal anguish and agony of bereaved children and parents.

The U.S. elect body's deficient human sensibility is evident not only in its acts of commission but in its acts of neglect. By failing to respond to urgent appeals by General Romeo Dallaire, commander of the UN peacekeeping force, to intervene at the inception of the Rwandan genocide, it, along with the elect bodies of the EU, Russia, and China, shares blame as an accessory in the greatest humanitarian disaster since the Second World War. And then there is the ongoing carnage in Darfur, where, according to UN estimates, 300,000 people have died as a result of violence, starvation, and disease and 2.7 million more have been driven from their homes. The catastrophe in the Republic of the Congo is even worse, with over five million casualties since 1998. All of the above named offenders – the United States, the European Union, Russia, and China – are morally chargeable with negligent genocide for not intervening to prevent or halt these atrocities; however, the U.S. elect body, as the self-proclaimed global moral leader with the biggest and best-equipped army in the world and with the capability to rapidly deploy large numbers of troops, carries special responsibilities and must shoulder the greater blame for not preventing these crimes against humanity. It is appropriate to note that, at the same time as it refused to make a relatively small military commitment to prevent the atrocities in Rwanda and Darfur, the U.S. elect body was providing Ethiopia with weapons and military advisers to overturn an Islamic government in Somalia, killing many and creating 300,000 refugees.

At home, the U.S. elect body's deficient human sensibility is evident in a host of social statistics that describe ongoing violations of human dignity and assaults on the humanity of its own citizens. According to Amnesty International, the United States ranks third in state executions after China and Iran. The National Center for Health Statistics ranks the United States – the world's wealthiest and medically most advanced country – twenty-eighth in infant mortality; the Substance Abuse and Mental Health Services Administration has reported that, in a given year, 3.5 million citizens are homeless, of whom 39 per cent are children; the U.S. Census Bureau reported that, in 2007, 45.7 million Americans lacked health insurance, of whom 8.1 million were children; and the Department of Agriculture reported that, in 2008, 36 million Americans, including 17 million children, struggled with hunger.

The U.S. Declaration of Independence mandates an egalitarian society. It states, 'All men are created equal'; but the country's citizens are not born with equal opportunity, not treated equally, nor regarded as equals. The Federal Reserve Board's 'Survey of Consumer Finances' shows that the top 1 per cent of Americans owns 34.3 per cent of the national wealth, and the bottom 40 per cent owns less than 1 per cent; and the dispropor-tion is growing. Edward Wolf, managing editor of the *Review of Income and Wealth*, states that, among Western democracies, the United States has the greatest wealth gap between rich and poor. Under this system of inequitable distribution, ethnic minorities fare much worse than Caucasians. When these facts are considered with reference to nearly a trillion dollars spent annually for military instead of socially productive purposes, the picture suggests a profoundly deficient human sensibil-ity. In the nation that pretentiously and self-righteously proclaims its commitment to the equality of all persons, the idea of rectifying this unconscionable gap between rich and poor by redistribution of wealth is condemned as 'socialism' and stridently rejected by the elect body.

The U.S. elect body's dearth of human sensibility is given a particu-larly ominous significance by its global military pre-eminence and its history of self-exemption from international law; there is no external authority that can hold it to account for its crimes against humanity. People the world over are dependent on American citizens to control the militaristic ambitions and actions of an elect body in command of an arsenal that can annihilate civilization in a matter of hours, and whose readiness to wage war has been whetted rather than tempered by its military pre-eminence. This places an extraordinary burden of respon-sibility on American citizens.

Individually and collectively, Americans demonstrate as much human sensibility as citizens in other societies. This is evident in their generous humanitarian response to victims of disasters ranging from tsunamis and earthquakes to AIDS; millions of lives have been saved as a result. On the other hand, Americans celebrate military victories with little regard for the number of casualties inflicted on the inno-cent and defenceless civilian population of the 'enemy.' For instance, when Americans speak of the human tragedy caused by the invasion and occupation of Iraq, they dwell almost exclusively on the tragedy of four thousand and some U.S. military fatalities. They seem at ease writing off as 'collateral damage' the hundreds of thousands of Iraqi civilian casualties, the millions of persons displaced, and the ongoing societal and physical devastation the invasion and occupation have caused. In the same vein, when the International Committee of the Red Cross reported testimony from soldiers who had witnessed or participated in the torture and abuse of detainees as young as eight years old, Americans did not protest and demand accountability from their government, as they do when their taxes are raised; there was no acknowledgment of guilt and no disposition of atonement; they appeared content to file such crimes of war by their military under the heading: 'It won't happen again.'

American citizens, generally, may be more righteous than their elect body, but are their human sensibilities profound enough, and is their control of the mechanisms of government sufficient, to restrain their elect body from deploying its lethal arsenal when globalization seriously threatens its authority? The answer to this question is a matter of supreme concern for all of humankind. It also raises some complex issues about the moral accountability of an electorate in a democratic nation for the actions of its elect body. I will address these issues in chapter 5.

Prospects

Every geographic region of the world is afflicted with historical interstate distrust and enmities. Since the end of the Second World War, the U.S. elect body has been able to exploit this intraregional volatility to extend its strategic hegemony by guaranteeing the geopolitical security of states if they cooperate with U.S. policies. For instance, NATO, which was created to guarantee the geopolitical security of Western European regimes against the USSR, has, by reason of U.S. military dominance, functioned as an agency of U.S. strategic hegemony in Western Europe. However, the collapse of the USSR and the emergence of the European Union have effected a reduction of national-security concerns in Europe. This is diminishing NATO's role as an agency of European security and dwindling the U.S. elect body's sway in Europe. We were witness to this when several European NATO members sided with Russia against the U.S. invasion of Iraq.

The EU, having dealt with a number of sovereignty issues, has a head start in the development of institutions and structures capable of easing historical interstate enmities and intraregional security concerns.

However, the growth of global economic interdependence is giving rise to supranational organizations and alliances the world over. Although all national societies greatly prize their identities and autonomy, their sense of nationalism is changing from a defensive parochialism to an outwardly oriented aspiration for regional acknowledgment and status; they are ready to yield selective elements of national autonomy to gain global economic and political influence and advantages through membership in regional institutions and alliances.

Currently, this is the case in east Asia, where economic and political relations between neighbouring countries are being transformed by their growing reliance on each other for imports and exports. A significant feature of this development is a web of bilateral and multilateral regional agreements that ease trade and access to essential resources. The next logical step is closer diplomatic relationships and the development of a regional free-trade zone. Economic integration facilitates political and social integration, and, as east Asian countries negotiate trade and investment agreements, the process will begin to blur national lines, as it has in the EU, further easing inter-nation distrust in the region.

New organizations such as the Association of Southeast Asian Nations (ASEAN) and the East Asia Summit, a forum of sixteen Asian states, signify progress towards regional institution building and cooperation that prefigure Asian alliances capable of performing regional security, peacekeeping, and humanitarian functions. As the assimilation and realignment of national jurisdictions of authority into larger regional trade associations and alliances proceeds apace, intraregional enmities, distrust, and national-security concerns will wane. Moreover, the decline of the U.S. economy and the fiascos in Iraq and Afghanistan have undermined confidence in the security guarantees by which the U.S. elect body binds its client states in east Asia.

The erosion of this strategic hegemony bears directly on U.S. economic prospects. Until recently, U.S. hegemony has served to enlarge its treasury at the expense of its client states and allowed U.S. citizens to live beyond the sustainable means of their domestic economy. The impending 'end of empire' heralds the end of appropriated prosperity. Already the elect body has resorted to borrowing from foreign governments, principally China, to make up the difference. Burdened with a colossal national debt, record budget deficits, unprecedented current trade deficits, and a depreciating currency, Americans face a dismal economic future of higher inflation and interest rates, a significant decrease in personal wealth and income, and higher levels of unemployment as many U.S. multinational corporations move their manufacturing enterprises and millions of production jobs abroad to take advantage of cheaper labour and foreign markets.

The dismal economic prospect is exacerbated by the fact that decades of living on the spoils from hegemony resulted in the neglect of domestic manufacturing and other production, which creates many jobs and supports a large labour force. Manufacturing was supplanted as the primary 'engine' driving the U.S. economy by the financial sector, which makes profits from buying and selling securities and greatly enriches only a few wealthy people. Dubbed 'Wall Street,' the financial sector, a top contributor to U.S. political campaigns, has gained dominant influence within the state oligarchic structure, and it effectively dictates the political agenda. This was evident in the government's ready expenditure of enormous sums of taxpayers' money to bail out financial institutions, a move that has created few jobs and done nothing for the manufacturing sector, even though production and exports are in a recession and unemployment is at a high level.

The performance of the financial sector is profoundly vulnerable to speculation and graft and when it fails the result is a cascade of other failures, causing major economic disruption, a huge depreciation of national wealth, and the loss for many citizens of livelihoods and homes. An indication of U.S. prospects for the future is provided by a study commissioned by the U.S. Treasury Department. It shows that, in terms of present values, the fiscal gap between contractual social-service costs and expected revenue will bring about bankruptcy and a default in the government's obligation for entitlement programs such as Social Security and Medicare by 2020. Already the payouts to retirees from Social Security exceed the program's revenues from payroll taxes and require infusions from general revenue funds. Moreover, the inevitable slashing of vital social programs such as Medicaid, food stamps, and other 'safety net' programs will leave many U.S. citizens in destitute circumstances, placing them in worse social-psychological straits than citizens of developing countries accustomed to lower standards of living and more modest consumer expectations, needs, and demands.

For a large majority of Americans, a steep reduction in their standard of living has been unimaginable. Depending on the scope and speed of economic decline, U.S. citizens may be disposed to abandon the partisan Republican and Democratic self-identifications and loyalties that currently divide them into rival camps and unite in a populist 'rainbow coalition' to democratize the oligarchic authority structure responsible for their social/economic distress and deprivation. The Internet and cognate technologies, such as cellphones, Facebook, and Twitter, enable citizens to circumvent the oligarchy's monopoly over mass communications and give them the means to organize a mass movement against the arrogance, extravagance, greed, and fraud of their elect body. They can halt the vast and senseless expenditure on weaponry, bring to an end their elect body's nefarious hegemonic stratagems, and facilitate a peaceful assimilation and realignment of U.S. national authority into a global jurisdiction.

On the other hand, a worse-case scenario could ensue if unemployment escalates to Great Depression levels and the economic collapse is so precipitous that public and private pension plans on which citizens depend no longer have the assets to meet the payouts and the govern-ment is unable to meet the basic needs of its citizens. The consequent public disillusionment and outrage may strip away their sense of destiny and their illusions about moral exceptionalism and bring the meaning of patriotism into question. The endemic predisposition of U.S. citizens to paranoia, referred to earlier, which heretofore has served to unify Americans against 'foreign enemies,' real and contrived, may mutate into a domestic mood of fear, betrayal, and loss of faith in their leadership and government. Social media offer a means of communication beyond the control of the state oligarchy, making it easier for protestors to organize and for the unrest to spread. Inflamed by sensationalist political provocateurs and demagogues spouting paranoia-inducing conspiracy theories, they may decide that the enemy is 'within'; anger could factionalize their patriotism and splinter national unity into reactionary populist movements. Taken to an unthinkable extreme, it could erupt into a craze of radical political and social turmoil and undermine the legitimacy of their system of government. Like religious extremists who selectively apply their scripture according to their self-serving interpretations, disgruntled Americans may selectively apply their constitution according to their self-serving interpretations. In a country that guarantees the individual right to keep and bear arms, militias could spin out of control and necessitate martial law to quell 'patriot' insurgencies.

The ultimate resort of most hegemons when confronted with the loss of their empire is the use of force to maintain their authority. In view of its extensively mortgaged economic future, its seemingly ingrained lack of sensibility, its sixty-year history of massive investments in its military arsenal, and the susceptibility of its nationalistic and patriotic citizens to deception and manipulation, a reasoned assessment suggests the possibility, if not probability, that the U.S. elect body will resort to desperate and extreme measures to preserve its hegemonic and national authority against the forces of globalization. Given its documented disregard for international law, the U.S. elect body could resort to the one defence where its supremacy is undisputed – its military might; and neither the international community nor its citizens will be able to stop it.

With its huge land- and sea-based arsenal of long-range nuclear missiles and the means to deliver them with reasonable accuracy, it is conceivable that the U.S. elect body could use them to bully and intimidate other nations to do its will; it has given itself that option by creating its lethal arsenal. Shielded by a 'Star Wars' missile-defence system, it could decide that its long-range 'stealth,' 'smart,' and 'user-friendly' nuclear weaponry, launched by remote control by strategists sitting behind computer screens in air-conditioned bunkers, will assure 'victory' with practically no risk of harm to itself. Humankind has reason to fear that an elect body that can justify maintaining a military budget larger than the military expenditures of all other nations combined is capable of rationalizing the deployment of its massive lethal arsenal as 'the lesser evil' to preserve its authority. This possibility is given immediacy by the fact that the U.S. elect body's foreign policy is significantly determined by its military dominance and amoral 'realist' mentality.

A forced retreat from hegemony is often followed by a heightened feeling of vulnerability and a widespread sense of being under assault. This sensibility usually generates an intensified nationalism and protectionism. In the United States, this mood was fuelled by the events of 9/11 and has been sustained by a continuing fear of terrorist attacks. History records that the time of greatest danger is when the rulers of a dying empire face its demise. In the past, the U.S. leadership has detonated nuclear bombs on human targets when there was no imminent threat to its authority.

Although the U.S. elect body cannot control the world with its military might, it can destroy much of it. The imagery that comes to mind is that of a dying star: in its last stages, a star implodes, forming a black hole that pulls everything within its range into its destructive vortex. Humankind must hope that, when the U.S. elect body is confronted with the inevitable reality that it must yield its hegemonic and national authority to the deterministic forces of globalization, it will have a leadership that will understand the need for global cooperation and have the human sensibility to concede its authority peacefully.

Summary

In the world today, globalization is manifested by international investment, trade, and monetary institutions; numerous bilateral and multilateral free-trade agreements; a growing corpus and jurisdiction of international law; an expansion and increase in global communication; and internationally shared social-psychological concerns over various global problems.

My theory of globalization posits that social-relational interdependence generates power which is always actualized as social-order authority to meet the need for social regulation. The expansion of social-relational interdependence and growth in shared knowledge and understanding into larger spheres involve the realignment of social-order authority into ever larger unitary jurisdictions, coextensively with the growing scale of power. As human societies expand social-relational interdependence and shared knowledge and understanding to global dimensions, the inevitable outcome will be the merging of all primary spheres of power and the assimilation and realignment of all social-order authority into a unitary global jurisdiction. Although globalization does not proceed in a linear or predictable mode – in the past, its progression has often been halted and even reversed by colonial occupations, world wars, cold wars, invasions, economic crises, protectionism, and other dysfunctional actions by elect bodies – globalization is the past, present, and future of humankind.

When I describe the forces of globalization as 'deterministic,' I do not mean that they are beyond human control. We can choose how we will respond to the forces of globalization, whether constructively or dysfunctionally; we can choose whether the assimilation and realignment of national and hegemonic authority will be accomplished by violent or peaceful means. In this regard, I have cited the non-violent dismantling of the USSR as a hopeful model of positive accommodation to the deterministic forces of globalization. Similarly, the peaceful emergence of the European Union and the ongoing diplomatic negotiations and progress on international trade, investment, and monetary agreements – although both developments are tentative and beset with avarice, distrust, deceit, and self-serving scheming on all sides – provide another hopeful indication that national elect bodies can work cooperatively to peacefully negotiate the globalization of their economic and political authority.

Our quest for the Good Society requires that we acknowledge and understand the deterministic forces of globalization so we can respond to them in a reasoned and thoughtful way. Obviously, the U.S. elect body is not the only perpetrator of dysfunctional responses to the deterministic forces of globalization; the list is lengthy, and it prominently includes the elect bodies of China, the EU, Russia, and many other lesser nation-states. I have used the U.S. elect body's policies and actions as a case study because of its global economic and military dominance; the future of humankind depends significantly upon how the U.S. elect body responds to the forces of globalization. My review showed a consistent pattern of dysfunctional domestic and international responses by the United States. Currently, by its domestic fiscal irresponsibility, the U.S. elect body is placing the world on a trajectory that threatens an unprecedented global economic disaster of unpredictable outcome. Its post-Second World War ventures to expand or secure its hegemony by military intimidation and force have resulted in appalling and costly quagmires, with bad outcomes for all of humankind.

The U.S. elect body's enthusiasm for war cooled briefly following its disastrous and ignominious defeat and forced withdrawal from Vietnam, an impoverished developing nation. Unfortunately, this chastened attitude changed upon the economic collapse of the USSR. Instead of conducting itself as a peer in the world community of nations and taking this as an opportunity for mutual cooperation within the framework of the UN to advance global disarmament, the U.S. elect body construed the disintegration of the USSR as a bloodless military victory and chose to establish itself as the world's sole superpower. This rekindled its propensity to achieve strategic hegemony by military stratagems, and it has generated an ethos of non-compliance with international treaties that is engendering regional militarization. In the Middle East, the U.S. elect body's military stratagem to establish its hegemony has intensified Muslim antagonism against the United States, playing into the Israeli-Palestinian conflict and destabilizing that region at a time when the forces of globalization create an urgent need for international trust and cooperation.

Although its global ascendancy is in decline, the United States remains a dominant political, economic, and military force; its elect body is still in a preferred position to play a vital role in a constructive accommodation to the forces of globalization and lead the world to the Good Society. Alternatively, it can bring about the annihilation of civilization. It is this reality that gives immediacy to the question I posed in the opening paragraph of chapter 3: How will the U.S. elect body respond to the forces of globalization? To realize a constructive accommodation to the forces of globalization, the U.S. elect body must be guided by a conception of history as a deterministic journey towards a unitary global jurisdiction; it must understand and accept that it needs to surrender its authority; and its policies and actions must be designed to facilitate a peaceful passage.

In the past, the dimensions of spheres of power and jurisdictions of authority were relatively small. However, as we journey towards the global world, the progressive merging of power into ever larger spheres, the consequent assimilation and realignment of authority into ever larger jurisdictions, and the exponential increase in lethality of weaponry are creating a potential for future conflicts of unprecedented magnitude. Every elect body in possession of nuclear weapons will pose a serious risk when its authority is directly threatened by the forces of globalization. In this regard, the U.S. elect body has put the future in greater jeopardy by flouting international law and undermining the UN's credibility and capacity to serve as an effective forum for mediating future potentially devastating confrontations.

Currently, we are in the very early stages of a worldwide merging of power into a unitary primary sphere which will bring the era of hegemonic and national authority to a close. The Millennial Generations can and must choose whether this realignment of authority will proceed peacefully and humanely or by wars, genocides, ethnic cleansing, and forced population transfers. We need to recognize violence as a dysfunctional response to the forces of globalization or we will be destined to repeat the disastrous conflicts of the past, only on a much larger and unprecedented lethal scale. This is the essential lesson of history that must inform and guide our quest for the Good Society in a globalizing world.

PART TWO

Social Order in Theory and Practice

4   A Theory of Social Order

Social order as I use the term in the following discussion comprises two elements: a structure of authority, and a set of social-relational values. Social order can provide stable and predictable social relationships, and it has the potential to humanize or dehumanize its subjects.

In chapter 1, I described social-order authority as the actualization of power for the purpose of governing social relationships, and I stated that the transformation of power into social-order authority is a subjective process, meaning that every social grouping has the capacity to self-determine the mode and form of authority by which it will govern its social relationships.

How can we actualize our power in a form of social-order authority to realize the Good Society? A full answer requires not only that we discuss the structure and social-relational values that constitute social-order authority; it also calls for deep reflection on human nature, humane principles, and morality. I will defer my discussion of social-relational values and the other important elements of social-order authority to later chapters. Here I will describe two basic structures of social-order authority: 'diffused' and 'centralized.'

Diffused social-order authority implies consensual self-regulation that corresponds with a people's need for social order; centralized social-order authority implies imposed regulation that corresponds to an elect body's ambition to achieve social control of the people. My discussion of these two structures of social-order authority is organized under two ideal types, which I term the 'moral mode' and the 'amoral mode.'

The Moral Mode

The term 'morality' carries a religious connotation; however, morality can and does function independently of religion. As it is used in the following discussion, morality has no religious subtext; its defining feature is an ethically premised consensus as regards mutual duties and responsibilities for governing social relations. Our knowledge of the earliest societies indicates that their social relations were regulated by a moral mode of social-order authority. That is, they lived in some form of primary social grouping such as the family or kin group in which social relations were governed by an ethical system of mutual duties and responsibilities. As these primary social groupings developed, functional social-relational interdependence and intergroup shared knowledge and understanding of their respective primary spheres of power merged into larger dimensions, and their particular social orders were assimilated into a corresponding, larger, unitary jurisdiction of authority. The integration of distinct social groupings under the new unitary social-order authority was accomplished within the moral mode.

My idea of the moral mode can take two forms: 'authentic' moral order, signifying diffused authority; or 'synthetic' moral order, signifying centralized authority. An approximate form of authentic moral-order authority is exemplified by what anthropologists have labelled acephalous societies, described as 'societies without rulers.' In such societies, social order is created through a process of consultation that involves all stakeholders, and the resulting normative values, mutual duties, and responsibilities regulate all social relationships within the group. Such a process of creating social order diffuses authority and the duty to monitor social behaviour throughout the social body; this form of 'rule of everyone by everyone' leaves a greatly diminished scope and role for centralized authority structures in the regulation of social behaviour.

Authentic moral order is based on the premise that power, a social-relational phenomenon, is a generalized resource and that authority, which derives from power, is a prerogative of the people. This implies that every member of a functionally interdependent group is entitled to equal agency in originating moral-order authority and bears corresponding accountability for its authenticity. Therefore, to qualify as authentic, the system of normative values, duties, and responsibilities that constitute moral-order authority must be created by democratic discourse. Democratic discourse is a design for transmuting the power of the people into authority of the people by a process of open, inclusive, and free public discussion that honours the views of all stakeholders equally. When every affected person becomes a maker and judge of social order, that order is perceived by individual members as a justified and fair collective expectation, not as an arbitrary or externally imposed limitation on individual autonomy and freedom. The resulting self-determined social order harmonizes individual and collective aspirations, thus diminishing selfish concerns and bridging the 'individual versus collective' divide.

Democratic discourse elevates human agency to the highest level and facilitates humankind's aspiration to the fullest development of their potentiality for humanity by involving everyone in a process of evaluation of the society's customs, laws, institutional practices, and constitutions. It provides an opportunity for those who currently are most victimized to eliminate any moral and legal codes that deny or violate the principles of universal and equal human dignity, and thus end the legacy of racism, sexism, homophobia, economic and political oppression, and other offences against humanity that are evident in all societies.

Democratic discourse features the opportunity for ongoing feedback and amendment to prevailing normative values, duties, and responsibilities as the needs of the group for social order evolves and changes. Since the rules of democratic discourse must be established by democratic discourse, the creation of authentic social-order authority is a dynamic process; it progresses to a stable social consensus on appropriate mutual duties and responsibilities through trial and error and is subject to ongoing re-evaluation.

An approximate version of democratic discourse was practised by the Blackfoot people of North America prior to colonization. Once a year all band members gathered to recall, reflect on, and evaluate shared social-relational experiences of the previous year, with the purpose of informing their collective moral knowledge and understanding. In these gatherings, the normative values, duties, and responsibilities that the members agreed had yielded positive results for their nation would be formally extended to all of their social relations. This ongoing process of democratic discourse provided each generation an opportunity to update the prevailing social order in accordance with accumulating social-relational experience, evolving knowledge, understanding, aspirations, and needs.

It is worth noting that our definition of authentic morality does not disqualify so-called received morality. Arguably, some of the moral codes of the world's great religions were established by an informal process approximating democratic discourse. For instance, it seems plausible that the rules of moral behaviour prescribed by the Ten Commandments followed from centuries of informal open, inclusive, and free discourse long before Moses vested them with sacred significance.

Synthetic moral order signifies a radically different process by which the system of normative values, duties, and responsibilities that regulate social behaviour is created and implemented: it is created by an elect body, and it is implemented by means of official indoctrination and sanctions. The moral rules are generally given sacred and/or legal standing. Synthetic moral order serves a profoundly different purpose than authentic moral order; it is contrived to centralize authority and legitimate control by the few over the many. Oppressive systems such as fascism, fundamentalism, sectarianism, and patriarchy exemplify synthetic moral-order authority.

Most elect bodies invest their synthetic moral order with a sacred significance to give greater force and legitimacy to their authority. In theocratic states, elect bodies exercise centralized authority over their subjects primarily through religious synthetic moral order. In Western societies, elect bodies use religious synthetic moral order in the guise of law, custom, and culture to fortify the legitimacy of their centralized oligarchic authority. Religious synthetic moral order is also a device employed for bringing communities constituting distinct spheres of power and jurisdictions of authority under hegemonic rule. For instance, European colonizers converted and indoctrinated diverse ethnic-religious indigenous peoples in their empires into a Christian synthetic moral order to facilitate centralized control.

The Amoral Mode

'Amoral' means outside the scope of morality. It differs from the term 'immoral,' which implies a violation of moral standards, and from 'moral anomie,' which means alienation from moral standards. The amoral mode of social-order authority has its roots in Enlightenment thought. Seventeenth-century European philosophers, in their quest for the Good Society, broadened the Reformation initiatives against the totalitarianism of the Roman Catholic Church from a purely theological discourse to one focused on securing everyone's human dignity and humanity through liberty and social justice.

Prior to the Enlightenment, most European elect bodies justified their governing authority as divinely sanctioned by God through the church. The Enlightenment *philosophes* discredited this rationale and advanced the idea that social-order authority was the prerogative of human, not divine, agency. However, the legacy of the *philosophes* is not only emancipation from the divinely sanctioned authority structures and dynastic rule of the church state. The revolt against the church state's religious doctrines of divine rule and divine law gave rise to a secular social order based on the legal authority of the state, which creates and enforces the law. Another consequential legacy is that the Enlightenment ushered in an era in which the Western world's quest for the Good Society was transformed from a moral to an amoral endeavour. As heirs of the Enlightenment, Western societies have undergone a continuous social-philosophical transformation from moral to amoral assumptions, with profound implications for their systems of social-order authority.

It is a key proposition of my thesis that this fundamental change in the mode of social-order authority in Western societies is the result of a crucial misapprehension that the tyranny of the dynastic rulers, who derived their authority from the church doctrines of divine rule and divine law, was a function of the moral mode of social-order authority. Reasoning from this assumption, philosophers of the Enlightenment concluded that the moral mode was inimical to liberty and social justice. Then, proceeding from this misapprehension, they advocated the amoral mode of social-order authority instead of championing moral reform as the way to enhance liberty and social justice. It is important for my later discussion of human rights to stipulate that the *philosophes* advocated the amoral mode only for governing individual-to-state relations. The extension of this mode of social order to all social relationships is a twentieth-century development.

The immediate experience of emancipation following the end of the church state's synthetic moral tyranny served to affirm the judgment that the social-political oppression under the church state was indeed a function of the moral mode of social-order authority, and that the amoral mode was required to achieve liberty and social justice. Latter-day disciples of the Enlightenment have uniformly adopted this evaluation of the two modes of social-order authority. Leading philosophers, social thinkers, and theorists like Marx, Nietzsche, Freud, and Durkheim, from their respective economical, philosophical, psychological, and sociological perspectives, all perceived the moral mode as antithetical to individual autonomy, freedom, and self-realization and advocated amoral models of social order.

This fundamental misapprehension of the moral mode persists in Western liberal thought to the present time and is embodied in social-contract theory as the legitimating philosophy of the secular state. Social-contract theory proposes that, in the 'state of nature,' humankind lived as autonomous individuals who were in constant fear of each other. Contract theorists imagined that, for self-protection, these autonomous individuals entered into a secular-legal 'social contract' with each other to establish social-order authority (the contract state) that would guarantee the security of their lives and property.

It is not my intention to dwell on the implausibility of social-contract theory as an explanation for the origin of the state; however, it is appropriate to note that the facts as we know them tell us that in the 'state of nature' individuals were not autonomous but lived as members of primary social grouping such as the family or kin group, which were regulated by some form of moral social-order authority. Moreover, the social-contract theorists' idea that these prototypical individuals valued their autonomy and insisted on contractual protection for their individual freedom disregards an essential fact of human nature: the desire for freedom becomes important through the experience of social-political oppression. If the imagined individuals in the 'state of nature' existed autonomously and independently of each other, then, logically, they would have taken their freedom for granted. Western intellectuals, however, have embraced this theory as the primary legitimating philosophy of the modern secular state.

The nineteenth-century French sociologist Emile Durkheim made a searching analysis of the decline of moral social-order authority in European society. He observed that in European societies the moral mode of social-order authority declined as the social scale and density of a society increased from small communities to large industrialized and urbanized societies. As a descriptive account, Durkheim's observations of European societies in his time were perspicacious. The correlations he offered as evidence are real. Based on an analysis of his systematic observations, he reasoned that industrialization and urbanization brought about a division of labour that differentiated people socially and psychologically. He posited that this development brought about the transformation of society from a 'mechanical' system of morally ordered relationships to an 'organic' system of amorally ordered social relationships. Durkheim concluded from his data that the moral mode is unsuitable for maintaining societal order in modern societies and that its displacement by the amoral mode is a natural, necessary, and inevitable outcome of industrialization and urbanization.

Various philosophers of the Modern Age have characterized the change in social order observed by Durkheim in different ways. Auguste Comte outlined a positivist science and described the change in terms of a shift from religious to scientific humanist premises; Herbert Spencer viewed it as a passage from homogeneity to heterogeneity; Max Weber regarded it as a metamorphosis from traditional authority to legal-rational authority; Ferdinand Tönnies described it as a transition from community to society. Underlying all of these diverse characterizations is the idea of inevitable change from a moral to an amoral mode of social order.

Contemporary Western thought embraces the premise that the moral mode is inimical to liberty and social justice as well as Durkheim's conclusion that it is untenable for social-relational order in a modern industrial society. Western intellectuals hold that the change to an amoral mode is essential to ensure liberty and social justice and to maintain social order. I propose that both the Enlightenment *philosophes'* premise and Durkheim's conclusion are reasoned from erroneous assumptions.

An Appraisal of the Modes

Which of the two modes – moral or amoral – best meets the needs of the Good Society? The Good Society needs a mode of authority that ensures individual freedom, social order, and social justice. Social order always necessitates the surrender of a measure of individual freedom. An appraisal of the two modes requires a consideration of which best maintains social order and secures social justice with minimum infringement on individual freedom.

The two modes of social order imply forms of authority with profoundly different implications and possibilities for individual freedom, social order, and social justice. Under the moral mode, based on authentic morality, social constraints are self-determined and harmonize with society's need for regulation of social relations. The individual is required to sacrifice only those freedoms deemed necessary by members for securing social order; that is, the moral mode establishes narrowly delimited social constraints, leaving alone the citizen's residual social space and life. Created by democratic discourse, the normative values, duties, and responsibilities secure social justice in harmony with citizens' aspirations; this gives rise to a sense of authenticity and ownership which translates into a widespread societal expectation and vigilance for individual compliance.

Under the moral mode, individuals are socialized into a system of normative values, mutual duties, and responsibilities from birth. Thus, the social-relational standards take root at an early age, before individuals achieve independence. The standards are received and experienced as a natural definition and as an inner guidance system to what is 'right' and 'normal' in social relations. To quote Ralph Waldo Emerson's dictum, the child 'acts it as life' before he or she 'apprehends it as truth.' The inner guidance system, the sense of authenticity and ownership, and the shared societal expectations, together, function as a structure of social-psychological support and affirmation for individuals. By determining virtually every aspect of social relations, this structure acts as an effective behavioural guide, especially for those who have difficulty navigating on their own, to an individual's duties and responsibilities.

Our experience with authentic moral social order is limited to relatively small pre-modern societies. As a result, many believe that the moral mode of social-order authority is inadequate for ordering social relations in large-scale, modern societies. Some social scientists point to the steep increase in crime and social pathology that occurred in Western societies concurrently with industrialization and urbanization as evidence that the moral mode cannot accommodate the social complexity associated with large social scale and modernity. This analysis, however, neglects the fact that both the Industrial Revolution and the cited increase in crime and social pathology occurred under the amoral authority of the secular-legal contract state. A better-grounded explanation than failure of the moral mode for the escalation of crime and social pathology in Western societies can be inferred from the displacement of moral duties and responsibilities, extending to the erosion of traditional moral affirmation of obedience to the law, which occurred under the amoral authority of the secular-legal contract state.

There is no cogently reasoned basis for the assertion that the moral mode of social-order authority is inadequate to guarantee individual freedom, social order, and social justice in large-scale modern societies; on the contrary, the blending of 'inner' and 'other' sources of guidance engenders an attitude of vigilance in the enforcement of social-relational duties and responsibilities that need not diminish when social scale increases.

Clearly, urbanization, modernization, and growing social scale pose a significant challenge to creating authentic moral social order. However, advances in communication technology and universal education make it possible to meet any logistical challenges to the requirement of democratic discourse. The Internet, with its various networking applications and cognate technologies, offers a medium and the means for democratizing discourse; it can inform all affected persons and provide them with the opportunity to participate in establishing authentic moral social order; it can ensure full transparency of the process and provide provisional characterizations of any emerging consensus. Such feedback and transparency will give citizens a sense of being listened to, motivate them to participate, and provide them with confirmation that the emerging consensus acknowledges their aspirations to the Good Society.

The amoral mode is a design for state control of citizens. Under this mode, the individual is permitted only those freedoms that do not threaten the authority of the state; that is, it establishes narrowly delimited spaces of legal rights, with the residual social space and life of citizens regulated by state laws that severely limit individual freedom. Unlike moral norms, state laws come into an individual's life only after the formative years of childhood, and they are abstract, ambiguous, and complex, with significant gaps between theory and practice. Whereas the moral mode relies significantly on internalized self-control, the amoral mode relies entirely on external legal control.

The amoral mode of social order and the secular contract state as the legitimating authority describes a system of 'synthetic democracy,' signifying centralized authority. Synthetic democracy functions as legal/administrative control with ultimate authority vested in an elected legislature constituted as a state oligarchy. Under synthetic democracy, state laws are created by an elect body to control the behaviour of citizens; they lack authenticity and citizens are disposed to view inconvenient laws as alien and problematical limitations on their personal autonomy. This produces a social-psychological dynamic very different from the moral mode. It fosters a pervasive mentality of searching for loopholes instead of a genuine regard for the law as a standard for social relations. The broad-based public cynicism about the law is heightened by the fact that the rich and influential, who can hire skilled lawyers and buy influence, often circumvent the law without negative consequences for themselves.

The amoral mode of social-order authority relies primarily on the fear of being caught and punished to motivate individual conformity. This necessitates an extensive, intrusive, and costly system of state laws and enforcement institutions. Moreover, it creates a vicious cycle of diminishing freedom because any increase in violent behaviour or even a particularly sensational crime incites a mass psychology of uncertainty and fear, and when citizens feel threatened they petition the state for more 'law and order,' that is, stricter laws and enforcement measures. Under the pretext of complying with citizens' demands, the elect body exploits this situation to expand the scope of its legal authority and control through various measures such as more intrusive search and surveillance, lowering the age of accountability, and increasing penalties for violations of the law.

Citizens consent to state encroachment on their liberty and expanded control over their lives because, absent moral authority, it is the only recourse available to maintain social order and protect them from crime and other social pathologies. They draw comfort and reassurance from the idea that 'law and order' is working whenever one or another crime statistic is reported to have decreased from a new crest level. This is the case even when the system cannot protect them from violence in their own neighbourhoods. Citizens lament the erosion of traditional moral standards of social courtesy, trust, and cooperation, attendant upon amoral social order, but they adapt and accept the evolving state of affairs as 'normal.' They have learned to live under an amoral social order.

This brief appraisal indicates that, in a globalizing world, the moral mode of social order, based on democratic discourse, is the best option for maintaining social order and securing social justice with minimum infringement on individual freedom. As such, it meets the needs of the Good Society. Yet it should be noted that, in the practical context of the real world, all societies need to govern with a mix of the two modes. I will elaborate on the appropriate mandates for the respective modes of social order in chapter 9.

5   Social Order in the Modern Age

When the *philosophes* discredited the church's doctrines of divine rule and divine law, and delivered social-order authority into human hands, they brought about the displacement of the prevailing system of government (and the associated legitimating sacred doctrines) by a new system and new, secular rationales for state authority. It ended the hegemony of the church and, as described in chapter 4, inspired the idea of a social contract as the legitimating authority and basis of the sovereign nation-state. This fundamental change in principle of social order ushered in the Modern Age.

Social-contract theorists rationalized and legitimated the centralization of authority on the basis of two ideas: 1) the original state acquired its authority by the voluntary contractual consent of autonomous and free individuals; and 2) the state is the indispensable foundation and condition for the social-order authority required for the protection of life, property, and liberty. Various advocates of social-contract theory have advanced different ideas and rationales concerning state authority. Thomas Hobbes envisioned a strong state because he considered humans to be basically selfish and in need of stringent control. Jean-Jacques Rousseau envisioned a strong state because he regarded it as representing the 'general will.' John Locke favoured a weak state with authority limited to functions essential for the preservation of life, property, and liberty. All endorsed the displacement of ecclesiastical and monarchical dynasties by a secular state and representative assemblies as the primary system of government, and all envisioned a state that would serve to safeguard liberty and social justice. However, recognizing the possibility that the secular authority of the state could evolve into a tyranny, the philosophers of the Enlightenment incorporated two fundamental principles into the social contract: the natural rights of man and rule by representation.

While the two principles are conceptually distinct, the philosophers of the Enlightenment saw them as reciprocally confirming and sustaining elements of social order to protect the individual from state tyranny. They envisioned the natural rights of man as an inviolable foundation for self-determination, and they imagined rule by representation as diffusing authority throughout the social body so that citizens could insist on their natural rights. In Western societies, rule by representation has evolved into a doctrine of synthetic democracy, and the natural rights of man have evolved into the doctrine of constitutional human rights. Respectively, these two doctrines have been adopted by Western societies as the principal foundations for governance and social relations. Let us consider how well they have met the *philosophes'* expectations.

A productive discussion of the two doctrines and the derived Western governing and social-relational systems requires that we free ourselves from the constraints of what Michel Foucault has called a 'totalizing discourse.' By this he means an encompassing system of prescribed truths which precludes any contrary ideas, knowledge, or perspectives. This describes the current state of discourse on democracy and human rights in Western societies. To criticize these doctrines is to go against powerful currents of Western intellectual thought and prevailing popular sentiments and convictions. Western democracy and constitutional human rights are declared to be exemplary and essential social-relational doctrines, and all other perspectives are left out.

The two doctrines have become so embedded in Western political and societal beliefs that not only ordinary citizens but also Western intellectuals are blinded to their fateful inadequacies as a guarantee of liberty and social justice. Western intellectuals' enthralment with these doctrines numbs their critical faculties and stifles meaningful discourse about their authenticity. Systematic, extensive, and grave deficiencies in the performance of Western democracy and constitutional human rights as a guarantee of liberty and social justice are routinely rationalized by Western intellectuals in terms of 'gaps in the law' or 'lapses in execution,' and so on. The fundamental doctrinal principles are virtually never questioned. Instead, they are aggressively prescribed for all societies as the imperative blueprint for social order in the Good Society.

Western Democracy

As discussed, the contemporary Western doctrine of democracy is rooted in the Enlightenment. The origin of the idea of securing freedom and liberty by means of rule by representation is a matter for conjecture. Various scholars have traced particular aspects to Greek notions of democracy, to ancient Rome's model of rule by law, and to the cultural traditions of the American Indian. With a bit of imagination, contributions to the idea of democracy can be teased out of various historical intellectual and cultural traditions. Whatever the source of inspiration, the *philosophes* idealistically conceived representative democracy as a device for diffusing authority throughout the social body by subordinating the authority of the state regime to the general will. They generally envisioned a form of government in which all are given consideration in the decision-making process, thus bringing about freedom through self-determination.

History records that the *philosophes'* ideal of democracy as rule by the people was stillborn. While rule by representation served to emancipate Western societies from the synthetic moral tyranny of the church-state, it did not liberate citizens from the oligarchic authority of elect bodies. What actually happened was that the petty nobility and merchant class of the time exploited the *philosophes'* ideal of democracy to marshal mass support for a rebellion against the authority of the church and dynastic rulers. When this objective was accomplished, instead of diffusing the authority of the old oligarchy throughout the social body, they subverted the *philosophes'* ideal by constituting a new oligarchic structure which they misrepresented as authentic democracy. In effect, rule by the few over the many continued seamlessly in the transition from the church-state to synthetic democracy as we know it in Western societies today. Western synthetic democracy centralizes authority and control in the hands of a hierarchically organized elect body and thus betrays the Enlightenment *philosophes'* expectation that rule by representation would diffuse authority throughout the social body and subordinate government to the will of the people.

Every Western democracy conceals an oligarchy, with the controllers of industry, commerce, and finance playing a dominant role. This assertion is exemplified by the Canadian and American legislative systems of government. In Canada, with a parliamentary system, the political-economic-social agenda for the nation is fixed behind closed doors by a cohort consisting of the Prime Minister's Office (PMO), cabinet

ministers, senior bureaucrats, contracted consultants, and a clutch of
lobbyists for major financial and corporate interests. When the PMO
presents its agenda in Parliament for a vote, elected members of the
governing party are not free to represent their constituents' wishes.
They confront a choice between voting for the PMO's agenda or banish-
ment from the party caucus, the latter being tantamount to political suicide. Almost without exception, they follow the directive of the PMO.
This rule-by-oligarchy is touted as 'representative democracy,' implying meaningful engagement and informed consent by the electors. It
should be added that the elected candidates in opposition also follow
the directive of their leadership, not their constituents.

In the United States, with its presidential system, the political-
economic-social agenda is set by an oligarchy (popularly referred to
as 'Inside the Beltway') comprising the administration, senior congressional legislators and bureaucrats, well-connected lobbyists, well-
heeled election-campaign contributors, and a consortium of influential
special interests. This clique effectively sets the U.S. national political-
econommic-social agenda. The charade of democracy was reduced to a
farce in the year 2000 when the U.S. Supreme Court superseded a full
and fair count of votes in the state of Florida and decided the election
of the president by a ruling based on the swing vote of one politically
appointed justice who judged the case on partisan lines. The farce is
magnified by the fact that the U.S. president, vested with the executive
authority to veto legislation, can override the will of a majority of the
elected Congress and Senate. It is fair to say that any unfriendly foreign
government installed and operating in this way would be labelled autocratic and illegitimate by the U.S. elect body.

Both the Canadian PMO and U.S. Beltway oligarchies cite 'democratic elections' as evidence that their agendas have the 'consent of the
governed' and that they represent the 'general will.' Western elect bodies exploit the concept of 'general will' much as the erstwhile church
exploited the concept of 'divine will': they proclaim their own interests
as representing the 'general will'; then they cite the 'general will' to
legitimate their self-serving policies. They also use the pretext of doing
the 'general will' as a buffer against citizen resentment of their abuse of
authority.

In the following discussion, I examine several significant issues that
bear on the fitness of Western democracy as a blueprint for social order
in the Good Society; I make suggestions for authentic democracy; and I
conclude with a look at the future of Western democracy.

Western Elections

Advocates of Western democracy promote the idea that the secret ballot, the principle of one-person-one-vote, and periodic elections for one candidate among several who bid to represent voters in the legislative assembly effectively diffuse authority, subordinate government and the bureaucracy to the will of the people, and produce self-determination. They back up their claim by citing electoral reforms which have extended the franchise to non-property holders, to women, to non-white minorities, and to younger persons. There can be no doubt that the cited electoral reforms have accomplished beneficial social consequences by obliging the oligarchy to take into account a wider electoral base, but they do not constitute evidence of diffused authority and self-determination. (Champions of Western democracy also point to political-administrative formations that ostensibly 'divide,' 'balance,' or 'distribute' authority as evidence of diffused authority and self-determination; however, these formations merely diffuse authority within the elect body, not the social body.)

Western elections are elaborate rituals that give the oligarchic structure a facade of authentic democracy, but it is sheer sophistry to proclaim that elections diffuse authority and signify 'consent of the governed'; at best, they signify citizen consent to be ruled by the winning faction. And even this statement must be qualified because, typically, only 60 per cent of eligible electors vote in elections; in a close election this means that as many as 70 per cent of the electorate have not given their consent to be ruled by the winning faction.

If Western elections do not diffuse authority and yield self-determination, then what is their purpose or function? Primacy in the state oligarchic structure carries the authority to devise and implement the legislative-policy agenda in such a way as to benefit particular interests. It also involves control over who will have access to highly lucrative government contracts, prestigious appointments, and other major advantages and rewards. Individual ambitions and avarice within the elect body cause disagreements over whose interests will prevail in the oligarchy. To maximize their leverage within the oligarchy, individual members of the elect body with shared interests and goals have organized themselves into political factions. To avert the contingency that rivalry among the factions might escalate into destructive internecine feuds or even violence, they have contrived political elections as an artifice for peacefully establishing factional dominance within the oligarchic structure. In short, the primary purpose of Western elections is not to diffuse authority throughout the social body but to establish factional primacy within the state oligarchy.

In Western societies, elect bodies have developed their factions into a stable multiparty political system, and they have entrenched the secret ballot and periodic multiparty elections in constitutional law as the procedure for establishing factional primacy within the state oligarchic structure. To simplify citizens' electoral choices, the factions distinguish themselves from each other by adopting broad ideological labels for their political parties, such as 'left' or 'right' and 'liberal' or 'conservative,' and by promoting contrasting stereotypical positions on various economic and social-value issues. They strive to foster voter partisanship and support for their faction by diligently promoting political party loyalty as a decisive act of individual economic self-interest and a meaningful expression of social-value self-identification. For many citizens, their party identification is so profound that they automatically endorse their party's position on an array of diverse, often contradictory, social policies.

Most Western elections are decided by the votes of independent or 'unaffiliated' elector. To attract these voters, the parties formulate opportunistic policies on basic issues such as national security, deficits, and taxes, and on controversial economic-ideological issues such as public versus private enterprise. They also appeal to segmental interest groups by taking public positions on controversial value-loaded social issues such as abortion, gay marriage, and gun control, and then they aggressively market these positions to the electorate. Invariably, their policies are devised primarily to promote partisan political interests, not to advance the common good. For their part, the media, which profit handsomely from campaign spending, incite and escalate controversy in public discourse by casting differences on contrived issues in terms of elemental self-definition, thus polarizing citizens into hostile camps. The result is that critical problems such as globalization, climate change, health care, education, homelessness, and hunger, which require citizen consensus and cooperation for solution, are neglected or become battlegrounds of partisan politics.

The assertion that Western elections are not about diffusion of authority but are essentially contests for deciding factional primacy within the elect body is oddly corroborated by the way Western mass media describe and chronicle election campaigns. Even as they extol the election process as a hallowed exercise of representative democracy, they format, chart, and market it as a sporting competition; it is all about victory – the public good is incidental. Media pundits and journalists seek to generate excitement with 'pre-game,' 'play-by-play,' and 'post-game' coverage and analysis. They identify selected candidates as 'star players,' review their past election 'performance records,' speculate on 'gaming odds,' dramatize close contests as 'face-offs,' and follow up with 'after-game' analysis. They pepper their commentary with a stream of sports metaphors: presidential primaries are characterized as 'Ballot Bowls,' close contests are 'horse races,' and candidates score 'touchdowns,' 'knockout punches,' 'three-pointers,' and 'home runs.' And, like most major sports competitions, Western elections generate a transitory emotional high or low for the 'fans,' and then life carries on as before. Some enthusiasts follow the election campaign from the beginning of 'the season,' others tune in just during the 'playoffs,' that is, the final days of the campaign, and some tune in only for the 'deciding game' on election night. For the customary 40 per cent of eligible electors who don't vote, the elections are mostly non-events.

Money is the lifeblood of Western election campaigns, and, with so much to be gained by achieving primacy within the oligarchy, the rival factions invest enormous resources in their campaigns. To acquire the essential funding, political parties and candidates promise political access and influence in exchange for large campaign contributions. The money is used to hire a virtual army of advisers, consultants, and 'spin doctors,' and to beguile, dupe, alarm, and otherwise persuade electors to vote for their party's candidates. Candidates are selected for their personal appeal to voters, and enormous sums are spent on media advertising to create an image of them as paragons of virtue, wisdom, and commitment to the public good. Any personal views or behaviour that belie the public image are vigilantly concealed. Because their true character is hidden, electors must evaluate candidates on the basis of a concocted persona.

To avert the possibility that election rivalry might escalate into confrontations that could jeopardize the oligarchic authority structure, Western elect bodies have evolved a strict code to manage their competition for primacy in the oligarchy. Competing factions are free to accuse each other, in graphic language, of being stupid, dangerous, evil, incompetent, and dishonest, thus discrediting their rivals' personal, psychological, intellectual, and moral fitness to govern. This uncivil conduct extends to exchanges of personal insults in the hallowed chambers of the legislature. But, while their behaviour is often offensive, their accusations are always carefully nuanced to avoid any negative connotation about the essential legitimacy of the electoral process for determining factional primacy within the oligarchic structure. The efficacy of this code of conduct was demonstrated in the U.S. 2000 election: the losing faction charged electoral misconduct and expressed great dissatisfaction with the Supreme Court's ruling, but their public statements on this travesty of democracy were carefully nuanced so as not to raise any public doubts about the essential legitimacy of the electoral system. All are committed 'playing the game' so as to safeguard the foundation of oligarchic authority; after all, in Western elections, the 'losers' of today will have a chance to become the 'winners' of tomorrow, take charge of the oligarchic structure, and enjoy the major benefits and rewards it offers.

Western citizens, generally, know that elections do not create meaningful self-determination. Many cite this fact as their explanation for not voting. Many vote as an act of good citizenship, but, even as they vote, they feel disenfranchised and excluded from the policy-making process. (On a personal note, I have dutifully voted in no fewer than two dozen Canadian federal and provincial elections. My vote has 'counted' inasmuch as these contests have provided me a periodic opportunity to register my preference among the competing political faction for primacy in the oligarchy, but casting my vote has never yielded a sense of meaningful self-determination. Even when the candidate and party of my choice won control over the levers of government, I was left feeling disenfranchised. I believe my experience is typical of the great majority of Western electors, and it is accepted as normal.)

Although Western citizens are aware that their government functions as an oligarchy, virtually all of us, including the disenchanted 40 per cent who usually decline to vote, heartily endorse Western-style elections and democracy. How can we understand this phenomenon? Part of the answer can be found in the 'totalizing discourse' which indoctrinates citizens to venerate Western elections and democracy as signifying rule 'of, by, and for' the people. A more complimentary explanation is that, while our 'democratic' system of government is seriously flawed, when we contrast it with other existing systems, we have good reason to feel that it is the most benign form of governance currently available to us. Western elections are a better way to determine which faction will have primacy within the state oligarchy than are hereditary successions or bloody coups and revolutions with their attendant major disruptions to social order.

When things go bad in Western democracies, the anticipation of periodic elections serves to ease popular anger by providing an opportunity to 'punish' the incumbent political faction; they also give the illusion of a 'regime change' without incurring political instability. Furthermore, in Western democracies, the periodic requirement to win voter support for primacy in the oligarchic structure obliges the ruling faction to project a semblance of accountability and responsiveness to citizens' needs and aspirations. In the domestic arena, this yields a greater measure of liberty and social justice than any other contemporary system of government, and it deters the more flagrant misuse of authority, political misconduct, and mismanagement – as well as gross instances of corruption – found in most autocratic states. In the arena of foreign affairs, however, Western democracy does not give citizens enough control of the mechanisms of government to restrain their elect body from deploying its lethal arsenal when its authority is seriously threatened.

Constitutional Supremacy

The principle of 'constitutional supremacy' calls for each law to be interpreted by the judiciary in accordance with its understanding of the national constitution. Under this principle, the courts have the authority to strike down any law they deem 'unconstitutional,' that is, inconsistent with their interpretation of the national constitution. Traditionally, the role of the court was limited to ensuring that laws were applied correctly and fairly, in accordance with the elected legislators' intended meaning. However, under the principle of constitutional supremacy, the appointed judiciary has been transformed from independent arbiter of the law to autonomous arbiter of legal principles. Instead of referring problematical laws back to the elected legislators for clarification of their intent, they can reject laws and compel the elected legislators to amend existing laws and pass new laws that conform to the courts' interpretation of the constitution. In effect, they function outside the parameters of democracy and they do so virtually without redress from the elected legislators.

The U.S. federal court system presents many examples of rule by the judiciary. A notable instance is the action taken by the Supreme Court on the Communications Decency Act of 1996. This act of the U.S. Congress was conceived in response to widespread public demand for protection of children from exposure to pornography and other forms of offensive images and language being transmitted through cyberspace. The act was passed by large majorities in both houses of Congress and was signed into law by the U.S. president. Public-opinion polls showed that the act had the support of an overwhelming majority of citizens. However, upon its first challenge by the American Civil Liberties Union, the appointed judges of the U.S. Supreme Court ignored the will of the people and ruled that the act was an intolerable infringement on the constitutional freedom of expression. The court's ruling effectively suspended the enforcement of the law until elected representatives amended it to conform to the court's interpretation of legal principle and the constitution. Later, we will see that this case has special significance because, in their ruling, the judges implicitly rejected the validity of any community moral-value standard which infringes on individual human rights.

Even as advocates of Western democracy insist that the free election of legislators signifies government 'of, by, and for the people,' the traditional mandate of elected representatives is being progressively eroded by the ongoing transfer of significant areas of social-order authority from the legislative branch to the judicial branch of government. The courts profess to exercise their growing authority under the pretext of protecting democracy, but, however commendable the underlying motives and ethical justifications may be, the shift of authority over significant areas of citizens' daily lives to a simple majority of politically appointed Supreme Court justices, who deliberate in secrecy, unencumbered by any obligation of transparency or to do the will of the people, diminishes the elect body's accountability and responsiveness to its citizens. These are the very qualities that are cited as distinguishing Western democracy from autocratic systems of social-order authority. It is worth noting that this reorchestration of roles within the oligarchic authority structure, and the consequential erosion of the legislature's mandate to represent the electors, is being accomplished with the tacit collaboration of the legislative branch.

The Minimal State

Western elect bodies are further undermining the elected legislatures' mandate to do the will of the people by making a concerted move towards a 'minimal state.' This term refers to the downsizing of government infrastructure by subcontracting selected traditional functions such as statutory social services and other work to the private sector. By moving delivery of public services to the private sector and outside the control of government, the elect body shifts significant authority over these services away from elected officials to the corporate sector.

The minimal-state initiative has generated a factional political debate within the elect body, between the ideological 'right' and 'left,' framed in terms 'big government' versus 'little government.' The 'right' says that it champions 'little government' to free citizens from the inefficiency and oppression of government bureaucracy – an argument that glosses over the fact that this approach reduces government regulation over business and shifts sizeable public funds into corporate coffers. The 'left' says that it champions 'big government' to protect citizens from greedy, profit-driven corporations; but this rationale ignores the contradiction in the notion that 'big government,' which is controlled by the elect body, will protect citizens from the corporation, which is controlled by one and the same elect body – as if one-half a school of sharks will protect swimmers from the other half.

The move to a minimal state signifies another reorchestration of roles within the oligarchic authority structure to accomplish more effectively and efficiently the elect body's agenda for the protection and enhancement of its property, status, and privilege. Like the judicialization of legislative authority via constitutional supremacy, the privatization of government functions implied by the minimal state will erode the mandate of duly elected representatives and reduce the state oligarchy's obligation of transparency, accountability, and responsiveness to its citizens. To realize the ideal of democracy, it is essential that elected representatives be empowered to do the will of the people. It is ironic that Western elect bodies market the idea of the minimal state, which diminishes the authority of elected representatives, as 'liberation' of citizens – in other words, liberation from democracy.

Authentic Democracy

The Good Society needs authentic democracy, that is, government designed as a collective enterprise to serve the common good. This implies diffusion of authority throughout the social body and citizen control over the development of policies and decisions of government. Western elect bodies are quick to disparage and dismiss any move to expand the role of citizens in the process of formulating government policy and decisions as 'inefficient,' 'vulnerable to impulse or gridlock,' 'pandering to the lowest common denominator,' or 'susceptible to tyranny of the majority.'

To realize authentic democracy, we need to change the purpose of elections from their present function of establishing the elect body's factional primacy within the ruling state oligarchy to that of establishing the authority of the people. This requires that the existing dysfunctional system of partisan politics and its pervasive practice of lobbyists paid to suborn legislators be supplanted with a non-partisan governing system that works to achieve the consensual common good. It also requires effective interactive arrangements designed to inform and engage the electorate in a discourse designed to subject the decision-making process to the will of the people.

To accomplish this will require a fundamental remodelling of the political structure and culture of Western democracy. A comprehensive discussion of how we might achieve authentic democracy is beyond the scope of my thesis; however, we can make an auspicious beginning at creating such a political structure and culture by establishing an open, transparent, and non-partisan merit-based system of candidate selection. It requires, as a first step, meaningful involvement by all citizens in the process of selecting candidates for the legislature. In this regard, we can learn something from the process used historically by the Mohawk nation: candidates for their governing councils were selected by a consensus of 'clan mothers' who had watched them as growing children for qualities of honesty, generosity, wisdom, and leadership.

Restructuring Western democracy to achieve a workable system for vetting and selecting candidates, emphasizing personal qualities such as those prized by the Mohawk, is a realistic objective. In broad outline, this could be accomplished by mandating a non-partisan commission in each electoral constituency to conduct open, interactive, transparent, extensive, and intensive hearings regarding the credentials of potential candidates. Such a merit-based selection system would enable voters to choose their representative with full information about the people who are on the ballot. The electors of each constituency would fix the number of eligible candidates, set periodic election dates, and equitably finance the nominated candidates' campaigns. The resulting elected legislative assembly would periodically choose a head of state and cabinet officers, applying the criteria of honesty, generosity, wisdom, and leadership. A parallel system could be established for regional legislatures. Elected candidates as well as the leader and cabinet officers would be subject to official review and recall by their electors for predetermined grounds.

Authentic democracy requires that the authority of elected candidates to carry out the will of their constituents should be maximized by enlarging the legislative mandate. In particular, the lawmaking authority that has been appropriated by the courts under the principle of constitutional supremacy, and the legislative authority that has been eroded through privatization of government functions, must be restored.

Obviously, the suggested reforms involve profound complexities and formidable challenges; however, they are clearly within human capability. The engagement of citizens in a democratic discourse to establish a system of government that will meaningfully involve them in an interactive process of selecting candidates, determining the political agenda, and making decisions will enhance the legitimacy of elected government, create public confidence, and appeal to societies that currently reject Western synthetic democracy.

The Future of Western Democracy

Western democracy emerged within a national polity and evolved and reached its high point within the framework of the sovereign nation-state. The forces of globalization are bringing about the progressive assimilation and realignment of traditional nation-state authority. This trend is evident in the evolution of the EU and emerging regional organizations like ASEAN, the Gulf Cooperative Council, the African Union, and the South American regional-integration initiative, Mercosur. As discussed earlier, the authority of all national governments will be significantly reduced as these regional alliances develop political constitutions, governing structures, and institutions with capacities for making and enforcing laws, developing foreign policy, authorizing diplomatic relationships, and carrying out regional security and humanitarian functions.

How will Western democracy fare in the context of these emerging regional alliances? In the case of the EU, formerly non-democratic central and eastern European regimes have dutifully adopted the Western practice of holding periodic multiparty elections. But the shift of authority from national to regional jurisdictions will profoundly change the political dynamic that sustains Western synthetic democracy. In the Modern Age, national elect bodies were able to exploit state oligarchic structures for major personal advantages and benefits. The waning of the nation-state in the global age, however, will greatly reduce the role and authority of domestic governments. A plausible scenario is that they will be reduced to implementing and monitoring the terms of the international economic agreements and administering essential domestic social and civic programs.

In the global age, elect bodies will be able to increase their authority primarily by playing a bigger role in regional and global institutions. To maximize their authority, the various national elect bodies will be motivated to form new political alliances and factions and strive for primacy in the regional legislative bodies. In these circumstances, the incentive for partisan rivalry for primacy in the state oligarchy will languish, eroding the primary function and purpose of national elections. Regional legislative bodies, remote from domestic electors, will rule with even less accountability to the people they govern. This will be the case especially in regional alliances comprising states without a tradition of Western-style democracy. While some form of democracy may endure, the prospects for Western-style democracy in the global age are problematic, indeterminate, and gloomy.

Human Rights

Human-rights doctrine achieved prominence in Western societies following the Second World War. U.S. President Franklin Delano Roosevelt's famous speech on the 'Four Freedoms' (freedom of speech and expression, freedom of worship, freedom from want, freedom from fear) to the U.S. Congress in January 1941 provided inspiration and specified some principles for an international human-rights charter. A year later, on 1 January 1942, all of the Allied powers signed a declaration committing them to defend life, liberty, and religious freedom and to preserve human rights and justice in their own countries as well as in other lands. In October 1942 British Prime Minister Winston Churchill delivered a speech in which he anticipated a time when the world struggle would end with the 'enthronement of human rights.'

The Dumbarton Oaks proposal of 1944 for the establishment of the United Nations emphasized respect for human rights and fundamental freedoms. The crowning event in the history of the human-rights movement occurred on 10 December 1948, when the United Nations proclaimed the Universal Declaration of Human Rights. The thirty articles of the Universal Declaration stand as a global charter upholding the principle of universal, inherent, and inalienable human rights. Since the Second World War, this principle has become the pre-eminent civil doctrine in Western societies and has had a tremendous influence on Western social-political conceptions and justifications for individual freedom and social justice. The purpose and function of all political, economic, legal, social, and educational institutions and systems are founded on the assumption that universal, inherent, and inalienable human rights constitute the only valid doctrine for ordering human relations.

The logic of human rights has become so deeply imbedded in Western culture and consciousness that it constitutes the 'cognitive lens' through which virtually all of life is viewed, interpreted, and understood. Every sphere of living is increasingly governed by a social order predicated on this doctrine; it is the standard that orders citizens' relationships to the state, to the community, and, increasingly, to each other. It significantly establishes citizens' social and civic identity; it is experienced as the 'natural order' of life. The discussion that follows elaborate some significant inadequacies of human-rights doctrine as a blueprint for social order in the Good Society. I want to stipulate here that this discussion refers to the *constitutionalization* of human-rights doctrine, not to the idea of statutory human-rights laws as protection for liberty and social justice. I propose that human-rights doctrine lacks the authenticity to be accorded the status of constitutional supremacy that trumps all other laws and community moral standards.

Theory

The Western doctrine of human rights has its roots in the Judeo-Christian idea that humankind is created in God's image. By virtue of that distinction, every individual is said to be divinely endowed with a natural right to human dignity – a right affirmed by 'natural law,' meaning the immutable and pre-eminent law of God. This divinely endowed natural right is deemed to exist independently of any human legal, moral, or other authority and must not be violated by anyone or by society.

The philosophers of the Enlightenment needed a secular rationale for the existence of natural rights. To this end, they declared as self-evident that these rights resided in the nature of humankind 'by virtue of being human.' Although they were not all of one mind as to the precise meaning of natural rights, the Enlightenment philosophers agreed that these rights were universal, inherent, and inalienable; that they entitled every individual to liberty and social justice; and that they constituted an essential article of the social contract as the basis for governance.

Such a fundamental change of rationale for the existence of natural rights – from divinely endowed and protected by natural law to

self-evident and protected by contract – implied a radically new conception of human nature and called for an empirically grounded and
systematically reasoned theory for the existence of natural rights.
However, the secular-philosophical rationale for the existence of human
rights hardly ventures beyond a cosmetic makeover of the theological doctrine of natural rights. For the most part, it simply plagiarizes
theological axioms and gives them secular labels: 'divine endowment'
was characterized as 'the virtue of being human'; 'divine order' was
renamed 'the natural order'; 'the Garden of Eden' was labelled 'the
state of nature'; and 'divine law' was supplanted by 'constitutional
law,' signifying ascendancy over all contrary laws and customs. It provides no empirically grounded rationale as to what virtue uniquely
endows humankind with universal, inherent, and inalienable human
rights.

The want of an empirically grounded and systematically reasoned
theory of universal, inherent, and inalienable human rights has resulted
in practical problems in the application of the doctrine. Nearly every
identified human right is vulnerable to contradiction by some other
existing or arguable human right, and some of the contradictions are
impossible to mediate. In what must be deemed the summit of unrea-
son, the human right to freedom of expression gives measured constitutional protection to purveyors of hate literature which violates the
right to personal security and freedom from fear.

To salvage the authenticity of universal, inherent, and inalienable
human rights when two rights conflict, some scholars have advocated
a hierarchy of human rights. They conceive of 'core rights' and 'lesser
rights,' and assert that the former have primacy over the latter. But, if
we accept this proposition, we need a principled empirical basis for distinguishing 'core rights' from 'lesser rights.' Some hold that this determination should be made in accordance with democratic principles.
However, if 'core rights' are to be established by popular referendum,
then the determination becomes politicized and we risk 'tyranny by the
majority.' In the absence of an empirically grounded and systematically
reasoned theory of universal, inherent, and inalienable human rights,
the Western doctrine is readily transmuted into dogma.

Legislative and Judicial Practice

To comprehend the change from the moral mode to the amoral mode
of social order in Western societies, we need to understand how the

doctrine of human rights affects Western legislative and judicial conduct. Displacing the church-state by the contract- state called for the secularization of social order. However, to ease the transition from sacred to secular social order, the new elect body of the contract-state simply enacted many of the existing synthetic moral values, duties, and responsibilities prescribed by the church-state into secular law. This expedient served to meet the immediate need for seamless social regulation; it also served to legitimate the new elect body's authority by creating a popular perception that traditional sacred values and rules were still being honoured.

Initially, advocates of church-state separation focused on eliminating the authority of the church from government; they did not consider the codification of traditional religious values, duties, and responsibilities into secular law as a violation of the principle of church-state separation. A serious appreciation and acknowledgment that such religion-based statutory law constituted a violation of the principle of church-state separation came later, after the doctrine of human rights was elevated to constitutional status.

The constitutionalization of human rights raised to prominence two basic principles underlying legislative and judicial interpretation of the separation between church and state: constitutional supremacy and moral neutrality. The principle of constitutional supremacy, as previously explained, obliges legislators to conform new legislation to constitutional human-rights doctrine; also, it requires judges to give priority to human rights when they adjudicate conflicts between human-rights claims and statutory laws. It effectively authorizes and requires the court to declare unconstitutional (i.e., void) any law it deems inconsistent with its interpretation of human-rights doctrine. The principle of moral neutrality obliges legislators to conform all laws to secular standards and requires judges to exercise unfailing vigilance in the detection and voiding of any religious values, duties, and responsibilities in the adjudication of extant state laws. In tandem, these two principles have had the effect of morphing the standard of church-state separation from the elimination of church authority in government to the separation of religion and law. Since the end of the Second World War, Western legislators and judges have diligently striven to eliminate religious standards from all state laws.

The treatment of abortion in Western societies affords an example of how human rights have affected the adjudication of religious standards in law. Traditionally, prohibition of abortion was based on religious values in law and those opposed to abortion framed their opposition in a religious-moral idiom. This began to change when the right to abortion was framed as an issue of social equality, and laws restricting access to abortion were successfully challenged in court as a violation of a woman's constitutional human right to reproductive autonomy and choice. In response to this development, anti-abortionists renamed their movement 'pro-life' and transformed it from a religious-moral cause to a legal human-rights cause. They defined embryos as living human beings who, as such, were entitled to the same constitutional human right to life as any other living person. In terms of realpolitik, the debate over access to legal abortion in Western societies is now fully in the domain of amoral human-rights jurisprudence.

In the last two decades, Western court rulings indicate a progressive broadening in judicial constructions of what signifies a violation of the human right to freedom. Although neither the principle of church-state separation nor the separation of religion and the law require the elimination of moral standards from law, there is a growing judicial disposition to regard any societal moral standard in state law that constrains individual freedom as a constitutionally proscribed infringement and latent violation of individual rights. Evidence for such a judicial attitude is provided by the previously described U.S. Supreme Court ruling on the constitutionality of the Communications Decency Act of 1996. A more prosaic example is the 1994 ruling of a court in Ontario, Canada, on a human-rights-based challenge to a municipal bylaw prohibiting 'lap dancing.' (This oddly named activity involves a more-or-less nude female performer grinding her derrière against the groin of a clothed male customer.) Although the court upheld the bylaw, the judge pointedly disavowed that his ruling was based on moral considerations. He declared that the decision was impelled exclusively by the need to protect society from unhygienic activity.

This legal construction of moral neutrality is fortified by an influential judicial ethos, one that can be readily inferred from the tendency of judges to affect an air of judicial pluck, usually couched in terms of 'advancing the frontiers of liberty,' when they outlaw enforcement of constraining moral standards. Conversely, judges who make a ruling that might be perceived by colleagues, the media, and other significant parties as upholding enforcement of a constraining moral standard usually assume a defensive public posture; they feel obliged to stipulate, as did the Ontario judge, that their ruling does not invoke a standard of moral 'rightness' or 'wrongness.'

Western judiciaries rationalize their broadening construction of moral neutrality as accommodating evolving societal standards; they say that their interpretation of human- rights doctrine is 'keeping up' with the changing realities brought about by a societal drift to amoral standards. This rationale has some surface validity; however, it obfuscates the fact that the judiciary's broadened construction of moral neutrality leads and fosters the very amoral drift it purports to be accommodating. By exercising their legal authority under this expanded criterion of moral neutrality, Western judiciaries are changing the foundation of social order from moral standards to amoral legal principles. Moreover, the progressive emancipation of the individual from consensual moral restraints is creating an immuring dependency upon the state for social order; without moral tools, when citizens are confronted with social disorder, the only recourse available to them is to demand more state laws and stricter enforcement measures to control harmful social behaviour.

The judicial-legislative purging of moral values, duties, and responsibilities from state laws implies a profound change from the Enlightenment *philosophes'* idea of natural rights as a design for *civil* liberty (a guarantee of individual liberty vis à vis the state) to an emphasis on *social* liberty (a guarantee of individual liberty vis à vis the moral community). This change is bringing out the underlying opposition that exists between constitutional human rights and the moral mode of social-order authority: as human-rights legislation and adjudication progressively undermine moral standards, proponents of moral-order authority become radicalized or retreat into religious enclaves to protect their moral values. Former pope John Paul II, who hailed the UN's Universal Declaration as the 'conscience of mankind' and devoted much of his life to championing human rights as the universal standard for realizing social justice, in the latter years of his tenure condemned the human-rights movement's shift in emphasis from civil to social liberty as a change 'pitted against family and against man.'

Individual Liberty

Proponents of constitutional human rights conceive of them as protection for individual liberty and believe that every new or expanded human right enhances the individual's agency and freedom to construct his/her human selfhood. They confuse individuality with individualism; although human rights are individually held, human-rights laws are not individualized. All citizens are subject to the same set of state-mandated human-rights laws. Thus, the agency and freedom of individuals to construct their human selfhood is limited to uniform state-stipulated confines.

In practice, there exists a fundamental and irreconcilable contradiction between constitutional human rights and individual freedom. This is the case because every constitutional human right requires corresponding state laws to protect the implied freedom and these laws, in turn, require the extension of bureaucratic regulations for their implementation and enforcement. In effect, the liberty warranted by constitutional human rights is limited to narrowly specified freedoms circumscribed by a web of legal and administrative restrictions that constrain individual autonomy. In this regard, the clamour in Western societies for more 'law and order,' discussed above, places individual liberty in double jeopardy. Western citizens, habituated to counter any infringement of their freedom resulting from more 'law and order,' routinely demand offsetting constitutional human-rights protection for their civil and social liberties. The consequential expansion of the state's mandate to intrude on the daily lives of all citizens, and the associated legal and administrative exclusions, prohibitions, and limitations, result in a spiral of expanding state control and diminishing individual freedom.

In 1788 James Madison observed: 'Since the general civilization of mankind I believe there are more instances of the abridgement of freedom of the people by gradual and silent encroachment of those in power than by violent and sudden usurpation.' The evolution of human-rights doctrine in Western societies confirms his cautionary observation. Even as human rights are expanded in the name of civil and social liberties, the outcome is that more and more of a citizen's life and basic freedoms is being brought under the authority of the elect body's state oligarchy. Instead of advancing individual liberty, human-rights doctrine accomplishes the opposite; it serves as an instrumentality by which the elect body centralizes authority and controls the many.

Given its deficiencies, why do Western intellectuals continue to champion human rights as the best doctrine for ensuring individual liberty? Here we are witnessing an instance of what Foucault called a 'totalizing discourse': Western intellectuals' intensive indoctrination in human-rights doctrine has rendered them unable to think critically about it. This state of mind is reinforced by the protection of human rights in state constitutions and special charters. These influential symbols of the 'common good' invest the doctrine with a hallowed aura which deters serious scholarly critique.

Another explanation for the sanguine attitude of Western intellectuals about the erosion of freedom that results from the expansion of human-rights laws, regulations, and state enforcement may lie in their confidence that Western-style democracy will protect their liberty. However, in the wake of 9/11, we have witnessed in Canada and the United States, two citadels of Western democracy, how contingent and tenuous is the guarantee provided by democracy for human rights and individual liberty.

The Canadian Charter of Rights and Freedoms states explicitly and unequivocally that 'everyone has the right on arrest and detention to be informed promptly of the reasons therefore, and to be presumed innocent until proven guilty according to law in a fair and public hearing by an independent and impartial tribunal.' Yet, under the pretext of defending the nation against terrorists, the Canadian government expeditiously created the Anti-Terrorism Act (December 2001), which subverts democratic protection for constitutional human rights. The act authorizes the minister responsible for its implementation to issue a security certificate based on secret allegations which neither the accused nor the lawyer of the accused are allowed to see. Under authority of a 'security certificate,' police can make arrests and jail anyone alleged to have 'terrorist' affiliations without formally charging them with an offence. It also authorizes secret trials and indefinite imprisonment of suspects without possibility of appeal or release.

The issuance of a security certificate is subject to a judicial review but the terms mock due process. The presiding judge is limited to determining if the minister has 'reasonable grounds' for issuing the certificate. The judicial proceeding permits the presentation of evidence for 'reasonable grounds' to be kept secret from the suspect; it authorizes the withholding of contrary evidence; and it admits hearsay evidence without cross-examination of those making the allegation of 'terrorist' affiliations. The procedure makes it nearly impossible for the accused to refute the allegation.

In the wake of 9/11, the U.S. government subverted the constitutional guarantee of human rights provided by Western democracy under the pretext of 'safeguarding national security.' The Department of Justice authored legal interpretations that give the president broad constitutional authority to declare any attack on U.S. strategic interests anywhere in the world an act of terrorism. Subsequently, the president issued an executive decree authorizing the Defense Department to designate any suspected terrorist an 'enemy combatant.'

Under the executive decree, suspicion is enough to designate any person, including U.S. citizens, an 'enemy combatant,' who may be imprisoned and kept in solitary confinement without being charged with any offence, and who may be denied the right to challenge the validity of the allegation against him/her before a court of law. The accused is subject to a trial in which the panel of judges, the prosecutors, and the defence attorneys are all military officers assigned by, and subordinate to, the secretary of defense, who determines who will be tried. The trial rules are established by the Department of Defense and the procedural rights of the accused are granted provisionally by the panel of judges. The accused is denied lawyer-client confidentiality; denied the right to see the alleged evidence; and, if acquitted, can still be locked up indefinitely under a determination by the Pentagon. Moreover, the U.S. Department of Justice contrived a legal opinion and crafted a special protocol that permits the torture of detainees suspected of terrorist activities during interrogation and justifies the use against the defendant of self-incriminating evidence extracted through torture.

The legislative branch of the U.S. government responded to the events of 9/11 by passing the Patriot Act, the Protect America Act, and the Foreign Intelligence and Surveillance Act, authorizing a range of infringements of citizens' constitutional right to individual privacy, including: opening and copying personal mail; breaking into homes and carrying out secret searches; conducting warrantless electronic surveillance of individuals; wiretapping international communications; and compelling Internet-service providers, financial institutions, and telecommunications companies to turn over confidential client information. To facilitate these infringements of citizens' constitutional right to individual privacy, a secret court was sanctioned to issue warrants for search and seizure without 'probable cause,' and the citizen has no avenue of appeal or redress.

Even as the legislative branch was expanding the legal authority to intrude into the privacy of U.S. citizens by search, seizure, and surveillance, the administrative branch, by executive order, was greatly extending the range of government secrecy by implementing new rules that restricted public access and blocked disclosure of government information and documents. In effect, individual rights and freedoms were being eroded on two fronts. The judicial branch of the U.S. government collaborated with the administrative and legislative branches in this subversion of human rights by shielding their actions against legal challenges.

Under the pretext of protecting the national security, all three branches of government showed a readiness to override fundamental principles and values of human rights and to subvert the guarantee of individual liberty provided by Western democracy. This demonstrates the limitations of Western democracy as protection for the universal, inherent, and inalienable human right to individual liberty. In effect, Western democracy functions as a political-legal construct which can affirm or disaffirm constitutional human rights, according to the dictates of the elect body.

Social Justice

Constitutional human rights are assumed to protect citizens from social injustice but, inadvertently, they impair the quest for social justice. As discussed earlier, the human-rights-based legislative and judicial invalidation of moral social order by application of the principles of constitutional supremacy and moral neutrality is progressively disaggregating Western societies into singularities. This reality, in conjunction with the denial of constitutional collective rights, effectively places individuals into a relationship of duality vis à vis the state, which holds a monopoly over the administration of social justice. Thus, by eroding moral order, the doctrine of constitutional human rights undermines and impairs the capacity and motivation of citizens to organize and sustain a collective movement against social injustice by the state. As a result, victims of social injustice in Western societies are increasingly organizing themselves into special-interest groups to surmount their disadvantage vis à vis the state.

Special-interest groups differ from groups referred to as collectivities: a collectivity is a group held together by bonds of moral duties and responsibilities that transcend individual self-interest and subordinate its members to a collective purpose; a special-interest group, by contrast, comprises an aggregation of individuals held together by bonds of common individual self-interests. 'Minorities' may be constituted as either collective or special-interest groups. Although the members of a special-interest group may share the same goals and generic values, their relationship is primarily utilitarian, not moral. In this regard, it is akin to that of individual shareholders in a corporation: as in a corporation, the purpose of a special-interest group is reducible to the individual self-interest of any one of its members.

A variety of special-interest groups in quest of social justice are springing up in Western societies. A number of them are made up of members with a history of persecution and oppression under the synthetic moral order of the church-state. These victims of social injustice (e.g., women, homosexuals, and visible minorities) were excluded from the table when the synthetic moral values of the church-state were enacted into secular state law. Today, they aggregate their economic and social resources into a political force and mobilize their quest for social justice under the banner of human rights. Interest groups militantly exploit the vocabulary, ethical symbolism, public veneration, and constitutional supremacy of human-rights doctrine to enlist public sentiment in support of their particular agendas. They perceive human-rights laws, not moral reform, as the best instrument for achieving social justice.

When special-interest groups take conflicting positions on human rights, as in the case of pro-choice and pro-life groups, the outcome is the segmentation of Western societies into adversarial dualities. Thus, instead of promoting a unifying sense of shared social justice, human dignity, and humanity, human-rights doctrine generates antagonistic political-interest-group alignments. Western elect bodies exploit these antagonisms to 'divide and rule.'

Parenthetically, it is worth noting that special-interest groups generally do not represent a challenge to the oligarchic authority structure. They almost always pursue their goals within the existing political structure and system, where the most serviceable and effective levers of authority lie. In Western societies, a number of special-interest groups have evolved into a consequential political force; some have been recognized politically, juridically, and socially.

A major defect of human-rights doctrine for attaining social justice is that Western elect bodies have deliberately excluded economic justice from the list of constitutional human rights. This means that, when the courts adjudicate cases of economic injustice, they must treat them as ordinary legal cases, not as violations of human rights. The only remedy available to victims of economic injustice is to initiate civil suits for compensatory and punitive penalties; this mercenary system denigrates the idea of social justice. Moreover, few victims of economic injustice have the financial means needed to seek redress in the courts for such violations. This applies especially to the underclass, which lacks the ability to organize and finance an interest group to champion their cause. In this regard, the labour-union movement, originally a broad-based populist social-political alliance lobbying for economic justice for the poor, has virtually abdicated the role of champion for the broader constituency of victims of economic injustice. Union leaders have transformed and fragmented the movement into self-interested, occupation-specific, corporate-like hierarchical organizations, whose primary function and purpose is to negotiate better salary and other benefits for their dues-paying members.

Human Dignity

An evaluation of human-rights doctrine necessitates a discussion of its implications for human dignity. Wordsworth wrote: 'True dignity abides with him alone / Who, in the silent hour of inward thought / Can . . . still revere himself / In lowliness of heart.' Such a self-conscious sense of positive *human* worth cannot be self-created or derived from the trappings of social success such as wealth, authority, prestige, or even talent. The popular acclaim that such coveted social circumstances and qualities confers on the individual can nourish a sense of ego-worth or self-esteem, but not human dignity as described by Wordsworth. Individuals experience a sense of human dignity when they believe that their humanity is valued by others. Such a self-realization can originate only from social relationships which consistently affirm that one is unconditionally valued as an equal and worthy member of society.

The idea of human dignity is present in virtually all theological and philosophical traditions. In seventeenth- and eighteenth-century Judeo-Christian-Islamic theology, it was expressed as 'God in Man.' Theologians held as an axiom that, by virtue of God in Man, every person must be treated with dignity. The *philosophes* held as self-evident that everyone is endowed with the natural right to human dignity. With the advent of the secular contract-state, the justification for the right to human dignity changed from the sacred rationale of God in Man to the secular rationale of the 'virtue of being human.' Like God in Man, the virtue of being human embodies the principle of universal, inherent, and inalienable right to human dignity.

When the authors of the Universal Declaration of Human Rights formulated their manifesto, they explicitly affirmed the principle of universal, inherent, and inalienable human dignity. The Universal International Human Rights Covenant unequivocally states that human rights 'derive from the inherent dignity of the human person.' And the International Covenant on Civil and Political Rights explicitly requires that all people be 'treated with respect for the inherent dignity of the human person.' How well has this stipulation been realized?

Although 'true dignity' as described by Wordsworth is not a function of particular social-economic circumstances, the fundamental elements of quality of life such as adequate food, housing, education, health care, and employment serve as important societal indices of human worth and have a profound impact on a person's sense of human dignity. Horrific violations of human dignity, such as genocide and slavery, are readily recognized and condemned as crimes against humanity. However, the deleterious effects of extreme economic deprivation in the midst of celebrated, flaunted, and sometimes obscene extravagance also send an unequivocal message that an individual's human worth is not being honoured and as such constitute a violation of human dignity and an assault on humanity.

In Western societies, where the doctrine of human rights has been socially, politically, and constitutionally embraced for over half a century, the circumstance of the underclass is evidence that constitutional human rights do not prevent ongoing pervasive and flagrant violations of human dignity: structures of injustice, racial categorization, hunger, homelessness, poor education, unemployment, and lack of health care are common in the most affluent Western human-rights regimes. Robert Reich, former U.S. labor secretary, reported that in the United States, the wealthiest nation in the world and the self-proclaimed exemplar of democracy and constitutional human rights, 'there are millions of people desperately trying to stay afloat. One in five children lives in poverty. Forty-four million Americans have no health insurance . . . Americans are segregated by income as never before, so it is easier to pretend the worse off don't exist. They are out of sight.' Moreover, the gap between poor and rich falls on a racial fault line and a shrinking middle class is causing it to widen into a chasm. These statistics imply significant violations of human dignity. It is a fact that all Western human-rights regimes not only permit but commit flagrant violations of human dignity against their own citizens.

To understand why Western democracies and constitutional human rights are failing to afford the universal, inherent, and inalienable human dignity proclaimed in the Universal Declaration, we need to consider issues of access, relevance, and private property.

Access

Human-rights doctrine as set forth in Western constitutions and charters is worded to apply equally to all citizens, and no one can legally be denied human rights. However, the allegation of equal access to human-rights protection is disingenuous; in reality, the constitutions and charters provide only an abstract, rhetorical warrant for human dignity. Under these documents, human rights are a 'legal commodity,' and, accordingly, access to legal resources is crucial for the protection of human dignity. Those who can retain the best lawyers, command the respect of the court, influence enforcement officials, and manipulate public opinion can exploit human-rights law to protect their dignity. Members of the underclass lack the resources to use the law to achieve constitutional protection for their human dignity; when they experience a violation of human dignity, they are limited to futile expressions of indignation, frustration, resentment, and alienation.

Relevance

The enactment of human-rights doctrine into legal protection for human dignity is a political process, and, as is typical of all political enterprises, those most vulnerable to abuse of their dignity such as various minorities and the poor are left out of the lawmaking process. The elect body, in its role as legislator, creates human-rights laws that relate to the situations, possibilities, and interests of its class. As previously noted, Western elect bodies' enactment of human rights into law excludes socio-economic rights. As a consequence, basic necessities for a positive sense of worth and human dignity such as a job, health care, and adequate nutrition, housing, and education are not guaranteed by human-rights laws.

This bias in human-rights laws was demonstrated when welfare recipients in Ontario, Canada, brought a class-action suit against the provincial government for implementing a 20 per cent reduction in existing social-welfare allowances to balance its budget in 1995. The petitioners charged that the provincial government had violated the Charter of Rights and Freedoms, which guarantees the life, liberty, and security of the person. The Ontario court denied their petition, thereby averting a potential spate of human-rights-based legal challenges to other provincial and federal government social policies and programs which, in their effect, violate the human dignity of the unemployed, the elderly, and the incapacitated by failing to provide adequate levels of basic support.

Private Property

A crucial factor contributing to the violation of human dignity in Western societies is rooted in a deliberate distortion of the meaning of natural rights. The American and French revolutions both endorsed ownership of private property and wealth as a natural right of all citizens. Western elect bodies have self-servingly interpreted this to mean a legal contractual guarantee by the state to recognize and protect the right of the individual to acquire and own unlimited private property and wealth, and they have entrenched this construction of natural rights in their constitutions and charters, thereby giving rise to a legal system and culture that tolerates huge disparities in wealth and opportunity.

Through legal instruments such as patents and copyrights, Western elect bodies have broadened the construction of natural rights from the concept of individual private ownership of real property to include commercial ownership and exclusive legal control over public goods. They are transforming intangible goods formerly in the public domain, that is, owned collectively by all the people, such as airwaves, genetic materials, and knowledge gained over several generations through tax-supported research, into private property.

Western elect bodies declare that requiring the wealthy to pay the financial cost involved in providing the basics for human dignity for all would violate their constitutional human right to acquire and own unlimited private property and wealth. This interpretation of the doctrine of human rights turns the traditional meaning of natural right on its head; it accords a higher value to the right of ownership of unlimited private property and wealth than to the right to human dignity. The celebrated U.S. president Ronald Reagan gave worldwide voice to this interpretation of human-rights doctrine in a formal statement to the UN-sponsored World Food Summit in 1996. He declared that adequate food was 'a goal or aspiration but not a human right.'

Western elect bodies have agreed to meet the minimally adequate needs for biological survival. This, it is maintained, is their maximum constitutional responsibility as sanctioned by human-rights doctrine. The elect bodies of the West hold that the standard of responsibility and obligation for human dignity is fully met by social-welfare 'safety-net' programs which, on paper, provide that no citizen need die for want of the minimum daily requirement for physical survival. Often this standard is fudged, however, since these programs are chronically underfunded and, when revenues are tight, are among the first to be cut back. Under the pretext of protecting the human right to private property, elect bodies in the world's richest nations are rendering millions of their citizens homeless, jobless, sick, and hungry.

By construing natural rights as a constitutional guarantee by the state to recognize and protect the right of the individual to acquire and own unlimited private property and wealth, while excluding socio-economic rights from the list of constitutional human rights, the doctrine of human rights perverts the Enlightenment *philosophes'* meaning of natural rights and betrays the principle of human dignity. Professor John Rawls, a distinguished Harvard University philosopher, has provided an ethical rationale for this construction of natural rights. His 'Maximin Principle' holds that economic inequalities are justifiable if it can be shown that there is a 'trickle-down' benefit for the worst off. (It is noteworthy that, in their time, the practitioners of slavery, colonialism, and apartheid all defended their violations of human dignity by alleging that they were improving the lives of their victims.)

Western 'liberals,' hard pressed to rationalize the great gap between rich and poor in their democratic, human-rights societies, and eager to free themselves from an ethical and economic obligation to alleviate the plight of the poor, enthusiastically acclaim Rawls's principle. In this regard, they show a crass insensitivity bordering on moral blindness to the gross violations of human dignity that are implicit in the experience of homelessness, joblessness, want of medical care, malnutrition, lack of education, and other forms of social injustice in the midst of plenty. Current social trends indicate a disturbing physical and psychological retreat by the privileged class into 'gated' communities, where they are bound to become more insulated, disengaged, and impervious to the chronic violations of human dignity experienced by those living in slum communities.

Humanity

The genetic similarities between humankind and some other species come close to intra-human genetic similarities; and all other differences, such as intelligence, are rooted in nature and can be plotted as increments on the scale of biological evolution. The elemental quality that distinguishes humankind from other species is an intrinsic potential and aspiration for humanity that transcends nature. However, we are not controlled by our humanity as other life forms are controlled by instinct. Nor is humanity an attribute that we can ascribe to ourselves by virtue of a divine soul or human right. Our potential and aspiration for humanity can be realized only if we create knowledge, understanding, and a social order that fosters and affirms a regard for the equal human dignity of all.

Human dignity is essential for a sense of humanity; however, as we have seen, human-rights doctrine permits grave violations of human dignity and humanity. It also lends itself to an ethos that can be readily exploited by elect bodies to institute expedient social policies that derogate humanity. Evidence for this assertion can be inferred from the ongoing public debates and current legislative/judicial initiatives in Western societies regarding the human right to assisted death and to abortion. I will stipulate in advance that my discussion of these issues is not rooted in conventional theological-philosophical notions of the sanctity of life; nor whether God or Man is or should be master of life and death; nor whether assisted death or abortion are 'good' or 'bad.' Rather, my discussion focuses narrowly on the implications that a constitutionalized human right to assisted death or abortion portends for the valuation of humanity.

Classical natural rights held that the inviolability of life was fundamental to the protection of liberty, social justice, human dignity, and humanity. This philosophy was embodied in laws proscribing every form of deliberately induced death. Currently, Western legislators and judiciaries proceeding under the logic of human-rights doctrine are selectively nullifying the inviolability of life. For instance, they are incrementally creating a constitutional human right to assisted dying (euthanasia, mercy killing, suicide) without due regard for its effect on the valuation of humanity. They focus on ethical-legal procedures (e.g., free and informed consent); scientific issues (e.g., beginning or viability of life); and various pecuniary criteria (e.g., cost and profit of care). The idea of honouring the essence of humanity is virtually disregarded. In 2006 the U.S. Supreme Court sanctioned Oregon's Death with Dignity Act (which permits doctors to assist suicide) without even considering the issue of humanity. It based its decision exclusively on grounds of state rights.

Proponents of the human right to assisted death proclaim humanitarian motives; they contend that a free choice to assisted death will enhance human dignity and humanity. This argument ignores some important issues and perverts the meaning of human dignity and humanity. The decision to request an assisted death is usually made under conditions of unbearable anguish, both physical and emotional. It is ethically and intellectually dishonest to characterize a request for assisted death made under such circumstances as an act of free choice. Moreover, our human dignity and sense of humanity derive not from being kept alive or being euthanized, but from caring relationships. Even dying people draw their meaning of life from relationships, not from death; and life without humane relationships is anguish. Death is the cessation of humane relationships and the end of human dignity and humanity. Death may offer an escape from a life of unbearable anguish, but it is perverse to contend that the human right to assisted death confers a sense of dignity and humanity.

It is no mere coincidence that the human right to assisted death is coming into prominence and being promoted as a right to human dignity at a time when the public cost of medical care for a growing elderly population is steeply rising. Elderly people contribute almost nothing to economic productivity, but the per capita cost of government programs for those aged sixty to eighty years is approximately ten times higher than for those aged twenty to sixty. Increasingly, health-care professionals and government officials equate the cost of end-of life care with economic waste, and they are looking for 'respectable' ways to reduce the spiralling cost of maintaining these so-called negative-cost-benefit citizens. Some assert that enormous savings could be achieved if elderly persons were given the constitutional human right to an assisted death when they are judged to have attained a 'diminished state.'

The push to establish assisted death as a constitutional human right comes from various agents of a profit-driven industrial health complex keen to over-treat those who can pay but averse to treating patients who can't. At the World Conference on Assisted Dying held in Boston, Massachusetts, in September 2000, the conference organizers, consisting of government bureaucrats, hospital administrators, medical-insurance executives, and an assortment of health professionals, responded to a group of blind and wheelchair-bound citizens, who came to protest the conference theme, by hiring a photographer to videotape them and then called police to remove them for disrupting the peace.

There is no evidence of popular support by the 'negative-cost-benefit' population for the move to establish assisted death as a constitutional human right. The various organizations that broadly represent the interests of the targeted populations consistently declare that their members feel threatened by the aggressive and highly publicized social-political campaign to enhance their dignity by legalizing assisted death. Understandably, they are distrustful of the proclaimed humanitarian motive for the provision of a constitutional right to a physician-assisted death when they are being denied constitutional rights to an adequate income, appropriate health services, and a life with dignity.

Creating a constitutional human right to assisted death, and creating human-rights-predicated social policies that mandate the venerated medical profession to carry out this function under the euphemism of a 'medical decision,' conveys a powerful message to the 'costly' sick, the 'burdensome' elderly, the 'incommodious' disabled, and other 'negative-cost-benefit' citizens that we don't need them; that they should think of themselves as expendable; and that our society would function better without them. They are being programmed to see themselves not as human persons worthy of dignity but as perpetrators of an economic sin against society, and to recognize that it is unreasonable for some not to request death. This stigma, more than their 'disability,' causes them to feel that they should 'voluntarily' exercise their unsolicited human right to the services of a state-mandated euthanizer.

There are humane alternatives to assisted death, such as hospice care. The philosophy of hospice care is that the 'good death' is dying with the conviction that one is loved and valued; that the dying person is not looking for a future or an end, but for a positive sense of humanity. The hospice-care movement seeks to foster this by providing compassion and psycho-social support, and minimizing the dying patient's physical suffering with the best medical techniques. This humane approach provides the patient with a personal sense of dignity and being valued as a living person.

The combination of an aging population and increasingly sophisticated, costly technologies and treatment regimes raises some legitimate concerns about getting the most value from available health-care resources. These concerns involve some profound and difficult moral issues regarding quality of life and end-of-life decisions, issues that underline the need for a principled protocol that honours the dignity and humanity of patients. Clearly, for some patients, the quality of life may become such that even the best efforts cannot yield a positive sense of dignity. In these cases, humanity may well be honoured by an assisted death and the patient's decision about the best way to die should be respected on condition that the decision meets the standard of informed choice and self-determination.

The standard of informed choice and self-determination regarding the end of life must ensure that patients have access to appropriate professional advice and assistance in making their decision or in preparing an advance directive and appointing a proxy with authority to carry out the terms of their directive in the event they are incapable of making a decision. To meet the standard of informed self-determination, discussions between professionals, patients, and/proxies must go beyond medical prognoses and explanations of the available technological and therapeutic capabilities and options to prolong or end life; doctors can't know with certainty that death will occur – there may be a chance the patient will recover. The emphasis in these discussions should be on ensuring that the patient's and/or proxy's decision is being made with the utmost confidence that they are honouring their own and others' humanity; this will require a profound discussion with the patient and/or proxy about their conception of humanity. In short, the decision to terminate a life should be based on carefully thought-out principles and guidelines that honour the essence of humanity. It should not be influenced by technological and therapeutic capabilities, medical aspirations, or economic considerations; nor by human-rights policies that lead to social acceptance of assisted death without regard to its effect on the valuation of humanity.

Turning to the human right to abortion, the twentieth century began with a synthetic moral order that grossly violated the dignity of unmarried women who became pregnant. They were condemned as shameful persons, often cruelly punished, and their children were stigmatized with the label 'bastard.' To escape this humanity-destroying experience, many unmarried pregnant women were forced into illegal and unsafe self-abortions or 'back-alley' abortions performed by persons with no training. Many of these women died as a result and all survivors were permanently traumatized.

Western societies, influenced in part by human-rights doctrine, ended the twentieth century with the decriminalization of abortion and a diminished stigma against unmarried mothers and their children. However, this greater public tolerance of out-of-wedlock childbearing shows only an ambiguous regard for the value of humanity. Many women have abortions because they feel they have no better alternative; it is a last resort often resulting from poverty and poor physical and emotional health. Honouring humanity calls for more than the decriminalization of abortion, providing safe abortions, and public tolerance of unmarried mothers and their children. It requires genuine humane concern for their emotional and material well-being, which is not met by the prevailing minimally adequate and stigmatized provision for their biological survival.

To honour humanity, we need to give thoughtful consideration to how abortion affects the valuation of humanity. Aristotle reasoned that 'the nature of things consist in their end or consummation; what each thing is when its growth is complete we call the nature of that thing.' Following Aristotle's logic, the nature of human embryos is a potentiality for humanity. How can we honour this potentiality? In

the first instance, we have an obligation to prevent unwanted conceptions. Failing in this, the rightness of an abortion should be decided on
the principle of valuing humanity. On the seamless continuum from
conception to death, the mother and the embryo both have a potential
for humanity and to honour humanity this potentiality must be valued equally. This requires that, in every case, the determination for or
against an abortion must be subject to the principle of least injury to
the valuation of humanity. Such a determination involves consideration of situation-specific circumstances. Like assisted death, abortion
is a profound and complex ethical issue, fraught with moral ambigui-
ties that cannot be resolved by categorically defining it as a sin or a
human right.

The preceding discussions of assisted death and abortion describes
how the doctrine of human rights can lend itself to the creation of public
policies that justify violation and devaluation of the human dignity and
humanity of vulnerable members of society. Human-rights doctrine,
however, devalues humanity in a more general way: it is a philosophy
of personal entitlement and self-interest that gives rise to an ethic and
culture which legitimates an egocentric world view and consciousness
in social relationships that discourages responsibility for others. Human
sensibility deteriorates within the closed borders of egoism and I propose
a causal connection between the self-focused world view fostered by
human-rights doctrine and the diminished faculty of self-transcendence
and valuation of others' humanity observable in Western societies.

The effects of a diminished faculty of self-transcendence and valuation of others' humanity are manifested in various ways. A survey by
the Child Abuse Prevention Center in Baltimore showed a 54 per cent
rise over six years in the number of American children who died by
violence and other kinds of abuse. As distressing as this statistic is, the
survey reported the even more disturbing finding that in many of the
cases cited the violence and abuse were known to doctors, social workers, police, teachers, relatives, friends, and neighbours but no interven-
tionist action was taken. This phenomenon is not peculiar to the United
States; it occurs in all Western human-rights societies.

A diminishing sense of humanity in Western societies can also be
inferred from studies showing a steep rise in 'random' killings on the
streets, at workplaces, in public- service offices, and on schoolyards and
college campuses. The term random implies that the killer's actions defy
analysis in terms of a rational motive. This appraisal, however, assumes
that the perpetrator perceives the victim as a *human* being. Hunters, for

example, shoot and kill wildlife in a random pattern, but we don't consider them as lacking a rational motive. When acts of random killings (here, I include terrorist as well as piloted and drone bombings that kill civilian populations) are decoded, they send a message of nihilism that is rooted in the perpetrators' estrangement from their own and others' humanity. Members of societies with an impaired sense of humanity are insensitive to violations of human dignity and crimes against humanity.

The Individual and Society

As stated above, there is a fundamental difference between individual freedom as contemplated by the Enlightenment philosophers and that implied by contemporary Western human-rights doctrine. The *philosophes* envisaged individual autonomy within a framework of community, that is, consensual moral duties and responsibilities. They regarded the individual and community as 'of each other.' To the extent that they intended to liberate the individual from community moral restraint, their efforts were focused on the invalidation of particular moral laws that kept individuals subject to church control. Contemporary human-rights doctrine seeks to liberate the individual from community moral constraints and treat the individual and community as separate entities with competing or even antagonistic interests. Moreover, by vesting the individual with inherent, inalienable rights but denying such rights to the community as a body, contemporary human-rights doctrine effectively elevates the interests of the individual above those of the community.

The human-rights-predicated dualist conception of individual and community involves the idea that individuals have the autonomy to determine their own behaviour. Consequently, social problems such as domestic and street violence and racially motivated hate crimes are considered to be primarily *individual* behavioural pathologies that stem from personal values and motivations. This perception of social behaviour as an individual phenomenon permeates the Western world view and provides the foundation of all social policies. It obliges the judiciary to consider social deviance and criminality, even by children, as individual phenomena, independent of a societal moral context and societal accountability.

A notorious instance of this individualistic amoral world view was the 1993 British trial of two eleven-year-old boys who were convicted of the abduction and murder of James Bulger, a two-year-old child. The two boys, ten years old at the time, lured the toddler away from his mother at a shopping mall, then dragged and pushed him along a four-kilometre route to a secluded spot, where they beat the child to death with bricks and a metal bar. The pair then partially stripped their victim and left the body on a railway track where it was sliced by the wheels of a train.

The response by the British public to this gruesome act is revealing. An angry mob made up mostly of parents charged the police van carrying the two children to court, screaming abuse and death threats and calling on the guards to 'kill the bastards.' The judge, who tried the boys in adult court, described them as 'cunning and wicked' and charged them with having committed 'an act of unparalleled evil and barbarity.' Then he sentenced them to a minimum of eight years in custody; this was increased to ten years on appeal to the lord chief justice. Later, the British home secretary, bowing to a 300,000-signature petition demanding a stiffer sentence, increased the jail term to fifteen years before parole eligibility (this decision was subsequently overturned and the boys were eventually released after serving eight years).

The then British prime minister, John Major, followed up by legislating stiffer sentences and custodial terms for law-breaking children aged ten to fourteen years. Major also stated that 'society needs to condemn a little more and understand a little less.' Seven years earlier, in 1987, his patron-mentor, the famous British Prime Minister Margaret Thatcher, declared that 'there is no such thing as society . . . only individuals.' Taken literally, the statements by the two prime ministers seem at odds regarding the existence of 'society'; however, they express the same idea of individualism, and the philosophy that the individual and the community are not 'of each other.'

The judge, the home secretary, the prime minister, the media, and the public who condemned the children as morally depraved individuals seemingly were purblind to the correlation between the children's lack of human sensibility and a society in which a mob of adults screamed abuse and death threats at children. They seemed oblivious to the notion of a societal moral-social responsibility for the monstrous act committed by the children. They did not examine their collective morality or appraise the moral instruction of their children. They viewed the children as morally self-made, autonomous individuals, and their actions as products of their individual 'evil' minds. The then home secretary, Michael Howard, speaking on the BBC, echoed the sentiments of the trial judge; the murder, he said, was 'an unforgivable act from the heart of darkness.'

In Canada and the United States, some youths have turned school grounds into 'killing fields,' and, like the two ten-year-old boys in Great Britain, the youthful perpetrators of these horrendous acts have been widely portrayed as self-owned and self-created evil individuals. A recent U.S. national television newscast showed two African American youths, who had just been convicted of a brutal killing, being escorted in shackles from the courthouse to a waiting police van. One of the youths turned to the television cameras and, with a defiant middle finger 'salute,' accusingly shouted: 'We are the products of your society!' While this was not an endearing analysis of his actions and personal accountability, the youth was expressing a profound truth.

William Bennett, former director of the U.S. Office of National Drug Policy, an internationally prominent author and media pundit as well as a self-proclaimed moralist, echoed Thatcher's and Major's philosophy of the relationship between the individual and community in his assertion that 'incarceration is a failure of the individual, but it is a victory for society.' There is irony in the fact that the self-proclaimed 'moralists' in Western societies are the ones who clamour loudest for law and order as the solution to moral decline. In keeping with his philosophy, Bennett forcefully declared that the solution to the U.S. drug problem was 'more police, more prisons, and more prosecutors.' It is noteworthy that, under such a policy, the U.S. prison population during the period from 1980 to 2009 increased from 501,886 to 2,297,400 (U.S. Bureau of Justice Statistics); it included children under the age of thirteen and mentally ill offenders, with non-white minorities significantly over-represented. Yet the problem of crime continues to grow.

Western social scientists study social deviance as a function of social, political, legal, economic, medical, and educational disadvantages; they implicate poverty, unemployment, poor housing, dysfunctional families, a media preoccupied with violence, biased legal definitions and law-enforcement patterns, and social or biological determinism. They explain criminal behaviour as deviation from abstract standards of social-psychological normality, not societal morality. They have practically abandoned the idea of social deviance as a function of societal moral dysfunction.

Standards of Social Behaviour

Under the doctrine of human rights, the basis for judging social behaviour is changing from the moral mode to the amoral mode. In the church-state, social behaviour was judged primarily according to synthetic moral standards of 'right' and 'wrong.' In the secular contract-state, social behaviour has come to be judged primarily according to the amoral standards of 'legal' and 'illegal.' The shift from moral to amoral standards can be observed in current assessments of a wide range of aberrant behaviours such as domestic violence, sexually transmitted diseases, racism, and unrestrained greed. While still subject to vestigial moral reproof, these behavioural pathologies are perceived and explained primarily in amoral-legal terms; and public policy calls for legislative-administrative solutions, not moral reform. (I stress 'primarily' because, as indicated earlier, the change from moral to amoral standards is occurring incrementally; some moral standards reflecting basic values of the community are still evident in Western statutory laws, and often these laws supplement community forms of social controls.)

Currently, in Western societies the basis for appraising social behaviour is being expanded to include utility-rational standards. For instance, promiscuous sexual behaviour, once judged primarily by the 'moral/immoral' standard, then by the 'legal/illegal' standard, is now judged primarily by a utility-rational standard, frequently characterized in terms of 'smart and dumb.' Thus, protected sex is deemed 'smart' behaviour while unprotected sex is deemed 'dumb' behaviour. Similarly, corporate and political misconduct, while viewed with social reproof and liable to legal prosecution, is generally characterized in terms of 'smart/dumb' criteria, such as finesse of execution, sophistication of concealment, exploitation of legal loopholes and grey areas, and competency of prosecutors and defence lawyers.

The utility-rational 'smart/dumb' standard achieved international repute in the infamous U.S. 'Clinton-Lewinsky' affair. While many American citizens voiced moral disapproval of President Bill Clinton's sexual dalliance with White House intern Monica Lewinsky, U.S. public-opinion polls showed that a significant majority judged his behaviour primarily in terms of the 'smart/dumb' standard. In the court of public opinion, the majority of Americans judged Clinton guilty of reckless stupidity, not of behaving immorally or illegally. This was confirmed by the general reaction to independent counsel Kenneth Starr's September 1998 report to Congress on his investigation into the Clinton-Lewinsky affair. Editorial inferences of a moral tinge in the report's legal indictment of Clinton's lewd conduct prompted popular reproach and ridicule of the report's author for trespassing into the moral domain. Starr had to defend not just his report but himself against innuendoes that he was perpetrating a moral witch-hunt.

Western media, for the most part, dealt with the scandal in partisan political terms; a few political, academic, and religious commentators professed bafflement over the American public's apparent moral indifference to such a carnal debasement of the presidential office. This phenomenon, however, can readily explained by the shift from the moral to the amoral mode of social order in Western societies.

Western Social Institutions

Social institutions function as agencies of social order. Western elect bodies make the case for democracy as diffused authority by alleging that the social institutions in their countries function as independent, autonomous entities. However, the doctrine of human rights is undermining the autonomy of Western social institutions and is gradually transforming them into functional constituents of the oligarchic authority structure. I will briefly sketch how the doctrine of human rights affects the autonomy of four key Western social institutions.

The Judicial System

As a branch of Western democratic government, the judicial system traditionally functioned as an independent arbiter of state law; it was mandated to apply the law appropriately and fairly for all citizens. Yet, as we saw earlier, the judiciary, under its broadened construction of the principles of constitutional supremacy and moral neutrality, is gradually asserting itself as autonomous arbiter of legal principles. Furthermore, by exempting the individual not only from any religious moral constraint in state law but also from any unwanted societal secular moral constraint that violates personal autonomy and freedom, the judicial system is progressively invalidating the authority of moral order and establishing an amoral legal regime by which it is asserting itself as an autonomous arbiter not only of legal principles but also of culture and social order in Western societies. In effect, the judiciary is exploiting the principles of constitutional supremacy and moral neutrality to attain a doctrinal jurisdiction that rises above the level of the erstwhile church.

A noteworthy characteristic of this development is a more complete synergy between the court and the state than that formerly prevailing between the church and the state. Specifically, in the church-state, the ecclesiastical elect body and the monarchical elect body functioned under two distinct constitutions. Although they usually worked in a mode of reciprocal affirmation, there existed a state of chronic contention over jurisdiction by the two distinct hierarchical structures and regimes which served to limit their respective oligarchic authority and control over the people. In Western democracies, by contrast, the judicial and political regimes both function under the same supreme constitutional doctrine of human rights. This doctrinal fusion of political and judicial authority diminishes the susceptibility to jurisdictional clashes that existed in the historical church-state.

Although Western judicial and political branches of government do not constitute a monolith (jurisdictional conflicts do occur), the fact that both exercise their authority under the same supreme doctrine of constitutional human rights gives them a commonality of self-interest and purpose that renders the claim of institutional independence and separation of authority between the two virtually meaningless. For all intents and purposes, they function as two branches of the same structure of oligarchic authority and control.

The Media Complex

Western elect bodies equate the constitutional protection of freedom of the press with institutional independence of the media. This assertion had a measure of validity when control of the media was dispersed among many independent outlets for news and editorial commentary. Today, however, independent media outlets are few and far between; media ownership is significantly concentrated in the hands of wealthy elements in the elect body which control very big vertically integrated corporate conglomerates, comprising movie studios, television networks, publishing houses, and commercial websites. These media moguls have a compelling shared interest in using their influence to secure the oligarchic authority structure that guarantees their privileges. They are unified in building a narrative that legitimates rule by the state oligarchy. They generate supporting public opinion for the legitimating narrative through ongoing self-censorship involving selective reporting, remaining mute, and leaving out, ignoring, and giving biased interpretations of contrary information. Any events or voices that could potentially incite significant opposition to the essential legitimacy of the state oligarchy are shut out or discredited as naive or condemned as antagonistic to national security, and possibly seditious.

This is not to say that Western media refrain from censure of government or its officials. They frequently feature harsh criticism of government policy and actions, and they diligently investigate and inform the public about personal foibles, eccentricities, and political misconduct by elected and appointed officials. This exercise in public criticism of government policies, actions, and officials is featured as signifying an independent voice and an institution outside the oligarchic authority structure. Those who allege separation of the media and government are wont to tout publication of the Pentagon Papers as proof of press independence from government. By way of background, in 1971 Daniel Ellsberg, a senior policy analyst for the U.S. Defense Department, risked life imprisonment by leaking to the media top-secret documents which exposed over a decade of public deception by five U.S. presidents about the purpose of the Vietnam War. The media published these documents, dubbed the 'Pentagon Papers.' Clearly, in so doing, the media defied the government, more particularly the Nixon administration. But any claim that this act signifies press independence from government is tainted by other evident motives. In the case of the *New York Times*, which broke the story, editorial concerns that another media outlet might publish the documents – and that the *Times* would be perceived as cowardly for failing to protect free speech against government encroachment – played a prominent, if not decisive, role in the decision to publish.

The claim that publication of the Pentagon Papers signified press independence from government was also belied by the fact that, even as the corporate media portrayed themselves as guardians of the public interest, independent of government, they censored their own accounts of the Vietnam War and intimidated commentators into self-censorship by threatening and even firing some who dared to condemn the government for perpetrating unconscionable violence against the civilian population. Following publication of the Pentagon Papers, they refused to report Ellsberg's press conferences on the government's continued massive bombing of Vietnam's urban civilian population ('One Hiroshima a week'), thus defeating his primary purpose for smuggling the documents: that is, to inform and motivate the American public to bring about an end to their government's ongoing crime against humanity.

The Western corporate media complex exercises its constitutional protection of freedom of expression principally to advance its corporate economic interests, not to establish itself as an independent institution outside the oligarchic authority structure of the state. This fact was curiously demonstrated by the media's role in the protest movement initiated by draft-eligible U.S. college students opposed to the Vietnam War. The movement started out as a protest against the authority structure. To forestall the possibility that it might grow out of control, the corporate media deftly co-opted the movement and channelled the protest against the oligarchy into a protest against prevailing societal moral standards, and labelled it the 'counterculture movement.'

In the 1960s, prevailing societal moral standards inhibited the corporate media from engaging in a potentially lucrative traffic in socially proscribed words and images. Keen to promote a change in mass culture that would eliminate this moral proscription and foster a societal ethos of leniency and tolerance for their ambitions, the corporate media proceeded to transform the anti-authoritarian disposition of the protesters into a rebellion against the restrictive societal moral standards of the day. It accomplished this by portraying and promoting the protesters' attention-seeking antics (a sideshow of puerile violations of moral convention involving public expressions of scatological invective, sexual promiscuity, and experimentation with drugs) as a bold, if not noble, assertion of the human right to freedom of expression, and as the primary reason for the movement's existence.

This portrayal appealed to the imagination and vanity of the juvenile protesters and, like candy held up to distract children, completely diverted them from their original purpose. Arguably, the counterculture movement hastened the end of the Vietnam War and promoted some idealistic aspirations (e.g., the hippie mantra of peace and love); however, it did not inspire a humanitarian socio-cultural consciousness, as did the civil rights movement. The counterculture never threatened nor did it effect any change in the oligarchic authority structure. Its most notable legacy is that it served the corporate media complex as a proxy in a culture war that subverted traditional community value standards, thereby freeing it to establish a multibillion-dollar tabloid industry dealing in salacious news and entertainment that violate traditional societal moral conventions on proscribed words and images. Today, any public initiative to enforce societal moral standards in commercial media programming, even by parents wanting to protect their children from exposure to pornography, violence, and other forms of offensive images and language, is denied by the courts as a violation of the constitutional right to freedom of expression.

In short, the corporate media complex exercises its constitutional protection of freedom of expression principally to advance its corporate

and economic interests, rarely as a guardian of public interest independent of government. The claim of diffusion of authority via institutional independence and autonomy is meaningless when the interests
of the media complex are best served by advancing and securing the
oligarchic authority structure of the state.

Organized Religion

As we have seen, a primary reason why the *philosophes* sought to separate church and state was to stop the church from exercising direct
authority over the affairs of the state. They did not anticipate the prospect that the state would exercise direct authority over the church. Yet,
in Western societies, the affairs of religious institutions are progressively being subordinated to the authority of the state. This is evident
in various legal rulings requiring religious organizations to conform
their hiring and employment policies, their membership criteria, and
various other organizational practices to the state's human-rights laws.

For instance, Canada's quasi-judicial Human Rights Commission
has ruled that requiring teachers employed by parochial schools to
conform their personal conduct to the standards of the sponsoring
religious community constitutes an infringement of the human right
to self-determination and freedom. The implication is that the authority of religious institutions over their moral province is subject to legal
prohibition when challenged in court. In the United States, religious
institutions that do not follow government employment practices and
regulations do not receive appropriate funds for their school and social
programs. As a result of these strictures, Western religious organizations have either already changed or are in the process of changing
their operating practices in a number of functional areas to conform to
state human-rights laws.

Significantly, the enforcement of constitutional human-rights laws on
religious institutions is causing a change in Western theologies. While
particular religious communities may vehemently object to specific
human-rights laws, nearly all Western churches proclaim constitutional
human rights as a fundamental 'good'; and, to avoid social marginal-
ization, they are adopting human-rights doctrine as an essential theme
in their theological-doctrinal practices. Even as they lament the trend
towards individualism, they are developing a theology of individualized spirituality and self-fulfillment in place of traditional consensual
moral duties and responsibilities.

Among other things, this theological development is changing the way many Western denominations explain and rationalize the great economic disparities that prevail in their societies. Traditionally, Western churches advocated the idea of a 'sacred' meritocracy; they explained and rationalized the coexistence of excessive wealth and desperate poverty in terms of individually merited divine blessings. Today, most Western religious denominations endorse the idea of a 'secular' meritocracy. They explain social-economic disparities in their societies in terms of individually merited achievement; and they rationalize the great gaps in wealth by referring to human-rights-based policies and laws purported to guarantee equal opportunity. They have virtually abandoned the social gospel; they hold that their responsibility and obligation to uphold human dignity is fully met by the state's provision of minimum daily requirement for physical survival. Some Western religious denominations incorporate human-rights doctrine into their theology in the form of a gospel of prosperity that encourages the individual to amass unlimited private property and wealth.

Organized religions are ceding to the state and the courts their traditional role as the primary source and guide of ethical standards and values. Rather than promote altruistic moral remedies for racism, sexism, homophobia, and other forms of social discrimination, they are satisfied to leave the remedy for all forms of social injustice to legislative-judicial action and secular human-rights-based state social policies. For instance, providing the poor with the essential requirements for survival is considered primarily a civil not a moral matter. The effect of changing their organizational practices and theology to conform to human-rights doctrine, then, is the gradual assimilation of Western religious institutions into the state oligarchic authority structure.

The Family Unit

Under human-rights doctrine, children, 'by virtue of being human,' possess the same inherent, inalienable human rights as adults. Consistent with this doctrine, the UN recently proclaimed the Rights of the Child Act, and it has mounted an international campaign to pressure all nation-states to ratify the act and extend constitutional human- rights protection to children. At present, there is no widely shared consensus on appropriate rights for children; however, freedom of choice in making decisions, freedom of speech and thought, freedom of association, freedom to access the media and receive and impart information, and protection of privacy are generally deemed necessary for children to control their own lives. The act treats children as abstract objects of a state human-rights-policy agenda. The UN has provided no evidence that the act will serve as an effective deterrent to major violations of childhood human dignity and humanity, such as poverty, hunger, lack of health care, and abuse.

Western legislative-judicial officials have begun to extend human-rights laws to children. The ostensible reason for doing so is that they need the protection of the law because their status disadvantage and dependence upon their parents and other adults place them at risk of abuse. However, the extension of human-rights laws to children makes children subject to state laws and regulations that impose exclusions, prohibitions, and limitations on their liberty. When they break the law, they can be charged and tried in state courts. Given that children lack the understanding, money, and political power (the vote) needed to influence the state, increasing their dependence on the state places them at an even greater status disadvantage than before.

The enactment of children's' human-rights laws is changing parental duties and responsibilities. It forces parents, when teaching their children, to redefine 'ought' and 'ought not' from moral-value principles to amoral legal principles. Instead of instructing their children about what is morally right and providing them with a moral compass for their behaviour, parents are obliged to instruct them about their human rights, along with the associated exclusions, prohibitions, and limitations on their liberty, and provide them with an amoral-legal compass.

The practical effect of expanding state legal authority over children is a significant erosion of the family as an autonomous institution of moral-value formation. In Western societies, children spend a majority of their moral-formative lives being taught in accordance with state-created curricula of instruction. This circumstance is magnified by the need for two incomes per family, which necessitates the delegation of family functions traditionally performed as a parental moral obligation to state-regulated daycare and nursery schools, often beginning as early as a few months after a child is born. The effect of extending constitutional human rights to children will be to transform the family unit from an independent morally based institution, which traditionally functioned largely outside the state's authority, into a subordinate constituent of the state oligarchic authority structure.

Summary

In the opening chapter of Part Two, I stated that humankind has the capability to determine its social order. And I posed the question: How can we actualize our power in a pattern of social-order authority to realize the Good Society in a globalizing world? I devoted most of Part Two to a discussion of how the question posed has been addressed by Western societies in the Modern Age. My thesis holds that the experience with the synthetic moral order of the church-state misled the Enlightenment *philosophes* to assume that the tyranny of their day was prototypical of the moral mode of social-order authority. Reasoning from this false assumption, they mistakenly concluded that the moral mode of social order was inimical to liberty and social justice. From this fundamental misunderstanding has followed the continuing transformation of Western social order from a predominantly moral mode to a predominantly amoral mode of social-order authority, signified by the secular contract-state.

The evolution of the secular contract-state in the Western world has been marked by transformation of the principle of rule by representation into the doctrine of Western (i.e., synthetic) democracy, and transformation of the principle of natural right into the doctrine of constitutional human rights. The *philosophes* idealistically envisioned that rule by representation and the legal acknowledgment of natural rights would diffuse authority and secure liberty and social justice. But, from the start, Western elect bodies have perverted the *philosophes'* idealistic vision. They have exploited the secular doctrines of democracy and human rights in the same way that the elect bodies of the church-state exploited the sacred doctrines of divine rule and divine law – that is, as a (civic) religion to enforce and legitimize their oligarchic authority over their citizens; and as an 'opiate' to numb the masses to their condition of deprivation and subjugation. Even victims of the system accept it as legitimate.

Western elect bodies have dressed these two doctrines in the garb of idealism and altruism, and they have 'sanctified' them by entrenching them in the pre-eminent emblem of the 'common good,' their national constitutions. By intensive and extensive indoctrination of the myth that Western democracy and human rights diffuse authority and guarantee liberty and social justice, they ensure that any legislative or judicial expansion of their oligarchic authority via expanded or new human-rights laws will be met by enthusiastic approval from a chorus of civil libertarians, lawyers, academics, and other influential voices that shape public perceptions and opinions.

My analysis has identified several crucial flaws in constitutional human rights as a basis for social order in the Good Society: human rights come into effect and are exercised as political spoils and legal commodities; they are construed by Western elect bodies as legitimation and protection for their wealth, property, status, and privilege; they foster an ethic and culture that promotes egoism and narcissism; and they provide a legitimating rationale for social policies that violate human dignity and devalue humanity. In Western societies, human-rights doctrine has proven to be divisive and ineffective in checking or redressing grievous violations of liberty and social justice for significant segments of the population.

Those who champion Western democracy and constitutional human rights as signifying a social order that diffuses authority and guarantees liberty and social justice seriously misunderstand humankind's future under these doctrines. Armed with these hallowed doctrines and a monopoly over legislation, adjudication, and law enforcement, Western elect bodies are transforming key social institutions into functional constituents of their oligarchic structure, and extending their authority over more and more of citizens' daily activities, behaviours, and social relations. Through legislative and judicial application of the principles of moral neutrality and constitutional supremacy, Western elect bodies can purge all vestiges of societal moral values from law and impair citizens' capacity to establish and convey moral standards, thereby making their oligarchic authority an indispensable condition for stable social order and subverting the citizens' capacity to organize and act collectively against violations of liberty and social justice.

Human-rights doctrine and individual liberty are inversely related: instead of liberating individuals, human-rights doctrine serves as a legal warrant for state control over citizens; it facilitates their incarceration in a cage of restrictive state legal, administrative, regulative, and enforcement structures. Even as constitutional human rights are being expanded in the name of civil and social liberty, the result is that more of an individual's life is brought under the mandate of the state's oligarchic authority. In allegorical terminology, 'the tree of constitutional human rights stands inside the garden of state oligarchy.' The human rights that Western citizens crave, savour, and celebrate today will become a prison they will curse tomorrow.

My appraisal of the two modes of social-order authority affirmed that, in a globalizing world, authentic moral order is the best model for securing social justice with a minimum infringement on individual freedom. I want to reiterate and underline that I do not advocate the elimination of statutory human-rights laws for the protection of liberty, social justice, human dignity, and humanity; rather, I propose that human-rights doctrine lacks the authenticity to be accorded the status of a constitutional supremacy that trumps all other laws and community moral standards. Under a state oligarchy controlled by an elect body, constitutionalized human rights imperil liberty and social justice. I advocate demoting human-rights laws to civil statutory status.

PART THREE

Social Order in the Global Age

6   Human Rights and the Global Good Society

The Enlightenment signified a crucial development in the history of Euro-Western societies. It achieved the end of the monarchic system of governance and the dogmatic authority of the church-state. It initiated the contract-state with a system of representative government and individual rights. It triggered a fundamental change in social-order authority: from a moral mode defined by synthetic moral order based on sacred doctrine to an amoral mode defined by secular-legal order based on human-rights doctrine.

Today, the Millennial Generations are witnessing the transition of the Modern Age to the Global Age. Impelled by the expansion of social-relational interdependence and shared knowledge and understanding, the merging of primary spheres of power has progressed to a point at which existing jurisdictions of authority are undergoing a major realignment from nation-state to global dimensions. Globalization heralds profound political and cultural developments, especially for non-Western societies which have not experienced the Enlightenment and are moving directly from the pre-Modern Age into the Global Age. To achieve the Good Society in the Global Age, humankind needs a humane global social order; Western elect bodies uniformly and concertedly proclaim human rights as the essential doctrine of social order for the Good Society in the Global Age. In this chapter I will assess the merits of this claim in the context of a global world.

Universal Authenticity

If human-rights doctrine is to serve as the basis of humane social order in the global Good Society, it must have universal authenticity. The vocabulary of human rights is certainly being used worldwide; yet, of all the claims made for human-rights doctrine, that of universal authenticity is the least tenable. Some Western advocates of human-rights doctrine seek to validate the claim for universal authenticity based on the classical utilitarian premise that it achieves the common good of liberty and social justice. In order to make this case, they need to establish that there is a worldwide uniform philosophy and consensus on the best way to achieve liberty and social justice. But there exist profoundly different understandings about this across cultures. In Western societies, where these concepts have evolved within cultures that esteem the value of individualism, human-rights laws are considered to be universally serviceable for enhancing individual agency and the best design for protecting liberty and social justice. In most non-Western societies, the meaning of these concepts have evolved within cultures that esteem the value of community; there, individual agency is an alien concept and consensual moral standards of mutual duties and responsibilities are considered to be the best design for protecting liberty and social justice.

Those who hold that human-rights doctrine has universal authenticity offer various other rationales to support their opinion. Some cite the 'self-evident truth' that inherent and inalienable human rights are intrinsic to the 'virtue of being human.' Some believe as an article of faith that the doctrine's universal authenticity exists independent of any cultural world view. Some circuitously infer that, since all human beings are vulnerable to violations of human rights, therefore the doctrine of human rights is by definition universally authentic as protection of those rights. Some cite the Universal Declaration and UN international covenants as authentication that human-rights doctrine qualifies as a universal ethical standard. Some argue that the aspiration to human rights is an authentic phenomenon of the Modern Age, and since the Modern Age is an inescapable reality, therefore, by implication, human-rights doctrine has universal authenticity.

The foregoing rationales for the universal authenticity of human-rights doctrine all rest on an intuitive intellectual-philosophical conviction that it is the supreme principle of liberty and social justice. However, this scholarly intuition is not empirically grounded, or confirmed by systematic reasoning from an independent ethical point, or affirmed by cross-cultural consensus. The rationales for universal authenticity of human-rights doctrine are beset by profound theoretical, ethical, and ideological disagreements over duties versus rights; individual versus collective interests; and the role of state law versus moral custom in regulating social relations.

Some scholars from non-Western societies, who endorse human-rights doctrine as the supreme ethical principle of liberty and social justice, argue that it is consistent with basic intellectual-philosophical ideas in their indigenous cultures. The practical reality, however, is that most non-Western societies would have to undergo radical and disruptive changes in the organization of their cultural, political, economic, social, moral, and legal institutions to accommodate the ethical principle of liberty and social justice implied by human-rights doctrine.

Widespread opposition to the claim of universal authenticity for human rights was expressed by delegates at the World Conference on Human Rights held in Vienna on 14–28 June 1993. The conference had been convened by the UN expressly to reaffirm the Universal Declaration, but, from its earliest planning stages to its conclusion, it was plagued by disagreements, objections, and division over the applicability, justifiability, and legitimacy of its essential doctrine. Conference delegates from non-Western nations including India, China, Malaysia, and Singapore, representing the views of two-thirds of the world's population, accused Western elect bodies of trying to impose incompatible principles on their societies; and they censured the Declaration on the ground that it disregards the historical and cultural realities of their nations and the traditions, beliefs, and values of their peoples.

At the July 1997 meeting of the Association of Southeast Asian Nations, Malaysian Prime Minister Mahathir bin Mohamad called for a review of the Declaration of Human Rights, which he declared was 'formulated by the superpowers.' The prime minister was alluding to the fact that the UN, with 192 members, started out with only 58 member-states and that a large number of these states were still under colonial rule in 1948 when the Universal Declaration was framed by Western or Westernized politicians, diplomats, and lawyers. This assertion was broadly supported by delegates from other non-Western states but drew sharp criticism from Western delegates who declared their categorical opposition to any attempt to change the Declaration.

The deeply felt opposition to the Universal Declaration expressed by non-Western elect bodies is motivated in no small measure by concerns over issues of sovereignty and the potential threat the Declaration poses to their synthetic moral- and social-order authority. Nonetheless, it demonstrates unequivocally that, by any reasonable criterion, the doctrine of human rights lacks the worldwide value-transcendence, meaning, and acceptance needed to meet the standard of universal authenticity; and, absent universal authenticity, human rights cannot be considered to be an effective doctrine for a humane social order in the global Good Society.

Some Western intellectuals acknowledge a Western bias in the Universal Declaration. However, they are convinced that human rights are essential for attaining universal liberty and social justice, and they insist that such a noble purpose cannot possibly be inimical to the welfare of any society. To promote its universal acceptance, they advocate reformulating the Declaration's articles into a 'generic' form to be interpreted in culture-specific terms to fit each society's unique values, history, philosophy, and meaning of liberty and social justice. To this end, they advance a 'minimalist' doctrine of human rights which would not involve social values and structural consequences that are disruptive for non-Western societies. But everything we know about the functioning of social values and social structures denies the viability of such a design. Every culture is a complex web of social values and structures involving unique understandings of human nature and human agency. No matter how human-rights doctrine is presented, the intrinsic principle of individualism and the amoral bias would disrupt the cultural integrity of historical civilizations that differ from Western societies.

The potential for disruption of historical civilizations is given immediacy by the collaborative insistence of Western elect bodies that, to gain their political and economic approbation, a state regime must adopt the Universal Declaration as the political and legal standard for nation-state governance and international relations. All developing societies are currently undergoing industrialization, urbanization, and modernization, and Western economic support is essential for their political stability as they go through these fundamental changes. By insisting, under threat of political-economic sanctions, that these state regimes must conform their domestic constitutions and charters to the doctrine of human rights, with or without the informed consent of their citizens, Western elect bodies are eroding the political, cultural, and moral autonomy of these societies and destroying the diversity of human civilizations. Their collaboration to coerce developing countries to conform their constitutions and charters to international human-rights laws is a reprise of seventeenth-century European hegemons who collaborated to fashion the 'law of nations' giving 'Christian' regimes a mandate to colonize 'heathen' lands and force the inhabitants to adopt Christian values.

True Believers

Antagonism towards human rights in non-Western societies is exacerbated by Western advocates who dogmatically construe the doctrine as a truth not to be questioned. These 'true believers' imperiously declare that human-rights doctrine signifies 'civilization and freedom' and denial of human rights signifies 'savagery and oppression.' They judge the virtue of all cultures according to their doctrinal orthodoxy; and, evocative of the oppressive images of the 'White Man's Burden' and 'Manifest Destiny,' they demand that all societies uniformly enact human-rights laws in conformity with their truth.

True believers in human-rights doctrine display many of the obsessive traits of religious extremists: they embrace the doctrine with unconditional commitment; they marginalize and demonize those with different views; they exhibit a high degree of self-righteousness, intolerance, and paternalism towards those with different ideas; they view life in black-and-white terms; they are impervious to any and all evidence and logic that challenges their truth; they declare that only corrupt regimes and popular ignorance stand in the way of universal acceptance of their doctrinal orthodoxy; and they wallow and glory in their dogmatic bias.

Western true believers have adopted the mindset of colonial missionaries who rationalized the imperialist goals of their church-state patrons on the grounds that they were bringing the ultimate benefit of 'salvation' to heathen societies. They manifest the same arrogant moralistic, ethnocentric, paternalistic, elitist, and cultural insensitivity as the proselytizers who once fanned out across colonial empires ravaging indigenous heritages, customs, and moral foundations and coercing subjected peoples to accept the synthetic morality of their church-state. They lobby for political, economic, and legal sanctions and other coercive tactics against some of the world's most destitute societies. Some approve of military intimidation and, if necessary, invasions ('holy wars') that kill hundreds of thousands of defenceless, innocent civilians to overthrow regimes that resist their dogma. These crusading 'modern missionaries' are absolutely certain they have the highest calling and a supreme mandate to subvert the independent evolution of indigenous humane social-relational blueprints of societies with different ideas about how to achieve liberty and social justice.

Through UN-affiliated NGOs and local agencies, true believers have parlayed human rights into a multibillion-dollar industry. Finding the money to grow their budgets and bureaucracies is a constant concern, and they have developed a schemer's sensitivity for the biases of their Western funding sources. Operating as propagandists, they promote human rights as the 'global culture' of freedom. They blend their message into popular forms of Western entertainment and fashions to provide the disaffected youth of non-Western societies with a motive for defecting from their oppressive and burdensome indigenous synthetic moral values, duties, and responsibilities. As an additional lure to citizens of developing countries, they misleadingly identify Western democracy and human rights with Western levels of material prosperity. This deceit conceals the reality of a growing gap between rich and poor, a growing problem of homelessness, destitution, and lack of health care, and a host of other serious endemic violations of liberty, social justice, human dignity, and humanity in the affluent bastions of Western democracy and human rights.

Internationalization of Human Rights

The Universal Declaration does not establish human-rights doctrine as an international legal obligation; it is a declaration of the principle and ideal – which all state regimes should teach, promote, and observe – that all human beings are born free and equal in dignity. In 1966, however, the UN initiated two human-rights-based covenants that are accorded the status of international treaties and, as such, are, hypothetically, legally binding under international law. The two covenants were not inspired by a commitment to freedom and equal dignity; they were conceived by Western and Soviet elect bodies to advance their respective hegemonic ambitions. Each of these Cold War contenders was determined that its political-economic agenda should prevail in international law, and they shaped the two covenants to advance their respective capitalist and socialist political-economic ideologies. The International Covenant on Civil and Political Rights was conceived by Western elect bodies to advance their capitalist ideology and agenda; the International Covenant on Economic, Social and Cultural Rights was conceived by the Soviet elect body to promote its socialist ideology and agenda.

The Western-capitalist-sponsored covenant includes the right to vote and hold political office; the right to liberty (i.e., freedom of thought, of religion, of assembly, of speech, of press, of movement); the right to due process; and the right to protection from torture and cruel, inhuman, or degrading treatment. The Soviet-socialist-sponsored covenant includes the right to adequate standards of living and economic security (i.e., food, shelter, health care); equal pay for equal work; fair and adequate compensation, leisure, and reasonable working hours; free development of personality; the right to an education; and freedom to participate in the culture of the community.

The provisions of the two covenants are legally binding under international law, but only on those nation-states that have ratified them; non-ratifying states are exempt from the legal provisions of the covenants. Even the ratifying states, however, are not all subject to legal sanctions for violations of the covenants. In the case of the Covenant on Civil and Political Rights, only those ratifying states that have approved an 'optional protocol' approving UN legal action on complaints of human-rights violations are subject to international legal action. In the case of the Covenant on Economic, Social and Cultural Rights, compliance is entirely on a voluntary basis.

Since the covenants were introduced, only a minority of UN member-states has ratified both of them and even fewer have signed the optional protocol. Moreover, the UN Human Rights Commission, which receives and evaluates the performance reports of member-states, is chosen by a system of regional rotation and includes members that are known to have committed flagrant human-rights violations. When such member-states sit on the panel, they can block criticism of their own performance and that of their allies.

The manifest ineffectiveness of international law to realize the Universal Declaration's ideal of freedom and equal human dignity is compounded by the fact that the covenants are not intended to protect the rights of *individual* citizens. While the UN has granted hearings to selected minority groups (such as Canadian Aboriginal peoples) charging their government with human-rights violations, it does not consider individual complainants to fall within its jurisdiction. Given that human rights are exclusively individual rights, this constitutes a fundamental breach of the Universal Declaration. In effect, the UN covenants and enforcement protocols favour the state perpetrators of human-rights violations, not the victims.

Until recently, the ambitions of Western elect bodies to internationalize human-rights laws have been impeded by the sovereignty provisions of Article 2(7) of the UN Charter, which protects the inviolability of domestic jurisdiction of all member-states. However, since the collapse of the Soviet Union, Western elect bodies have moved aggressively to weaken the sovereignty provisions so as to allow intervention in the domestic jurisdiction of a sovereign state when it is deemed to be in violation of international human-rights law. Bowing to Western political pressure, former UN secretary general Kofi Annan declared that Article 2(7) does not protect the sovereignty of a nation when a regime is guilty of pervasive and systematic violations of human rights. In 2005 the UN World Summit endorsed the principle of intervention on humanitarian grounds when a state fails to safeguard the lives and well-being of its own people.

The UN Charter's Articles 55 and 56 pledge all UN members 'to take joint and separate action,' in cooperation with the UN, to promote 'universal respect for and observance of, human rights and fundamental freedoms.' In reality, however, the UN is virtually helpless to stop violators or apply meaningful sanctions against them. Even with reams of evidence documenting appalling violations of human-rights laws including state-sponsored torture, executions, and slavery, the UN has been unable to act effectively. On the rare occasions when it can muster a political consensus of member- states for intervention, the UN lacks the competence and resources – legal, political, economic, military – to meaningfully regulate or force any state to observe international human-rights laws against its will.

Given the UN's incapacity to shield people from pervasive and systematic violations of human rights, it follows that any forceful humanitarian intervention will necessarily be performed by a 'coalition of the willing.' This has opened a loophole in the UN Charter's protection of national sovereignty, which is raising fears among some member-states. Although most UN members support the principle of collective responsibility to halt crimes against humanity such as genocide, ethnic cleansing, mass murder, rape, torture, and terrorism, many non-Western leaders view the Western elect bodies' proclaimed commitment to humanitarian intervention as suspect. Small, strategically important countries that are deemed to be unfriendly to Western interests worry that the pretext of humanitarian intervention will be exploited by Western elect bodies to legalize unilateral military operations against them.

A review of history shows that these apprehensions are well founded. Western elect bodies' have always cloaked their hegemonic motives in the guise of humanitarian crusades; however, their response to crimes against humanity has been very selective. When such crimes are committed by regimes hostile to the West, they are construed as a serious contravention of international law and as a pretext for aggressively applying strong-arm political and economic sanctions, or for mounting military operations, as in Iraq. When comparable violations are committed by friendly or collaborative regimes, they are disregarded, or, if the regimes are deemed to have a strategic value, they are bolstered with economic and military aid, as in the instance of Pakistan.

This hypocrisy of Western elect bodies has been underscored by their repeated refusal to respond to UN requests for humanitarian intervention to prevent mass atrocities. UN observers attested that, by sending a token force of 10,000 soldiers to the Darfur region of Sudan, NATO could have defused the conflict and prevented the murder of several hundred thousands of civilians, the rape of tens of thousands of women, and the displacement of over a million people perpetrated against Black ethnic groups by the Sudanese government and its Arab Janjaweed militia allies. NATO declined to intervene in this genocidal atrocity, but it expeditiously marshalled an international force of 70,000 troops to eliminate a terrorist cell in Afghanistan that posed only a potential threat to the security of its primary members.

The UN seeks to convey the impression that its undertaking to internationalize human-rights laws implies progress in its mission to extend the Universal Declaration's principle and ideal of freedom, social justice, and equal human dignity worldwide. However, as we have seen, this endeavour has been a profound failure. Even as all state delegates to the UN laud the performance of their own regimes for their record on human-rights protection, documented reports by NGOs indicate flagrant, ongoing crimes against humanity in a number of member-states; moreover, pervasive violations of human dignity and assaults on humanity occur in all states. These reports stand as irrefutable and tragic testimony that the UN strategy to internationalize human rights through legal means is not moving the world any closer to the Good Society.

The United States and the Internationalization of Human Rights

Any discussion of the internationalization of human rights requires that special attention be given to the role played by the U.S. elect body, the self-proclaimed global champion of internationalization of human rights. Every U.S. administration, regardless of party, ritually proclaims the American commitment to bringing human rights to every corner of the globe. President John F. Kennedy grandiosely proclaimed that the United States stood ready to 'pay any price, bear any burden' to promote and defend the human rights of all peoples. President Jimmy Carter made human rights a central moral theme of U.S. foreign policy. Carter declared that the United States would use foreign policy to promote human rights around the world. His declaration was given a high profile and applauded from every point on the U.S. political spectrum; it was perceived as a fitting expression of U.S. identity and global moral leadership.

Yet the reality is that the U.S. policy commitment to human rights is selective and always in the interests of U.S. strategic hegemony. Based on a review of formerly classified diplomatic and intelligence documents on U.S. foreign relations, the *New York Times* found that, under the Carter policy, human-rights principles were regularly trumped on grounds of political 'realism' by U.S. economic and military strategic interests. The *Times* reported that the administrations of presidents Carter, Reagan, and Bush, Sr wielded human-rights doctrine as a strategic weapon under the guise of a moral cause; they deliberately withheld information from Congress and the U.S. public about some of the worst human-rights abuses in countries friendly to U.S. strategic interests and objectives. Even as it castigated, threatened, and punished human-rights violators such as the regimes in Vietnam, Cuba, Venezuela, and El Salvador, which expressed criticism and opposition to U.S. policies, the U.S. elect body practically disregarded endemic and widespread gross human-rights abuses by a long list of compliant dictators, such as Augusto Pinochet in Chile, Reza Shah Pahlavi in Iran, Anastasio Somoza in Nicaragua, Fernando Marcos in the Philippines, Pervez Musharraf in Pakistan, and the al Sauds in Saudi Arabia.

Moreover, the U.S. elect body does not conform its own laws to its rhetoric on international human-rights law. It refuses to accept as domestic law any human right that does not fit its capitalist political, economic, or social agendas. For instance, it has refused to ratify the International Covenant on Economic, Social and Cultural Rights because it guarantees every citizen's right to a job, a place to live, health care, and education. Implementing the provisions of this covenant would correct a domestic history of endemic economic, political, and social violations of the human dignity of its own citizens, but the U.S. elect body refuses to commit itself to this international human-rights treaty because doing so would require a redistribution of wealth, income, commodities, services, and opportunities.

The suspect quality of the U.S. elect body's commitment to international human-rights laws was writ large in its policy authorizing the torture of suspects detained in its 'war against terrorism.' The UN Declaration of Human Rights, the Geneva Convention, and the U.S. constitution all prohibit torture of prisoners. To circumvent these strictures, and in direct violation of international standards and treaties, President George W. Bush requested, and the U.S. Department of Justice issued, memoranda giving legal justification for a wide range of cruel, inhuman, and degrading procedures (euphemistically named 'enhanced interrogation techniques') to extract information from detainees suspected of having knowledge about terrorist activities and plans.

To avoid domestic judicial scrutiny and legal accountability for these gross violations of domestic and international law, the U.S. Department of Justice crafted a special protocol affirming that its agents are not obliged to honour the principles of the U.S. constitution when operating outside the territorial United States, thereby freeing them to conduct extreme interrogation techniques involving simulated drowning, tortuous shackling, sleep deprivation, humiliation, and other forms of abusive treatment on U.S. military bases in foreign countries. According to investigations by the International Red Cross, this protocol gave rise to a widespread pattern of routine torture resulting in scores of deaths of detainees in U.S. prisons at Guantánamo Bay in Cuba, Bagram in Afghanistan, and Abu Ghraib in Iraq.

The Bush administration also mandated the CIA to perpetrate covert kidnappings of suspected terrorists and to transfer them (a practice termed 'rendition') for detention and interrogation to regimes that were known to be the worst violators of human rights. The *New York Times* obtained flight logs showing that the CIA sent terror suspects to Uzbekistan, whose ruling regime has been condemned by the UN and various international human-rights groups for systematic torture of prisoners in its jails, involving beatings, asphyxiation, scalding, electroshock, and plucking fingernails. In response to international censure of this violation of the UN Charter, the chairman of the U.S. Joint Chief of Staffs, General Richard B. Myer, responded: 'In my view, we shouldn't let any single issue drive our relationship with any single country.'

When pictures and accounts of atrocities by the U.S. military and the CIA were leaked to the media, setting off an international furore, President George W. Bush, commander-in-chief of U.S. forces, and his secretary of defense, Donald H. Rumsfeld, denied any accountability. Official blame for these atrocities was limited to a handful of low-level military personnel – called 'bad apples' – and civilian contractors. Although interrogation and prison policies were formulated and mandated at the top of the U.S. command structure, no high-level military officers or government officials have been held to account. Moreover, special protocols of the Justice Department, enshrined in the Military Commissions Act, exempted from war-crimes prosecutions any U.S. officials who implemented or had command responsibility for torture and transfers of suspected terrorists. Both the executive and legislative branches of the U.S. government turned a blind eye or acted in complicity with the military command structure in the perpetration of these crimes against humanity.

In his Fourth of July address in 2003, President George W. Bush reiterated the stock proclamation of U.S. global moral leadership. However, enlightened people the world over regard the U.S. elect body's breach of international laws, its refusal to sign and honour international treaties that would make the world safer, and its expedient violation of fundamental standards of human dignity and humanity by its torture of enemy combatants as representing a disqualification and forfeit of any claim to moral exceptionalism and global moral leadership. Beginning with the Vietnam War, U.S. elect bodies have wantonly squandered the inspirational legacy of humanitarianism symbolized by the Statue of Liberty and the international moral legitimacy earned by the Marshall Plan and other impressive humanitarian initiatives. Not only have they forfeited global moral leadership, but, by flouting international law at will, they have seriously undermined the UN's mandate to shield people the world over from genocide, ethnic cleansing, coerced flight, torture, and other gross violations of human dignity and humanity.

7 Globalization and Social Order

In the Modern Age, human rights prevailed as the dominant doctrine of social order in Western societies. However, as globalization progresses and the Global Age evolves, global free-market capitalism is setting off a political-economic dynamic that is rendering the doctrine of human rights problematical and spontaneously giving rise to a global doctrine and system of social order based on economic-utilitarian imperatives. I call this emerging post-modern doctrine and system of social order 'globalism,' and in the following discussion I will delineate the decline of human rights and the rise of globalism.

The Decline of Human Rights

Human rights, like Western democracy, emerged, evolved, and reached its crest within the framework of the sovereign nation-state. How will human rights fare in a borderless world? Whereas the future of democracy is obscure and open to speculation, the future of human rights is apparent in several contemporary trends.

Global free-market capitalism is bringing about a radical change in the way Western elect bodies deal with human rights. Under the rules of traditional corporate capitalism, Western elect bodies profited by insisting on including human-rights provisions in trade agreements that restricted the importation of goods and services from countries lacking basic human-rights standards. While they professed humanitarian motives, their primary intent was to eliminate any competitive advantage from lower costs of operations that might accrue to corporations located in such countries.

Globalization and the economic-utilitarian imperatives of global free-market capitalism are changing the dynamics of economic investment and moving human-rights doctrine into a new phase. In the emerging world, without investment and trade boundaries, countries with lower costs of operation have become lucrative investment targets. To take advantage of this new circumstance, Western elect bodies are adopting a 'realist' policy stand on human-rights provisions in trade agreements. At present, the rhetoric of human rights continues to have political and economic utility for Western elect bodies, and domestic sensitivities still require them to extol it. However, as human-rights principles get in the way of their own foreign-based multinational corporate investment and trade activities, their political support for international human rights is beginning to wane. For instance, they no longer promote World Trade Organization provisions that restrict the importation of goods, services, and investment because of corporate violations of human-rights standards.

The Canadian government exhibited this diminishing commitment to human-rights doctrine when it hosted the Asia Pacific Economic Cooperation Forum in Vancouver, British Columbia, in the autumn of 1997. The issue of human-rights violations was omitted from the conference agenda even though several of the eighteen member-states, including China, Indonesia, and Thailand, had been repeatedly condemned by NGOs for their grievous violations of international human-rights standards. When Canada's trade minister was confronted by human-rights activists demanding that he make a statement to the forum condemning the child-labour practices of some member-states, he explicitly asserted that Canada would not push human-rights principles because to do so could jeopardize profitable trade arrangements. In a subsequent television interview, then Prime Minister Jean Chrétien endorsed his trade minister's refusal to use the forum to promote human-rights principles and curtly dismissed his critics with the very odd comment that Canada should not act like a 'big shot' on the subject, because it was too small a country to have any influence.

The U.S. elect body has adopted a two-faced posture on human rights in its respective trade policies towards Cuba and China. On the one hand, the U.S. elect body imposes crushing political, economic, and trade sanctions against poverty-stricken Cuba, ostensibly to punish the government for its human-rights violations. On the other hand, it has granted its chief banker, China, the impenitent perpetrator of crimes against humanity in Tibet, of the Tiananmen Square massacre, and of other gross human-rights violations, 'most favoured nation' trading status. When President Clinton signed the bill granting China such status, he proclaimed that free trade is the best way to advance the cause of human rights and freedom; but not in Cuba. Evidently, the U.S. elect body considers profitable trade and investment relations with China to have priority over the human rights of oppressed people.

As free-market capitalism and the free movement of goods, services, labour, and capital achieve global scale, all corporations will have to compete head-to-head in the international marketplace. Corporations based in countries that enforce human-rights standards will be at a competitive disadvantage vis à vis others. To protect their investments in corporations based in Western countries, elect bodies will be motivated to erode and ultimately abolish human-rights principles and standards in their own societies. This prospect is given credence by the ease with which Western elect bodies abridged and compromised basic civil liberties and criminalized some forms of dissent in their own societies following 9/11.

In this regard, it may be significant that President George W. Bush, in his 2005 inaugural address, which was hailed by U.S. talk-shows, think-tanks, and op-ed and freelance media pundits as one of the most expansive manifestos of democracy, made only one cursory and oblique reference to human rights. Given that it is an alien and unwanted doctrine to many non-Western states, an ineffective warrant for liberty, social justice, and human dignity, and a hindrance to global free-market capitalism, the future of human-rights doctrine as the political and legal standard for nation-state governance and international relations is dismal indeed.

Globalism

The Global Age is characterized by the rise of globalism, a doctrine and system of social order based on economic-utilitarian imperatives. Globalism involves not only the decline of Western democracy and human rights but also a profound transformation of all currently prevailing forms of social-order authority the world over. Globalism differs profoundly from conventional social orders in its origination, purpose, realization, and attributes. Conventional social orders are originated by human beings for the purpose of regulating social relations, and they are realized as society-specific cultural blueprints for survival and sufficiency. Globalism, by contrast, is originating spontaneously as an

effect of global free-market capitalism's economic-utilitarian imperatives, and it is being realized as a universal lifestyle that transforms the
logic of living from survival and sufficiency to unrestrained consumption. Globalism beguiles individuals into self-motivated consumption
by promoting the newest stylistic variations in goods and services as
the primary criterion of individual identity, self-fulfillment, and one's
standing in the hierarchy of social status.

Whereas conventional cultures foster 'within-group' uniformity and
'between-group' pluralism in consensual values and identities, globalism fosters 'between-group' uniformity of social values by promoting a
universal aspiration to unrestrained consumerism; and it brings about
'within-group' pluralism by promoting income- and education-affected
aesthetic-hedonistic niche-style variations in personal consumption
(such as 'name branded' clothing, food, and music and broadcast programming) as meaningful and esteemed expressions of individual
identity and self-realization.

Globalism entails a world view and way of life that poses a threat
to traditional cultural values, and, usually, any threat to cultural values provokes strong social-political resistance. In Western secular-
amoral societies, resistance to globalism is largely muted because it
is experienced as a logical and natural extension of the capitalist pattern of consumerism and as a promise of a higher standard of living.
In non-Western societies, however, where social order is still based on
synthetic moral doctrines, often tinged with sacred significance, the
experience of globalism is quite different: it is perceived as alien and
detrimental because its secular-amoral principles affect a significant
change in lifestyle, especially in the younger generation. This is pro-
voking strong oppositional cultural-religious politics and engendering
an insular attitude, especially in Muslim societies, usually in the form
of a hostile and defensive religious fundamentalism or radical political
authoritarianism.

Opposition to globalism in non-Western societies is exacerbated by
a widespread belief that it is the new face of Western cultural imperialism, akin to Christian colonialism or human-rights internationalism.
This view of globalism stems significantly from the fact that Western
intellectual commodities such as movies, music, television shows,
and fashions currently reign in the global marketplace. Although
these commodities have Western origins and signify a Western lifestyle
(called 'pop culture'), they do not of themselves constitute culture in
the conventional meaning of collective values, duties, responsibilities,

purposes, and social identity. As a feature of globalism, the preponderance of Western intellectual commodities in the global marketplace is a consumer phenomenon of mass marketing and economic dominance; it signifies economic-political domination, not cultural imperialism.

To understand the domination of Western intellectual commodities in the global marketplace, we need to consider the influence of human-rights doctrine. As noted earlier, more than a half-century of constitutional human rights has practically voided all traditional moral meanings in Western cultures, giving way to an amoral economic-utilitarian doctrine. This has had the effect of depleting Western cultural properties of moral meaning and significance, freeing entrepreneurs from traditional moral constraints on the commoditization and commercialization of Western cultural properties. Abetted by the spirit of capitalism, they have taken these properties out of their cultural context and meaning and aggressively mass-marketed them around the world for profit. (Some Western entrepreneurs have extended the commercialization and marketing of cultural properties to the sacred and private artifacts of Aboriginal peoples, against their will.)

Most non-Western societies, on the other hand, are still inhibited by the traditional moral meanings and significance of their cultural properties from freely commoditizing and commercializing them. Their initial entry into the global marketplace has featured mainly manufactured commodities, ranging from textiles to computers. Non-Western societies have a huge potential for creative commoditization and commercialization of their cultural properties, both domestically and in the global marketplace. As global free-market capitalism's amoral economic-utilitarian doctrine takes hold in these societies, their customary inhibitions to the commoditization and commercialization of their cultural properties will diminish. And, when their own cultural properties achieve a proportional share of the global market, non-Western societies will comprehend that the present Western character of globalism is an economic phenomenon not cultural imperialism. This will depoliticize globalism, and non-Western opposition to it will diminish. Also, by reason of its promise of a better standard of living, non-Western societies will come to perceive globalism as a rational, natural, beneficial, even necessary adaptation for surviving in a globalizing world.

Globalism signifies the displacement of human agency by 'extra-human' agency as the originator of social order. By extra-human I do not imply a mystical or preternatural force. What I have in mind is akin to Adam Smith's 'invisible hand'; it can be readily apprehended in terms of the economic-utilitarian imperatives of global free-market capital-ism. Adam Smith saw the 'invisible hand' as a benefit to humankind; however, the extra-human agency signified by globalism diminishes humanity. It values individuals according to their perceived serviceabil-ity as units of competitive consumption and production, not for their intrinsic humanity. Those who cannot satisfy global free-market capi-talism's imperatives are devalued in their human worth. Thus, the rise of globalism portends an escalating evaluation of humankind's utilitar-ian qualities and a concurrent devaluation of humankind's potentiality for humanity. This regression from humanity can be readily observed in the pervasive layoffs of workers to achieve more efficient production; citing global free-market capitalism's economic-utilitarian imperatives, corporate owners and managers increasingly disavow moral account-ability for the devastating effects of the layoffs on the dignity and humanity of the affected employees and their families.

The economic-utilitarian imperatives of globalism also erode human-ity by fostering a technological revolution that objectifies and com-moditizes the human person. The growing sophistication of cybernetic technology is inverting the traditional functional dynamic between peo-ple and technology. Social theorist Marshall McLuhan anticipated the thought-changing effect of the computer ('We shape our tools and after-wards our tools shape us' [McLuhan 1994]); however, he perceived its effect in terms of a communications revolution and as an intermediary in the augmentation of human cognitive capability, similar to the aug-mentation of manual capability through tools and technology. He did not conceive of an age in which human cognition would become meshed with cyber technology and function as an extension of the computer.

In a growing number of endeavours, the capabilities of computers are surpassing those of their human partners. In such cases, human cognition is compelled to subordinate and adjust its reasoning/mediat-ing function to the economic-utilitarian logic of the computer so as to take full advantage of the computer's superior capability and efficiency. This requires the human partner to communicate, process, and contex-tualize information in the digital language of the computer. Computer language, like all languages, influences the fundamental patterns of human reasoning, imagination, and self-consciousness. In the human-computer partnership, the impact of language is augmented by the user's dependence on the computer's memory.

Computers oblige users to function in a stimulus-response mode. This mode differs from the stimulus-response pattern of instinct; whereas the latter is genetically fixed, human cognition can be repeatedly reprogrammed to conform to the evolving requirements and enhancements of cybernetic technology. However, the effect of an extensive and long-term partnership with the computer will be to progressively re-pattern and condition human cognition from a reflective to a stimulus-response mode.

Communication via the Internet and cognate technologies is increasingly fostering a lifestyle in which individuals relate to each other as proxy personas; that is, they know eath other as virtual, not real, human beings. This phenomenon progresses as cybernetic technology attains the ability to produce a visual digital world of virtual realism. In commerce this technology is being used to create digital proxy personas who conduct virtual 'face-to-face' business meetings in virtual office complexes. In some computer games this visual digital world involves players assuming proxy personas who simulate killing virtual human beings. In its military application, the technology assumes a more sinister form when army personnel are trained in interactive battle simulations to use proxy personas to kill a simulated enemy. And it assumes an extreme, malevolent form when military technicians, acting under orders, guide remote-controlled armed Predator drones to kill real human beings, whom they are programmed to regard as virtual people.

The impact of digital conditioning, and particularly the shifting of real-life experiences into the virtual realm, on the evolving human brain and human nature is still in its early infancy so we don't know how its growth and long-term effects will affect humankind. Its potential detrimental consequences for humanity are masked by its significant augmentation of our cognitive competence, its incredible efficiency, and the complex and entrancing creative challenges it affords. However, we know that cyber-technology diminishes personal connections and that, as we attain the ability to create a visual digital world of virtual realism, it takes on a dehumanizing aspect. The Global Age heralds a world increasingly reliant on cyber-technology, and reason indicates that, as the computer becomes the dominant partner and the principal vehicle in our communications with one another, its logic will condition human thinking and transform human consciousness and human relations in ways that erode human sensibility. Thus, the surrender of social-order authority to the 'extra-human' agency indicated by globalism foreshadows further regression from humanity.

Summary

In the Modern Age, social-order authority in Western societies was based on two primary doctrines: synthetic democracy, which defined the prevailing system of government; and constitutional human rights, which defined the dominant social-relational value system. Western elect bodies allege universal authenticity for Western democracy and human rights as doctrines of liberty and social justice; and, under the pretext of humanitarianism, they have collaborated in attempts to internationalize the two doctrines. Non-Western societies have resisted this initiative on two grounds: they consider moral duties and responsibilities, not amoral-legal standards, to be the best design for maintaining social order and warranting social justice; and they perceive the Western elect bodies' proclaimed humanitarian motive for internationalizing human rights and Western democracy as a sham and an expedient cover for hegemonic ambitions.

The Global Age portends a radical change for both Western democracy and human rights. The waning of the traditional sovereign nation-state's authority has the effect of diminishing factional rivalry for dominance in the oligarchic authority structure, thereby eroding the primary function and purpose of Western elections; and the economic-utilitarian imperatives of global free-market capitalism are rendering human-rights standards uneconomic and inexpedient for Western elect bodies, indicating the end of their support for these standards as the dominant social-relational value system.

Global free-market capitalism is spontaneously giving rise to globalism. Globalism is predicated on an economic-utilitarian doctrine of unrestrained consumption. Reason tells us that the planet's finite resources and fragile ecosystem cannot sustain unrestrained consumption. Reason also tells us that our prospects will deteriorate rapidly when populous societies like China and India endorse globalism as the primary standard of social order. This dismal prospect is exacerbated by the mammoth commercial-industrial projects made possible by the vast capital resources of global free-market capitalism. In the absence of effective global political-legal institutions with the motive and authority to regulate the conduct of mega-corporations and to mediate the anticipated conflicts over diminishing essential resources, globalism foreshadows the ultimate destruction of planetary life support and a Hobbesian post-state world.

Globalism signifies the transfer of social-order authority from human agency to the extra-human agency of global free-market capitalism. If globalism progresses to a fully subscribed global doctrine and system of social order, it will bring about the dystopian world imagined by Aldous Huxley and George Orwell: a world in which the 'worth' of individuals will be established by criteria of economic utility, not their intrinsic humanity; all human reasoning, imagining, creativity, and consciousness will be imprisoned in a technological stimulus-response mindset; individual human beings will become oriented away from their own and other's humanity and accept their lives as other species accept their lives. Ironically, human beings will feel no need for liberation, because globalism will beguile them to accept their economic-utilitarian-defined existence and worth as self-realization, freedom, and self-determination. But, even if there is widespread and grave discontent, there is no escape because the absence of moral integration forecloses the possibility of a social revolution.

Humankind exhibits a great variation of cultural heritages which have evolved over thousands of years. By constraining all societies to conform their value system to the economic-utilitarian doctrine of the global free-market capitalist system, globalism vitiates cultural self-determination and creates a convergence of social values, norms, and practices. Under globalism, all social, economic, political, and legal structures, all laws, rewards, and punishments, all social roles and relationships, all individual and collective values, sensibilities, and means and ends will be functionally configured into a uniform global utility-based pattern. All indigenous identities, customs, and institutions derived from diverse histories and ancestries and all cultural distinctions will be superseded and supplanted by the uniform and unitary economic-utilitarian doctrine of global free-market capitalism and globalism. Consumption will be the dominant means of self-expression;

variations in individual identity and self-realization will be expressed as styles of personal consumption. Civilization and humankind will be immeasurably impoverished.

Without intervention by the Millennial Generations, human beings will be conscripted and conditioned to perform as unreflecting, conforming, predictable, uniform, isolated functional units of efficient consumption and production; trade and capital will be liberated but humankind will be placed in servitude to the systemic totalitarianism of the extra-human global free-market capitalist system and the economic-utilitarian tyranny of globalism.

PART FOUR

Social Order and the Good Society

8   Social Order by Design

Globalization is like a river bound for the sea; although marked by eddies, backwashes, rapids, and waterfalls, its ultimate destination is never in doubt. However, the deterministic forces of globalization do not imply the inevitability of a Hobbesian world described by globalism. The future of humankind, although problematical, is open. We, the Millennial Generations, stand at the fail-safe point in history for determining the destiny of humanity. We can surrender our prerogative as originator of social order to the 'extra-human' agency of global free-market capitalism and reap globalism, which will transform social relations and human consciousness in a way that devastates humanity, or we can exercise our human agency to create a humane global moral social order that will place humankind on the path to the Good Society.

While the principles of natural rights and rule by representation as originally conceived by the *philosophes* imply humane goals, as discussed earlier, the Western doctrines of synthetic democracy and constitutional human rights do not fulfil our potential and aspiration for humanity. If we neglect to create and implement a humane social order, then our potential for humanity will remain dormant. In the following discussion, I will delineate a humane global moral social order in terms of a universal humane ethical principle and a social-relational system for implementing and nurturing authentic morality in a globalizing world.

A Humane Ethical Principle

Wendell Bell has provided a sober and disturbing representation of the morality that is currently culturally available in modern societies:

'a mish-mash of sometimes contradictory rules of thumb based on frag-
ments of religious and moral codes we have been taught, the laws of our
country, the lessons we think we have learned from our own experiences,
our personal preferences, the conventions and traditions of the group to
which we belong, our ineffable and intuitive gut feeling, and, of course,
myths and superstitions of all kinds' (Bell, 1997, vol. 1, 113). Moral values
have been replaced by religion, laws, egoism, fashion, and peer pressure
as primary determinants of individual behaviour.

To realize the Good Society in the global world, we need a morality
that is based on an authentic universal humane ethical principle that
will inspire common cause and commitment to individual liberty, social
justice, human dignity, and humanity for peoples the world over. How
can we discover such a principle? Philosophers have long sought to find
a universal humane ethical principle by means of intuition. Intuition
has been ambiguously described in terms of various forms of thinking:
imaginative, anticipatory, explorative, disembodied, inspired, independent, primitive, simple, unconscious, holistic, and so on. Scholarly intuition is characterized as a mental process of logical analysis, sometimes
involving an inner dialogue with imaginary interlocutors, or by means
of intellectual empathy with alter egos. The influence of scholarly intuition throughout the history of civilization is undeniable.

Some eminent philosophers have sought to determine a universal humane ethical principle by imagining a surrogate persona –
Everyman – a prototypical human being who is devoid of personal
biases and can stand as an intellectual proxy representing all of humankind. Sometimes Everyman is cast as a virtual superman. For example,
Rousseau speaks of a proxy with 'superior intelligence,' a capacity for
'beholding all the passions of men without experiencing any of them'
and 'knowing [human nature] through and through.'

More recently, Harvard professor John Rawls, in his quest for a universal ethical principle and philosophy of justice, imagined an intellectual proxy possessing the following attributes: the requisite powers of
reasoning; knowledge of the general psychology of human nature with
respect to fundamental passions and motivations; knowledge of what
primary goods every reasonable being wishes to possess to make life
meaningful; suitable knowledge of competing principles of justice; and
basic knowledge that the ethical principles selected will regulate real
life in the context of prevailing circumstances. In addition, he ascribed
to his intellectual proxy the capacity to be impartial, disinterested, and
equally responsive to the desire of everyone who will be affected by the
selected system of principles.

Scholarly intuitionists escape inconvenient empirical realities by situating their intellectual proxy in a fabricated pristine world, such as 'the state of nature,' 'the original position,' or a 'Garden of Eden,' and they ascribe a 'sanitized psyche' to their proxy. Following in this tradition, Rawls fabricated a pristine world and sanitized psyche by situating his proxy behind a hypothetical 'veil of ignorance.' Rawls assumed that the 'veil of ignorance' shields his proxy from all particular information about the self, such as age, gender, skin colour, education, personal history, and social status, and he denied his proxy any knowledge about how the principles of social justice he or she devised would affect their personal interests.

It is an engaging intellectual device, but, even if his proxy possessed all of the remarkable attributes Rawls imagined, it is delusory to suppose that a hypothetical screen or blindfold can cause total amnesia. Contrary to his fanciful notion, Rawls's proxy unavoidably carried all of Rawls's own experiences, interests, needs, aspirations, language, values, meanings, world view, understandings, conceptual premises, and other personal baggage behind the 'veil of ignorance,' and they profoundly influenced his proxy's conception of justice. Moreover, Rawls's proxy makes self-serving choices in a vacuum of humanity. This is evident in the principle of social justice which he intuits.

Rawls's principle of social justice, named 'Maximin,' is based on the ethical standard of impartiality within an individualist liberal system of meritocracy. It subscribes to the capitalist fiction of an expanding sum of wealth and the concomitant idea that an individual, regardless of social, economic, physical, and other inequalities, is limited in his or her ambitions only by the measure of their work ethic and talents. Under the pretext of maximizing individual potential, autonomy, freedom, and equality, Rawls justifies the elect body's entitlement to increase its wealth without limit if there is some spillover benefit for the poor, that is, if 'all ships rise.' This spurious ethical legitimation of the growing gap between rich and poor expresses the life experience, self-understanding, and world view of Rawls's own social establishment. It conveys a profound lack of humanity and an extreme insensitivity to the self-understanding that extreme poverty in the midst of superabundance produces in society's 'worst off,' even when their condition may be improving.

Intuition has a seductive appeal for scholars because it provides an opportunity to assume the exalting role of an intellectual surrogate or proxy for all of humankind. For example, the nineteenth-century English philosopher and political theorist Jeremy Bentham boasted that he could legislate wisely for all of India from the privacy of his study, based on his capacity to reason and his knowledge that human beings everywhere were like him. Also, as a process for discovering and validating universal ethical principles, intuition gives scholars free reign for intellectual speculations, unencumbered by inconvenient empirical realities. Liberated from any inconvenient facts that are inconsistent with their particular world views, scholarly intuitionists can readily achieve a logically consistent argument. Their rigorous attention to all sides of every question and logically consistent arguments in the context of abstract discussion gives their conclusions an appearance of substance and validity which can then be represented as 'universal truth.' However, it is naivety if not arrogance to assume that one can discover universal humane ethical principles from within the narrow, biased precincts of one's mind, or understand humanity via a proxy who is divorced from real life.

Parenthetically, some scholars have proposed aestheticism as a promising medium for ascertaining universal ethical principles. In its classical phase, aestheticism idealistically championed the concerns of disenfranchised humanity. However, Western aestheticism has progressively changed from an idealistic to a materialistic world view. A notable quality of contemporary aestheticism is that it serves primarily to open new dimensions of hedonistic self-fulfillment and self-indulgence which serve elect body possibilities and sensibilities, not the concerns of disenfranchised humanity.

How can we determine an authentic universal humane ethical principle? I propose that humankind's accumulated experience in living together can yield the social facts from which we can derive such a principle. Ideally, our social facts should be drawn from a systematically validated, comprehensive, and extensive cross-cultural database, including oral traditions, describing diverse human groups living together under different social-relational ethical principles. In the absence of such data, we are obliged to infer a universal humane ethical principle from the social-relational experiences and storehouse of shared knowledge and understanding of diverse groups that are readily available to us. Based on this information and affirmed by contemporary social sensibilities in all cultures, we know that in social relationships individuals uniformly and invariably develop a self-conscious need and aspiration to human dignity.

Although the need and aspiration to human dignity is experienced by the individual in culture-specific terms, the self-conscious awareness of this need and aspiration is a universal social-relational phenomenon. We can infer confirming evidence for this assertion from the cross-cultural similarities of values and morality regarding human dignity found in humanity's oldest oral traditions and in many important written texts. For instance, all of the great religious writings acknowledge human dignity as a common good: Buddhism stresses respect for all others and caring for the needs of the underprivileged; Islam has explicit provisions that promote the dignity of individuals; Hinduism emphasizes social responsibility for the dignity of others; Judaism's story of God's covenant requires Jews to treat all – women, children, domestic slaves, and strangers in their midst – with dignity; Christianity ordains that treating all others with dignity is a primary and universal moral obligation.

The idea of human dignity is also acknowledged in eminent secular manifestos: the Greek standards of justice acknowledged (albeit selectively) the dignity of human beings; Renaissance philosophies of humanism exalted the idea of human dignity; international laws and treaties such as the 1864 Geneva Convention enshrine human dignity; the U.S. constitution proclaims the right to human dignity as a 'self-evident' truth; the UN's Declaration of Human Rights and its international covenants recognize human dignity as an entitlement. All of the leaders of the great grass-roots movements for liberty and social justice, notably Mohandas K. Gandhi, the Reverend Martin Luther King, Jr, Bishop Desmond Tutu, and Nelson Mandela, were inspired by a profound concern for human dignity. In his 'Letter from Birmingham Jail,' King proclaimed his dream of 'a positive peace, in which all men will respect the dignity and worth of human personality.'

This extensive and important body of knowledge and understanding makes clear that esteem for human dignity has been universally acknowledged and proclaimed by all major cultural and ethical systems in recorded human history. It is present in the values, customs, norms, languages, and psyches of people of all types of societies (i.e., modern and traditional, individualistic and communitarian, theocratic and secular, etc.). It has persisted through great and profound social upheavals, such as wars, famines, plagues, natural disasters, industrialization, urbanization, and modernization. Moreover, it is in harmony with our self-awareness and personal sensibility of what affirms our own humanity: all individuals evidence a personal need for and aspiration to human dignity. Every affirmation of our human dignity has a humanizing effect while any violation of our human dignity has a dehumanizing effect on us. The uniformity and consistency of the data signify 'self-authentication' rather than 'self-evidence' of the universal need for and aspiration to human dignity.

It is worth noting that, by deriving our universal humane ethical principle from humankind's accumulated social-relational experiences and shared knowledge and understanding, we avert the tangle of infinite regressive speculation over a 'first' ethical principle, or the need for a hypothetical independent point of observation for verifying its universal authenticity. Some scholars of the intuitional school attempt to dodge these entanglements by resorting to a sophist process of logical deduction from unproven maxims and axiomatic assumptions or by imagining 'self-evident' facts to validate the universal authenticity of their stated ethical principle. To the same end, some theologians resort to assertions of divine inspiration or revelation or some other process involving meta-ethical validation for the universal authenticity of their ethical principle.

The universal need and aspiration of humankind to human dignity objectively authenticated by accumulated social-relational experience, shared knowledge, and understanding, and affirmed by contemporary social sensibilities in all cultures, constitutes a persuasive reason to adopt the ideal of universal and equal human dignity as an *absolute principle* and ethical foundation for global social order. It meets the required standard of a universal principle for the common good set out by Immanuel Kant: that is, it is logically possible to want everyone to follow the ethical principle of universal and equal human dignity under any condition; and any counterclaim cannot be justified, because fulfillment of anyone's aspiration to human dignity can be realized only by others' affirmation of one's own human dignity.

Here, I propose the *contingent* adoption of the absolute principle as the highest- order principle and ethical foundation for global social order. While it currently expresses a timeless universal principle, we do not yet stand at the end of humankind's knowledge, understanding, and experience in living together. Thomas Paine suggested that each generation should have the option of designing a new social order, while Edmund Burke envisioned each generation as an increment in the evolution of social order. A contingent adoption of the absolute principle accommodates both ideas. It is possible that the future may reveal a different and superior ethical principle of humane virtue and truth. By leaving open this possibility, we do not hold future generations captive to past generations' ethical understanding of humane virtue and truth;

we allow every generation to discover and invoke its own authentic universal humane ethical principle for social order. However, so long as the virtue and truth of universal and equal human dignity continues to be affirmed and confirmed by our knowledge, understanding, ongoing experience, and social sensibilities, it is to be regarded as the absolute ethical principle of global social order.

The notion of ethical absolutism is generally considered by enlightened people to be objectionable. This attitude arises from experiences with oppressive theistic-religious moral absolutes and from past crimes against humanity which were sanctioned by dogmas based on ethical absolutism, recently and most notably Nazism. However, the perpetration of crimes against humanity is a consequence not of ethical absolutism per se but of contrived ethical principles which lend themselves to the legitimation of violations of human dignity such as genocide, slavery, state executions, and abuse of children and women. Unlike past 'absolute' dogmas that were created and supported by sinister or misguided individuals or groups for self-serving ends, the absolute principle of universal and equal human dignity expresses the natural aspiration of all human beings to greater humanity.

In a culturally pluralistic world, it is not possible to make an objective evaluation of an ethical principle from the vantage point of our own ethical values; and revelations, inspirations, and innate moral sense have proven to be unreliable for ascertaining an authentic universal humane ethical principle. In this regard, the absolute principle provides an objective ethical standard that can guide and move all societies from ethical uncertainty to certainty in creating moral and legal codes that honour the humanity of all. We need such a principle as a reference point to guide moral development as new needs and new threats to human dignity and humanity emerge. It provides us with a horizon of moral possibility that can motivate us to attain the Good Society.

Humane Mutuality

A global moral social order needs a social-relational system capable of transcending the bordered social, cultural, religious, political, and national parochialisms that divide humankind. The idea of 'community' suggests itself. Community has various connotations; the particular meaning of community that has relevance for our discussion here is the *traditional* community, based on shared moral values, norms, and meanings.

Scholarly conceptions of the traditional community range from uto-pian to dystopian. In their literary, philosophical, and political visions of community, most pro- and anti-communitarians conceive of commu-nity primarily as a design for social regulation and in terms of dialectic between individual and collective interests. Pro-communitarians, such as the nineteenth-century 'Gemeinschafters,' championed the moral community as a promising concept to temper unfettered individual-ism and to balance individual rights with corresponding duties to the collectivity. Anti-communitarians, on the other hand, proceeded from the premise that the moral community is essentially illiberal because it subordinates individual autonomy to the will of the collectivity and, thus, unacceptably inhibits individuality, freedom, and individual self-determination. Some have associated the community with tyranny, fas-cism, jingoism, and fundamentalism. Only rarely or incidentally is it conceived of as a design for humanizing social relations.

In Western societies, community as a functional moral social-rela-tional network has virtually diminished to symbolic status. In an ear-lier discussion I stated that legislators and judges in Western societies, by their broadened construction and application of the principles of moral neutrality and constitutional supremacy in the service of human-rights doctrine, have facilitated the deterioration of traditional moral communities. The decline of the moral community, however, is not lim-ited to Western societies; it is a global phenomenon. Some attribute the observed decline to erosion of traditional patterns of social communi-cations and associations. If we reason that the traditional moral com-munity was a phenomenon primarily of social communications and associations, it follows that the emerging new networks and patterns of social communications and associations would originate new moral communities.

In this regard, we hear much these days about the Internet commu-nity. Through various innovative social networking sites, the Internet and various cognate communications technologies – like cellphones with text-messaging and, more recently, Facebook and Twitter – have put people the world round into immediate contact with each other. However, these advanced new networks of social communications and associations are not recreating the traditional moral community. Members of these networks may share generic values, concerns, and self-interests, but their relationships are not governed by shared moral values. I propose that the new networks of social communications and associations are not recreating the traditional moral community because the parochialism that is characteristic of the traditional moral community critically limits its functional scope to accommodate the increasing social scale and diversity associated with globalization.

I have stated that a global moral social order needs a social-relational system capable of transcending all bordered parochialisms. Furthermore, it must be able to accommodate the increasing social scale, urbanization, industrialization, social mobility, and other forces of modernization associated with globalization. My search for such a social-relational system led me to the idea of *humane mutuality*. In a sentence, humane mutuality has reference to an open and inclusive moral covenant of mutual duties and responsibilities based on the absolute principle and established by democratic discourse.

To understand humane mutuality, we need to distinguish between 'reciprocity' and 'mutuality.' Although they are often used interchangeably, reciprocity and mutuality imply two profoundly different functional forms of social relations. Reciprocity, generally, has reference to social exchange based on equivalence in giving and receiving of actions or things. That is, every action or thing received creates an obligation or justification (as in 'an eye for an eye') of approximate equivalent repayment. To ensure equivalence of exchanges, reciprocity requires formal or informal negotiation and monitoring. Not infrequently, it generates conflict over perceived or real inequities in exchanges. Because reciprocity requires symmetry between giving and receiving, it tends to place at a disadvantage those without or with limited resources, creating 'creditors' and 'debtors.'

Mutuality, as I use the term here, refers to carrying out obligations and duties unconditionally and without personal attribution. There is no negotiation and monitoring of actions or things, given or received, for equivalence of exchanges. Mutuality implies symmetry between giving and meeting other's human needs. Whereas reciprocity divides society into 'debtors' and 'creditors,' mutuality unites a society into a common support group. The Marxist slogan 'from each according to his abilities, to each according to his needs' eloquently expresses an economic version of the idea of mutuality. However, mutual economic relationships do not fully meet the standard implied by humane mutuality; for this we need a moral covenant based on the absolute principle, which stipulates the social obligation to meet everyone's need for human dignity and aspiration to humanity.

Traditional Polynesian culture approximated the idea of humane mutuality. Polynesians distinguished between social transactions that fell in the broad class of 'economic exchange' and those that fell in the category of 'human need.' Whereas economic transactions were judged by the criterion of reciprocity, requiring equivalence of exchange, transactions that occurred in the category of human need were performed as covenanted moral duties and responsibilities and judged by the criterion of mutuality: that is, symmetry between giving and the individual's human needs.

The traditional family manifests the idea of humane mutuality insofar as parents carry out their duties and responsibilities, unconditionally, with symmetry between giving and meeting their children's human needs. As we have seen, however, the passage of children's human-rights acts in Western societies is changing family duties and responsibilities customarily performed under a moral covenant of humane mutuality into a state legal obligation, thereby diminishing children's social-relational experience of humane mutuality. As the scope of morally covenanted family duties and responsibilities is gradually diminished, the effect is that less and less of the individual 'self' is moulded by the experience of humane mutuality.

Charity and social welfare generally do not qualify as humane mutuality because they place recipients of help in the subordinate position of supplicants, not equals. Voluntary mutual-aid societies, such as non-profit insurance societies, approximate humane mutuality insofar as they operate as consensual alliances for meeting a human need without personal attribution. However, they do not meet the standard of humane mutuality in that they are based on a legal-utilitarian contract, not on a moral covenant. Also, their benefits are limited to a particular need and to 'paid-up' members.

In their literary, philosophical, and political visions of society, the community utopians of the nineteenth and twentieth centuries advocated social relations based approximately on the concept of humane mutuality. Actual versions of such communities, such as those of the Quakers, Amish, and Hutterites, proclaim a moral covenant of symmetry between giving and meeting others' human needs in accordance with the criterion of mutuality. However, each of these versions function primarily as a parochial alternative to the prevailing regulative and administrative system of social-order authority, not as an open and inclusive moral covenant for nurturing the common good of universal and equal human dignity and humanity.

The concept of humane mutuality is not hindered by the parochialism that critically restricts the functional ability of the traditional moral community to accommodate the diversity and increasing social scale connected with globalization. The implied moral covenants of humane mutuality are not limited to any socio-cultural, political, and religious boundaries; they can encompass all of the diverse duties and responsibilities needed to nurture human dignity and humanity. Predicated on the absolute principle, the social-relational concept of humane mutuality has the potential to guarantee liberty and social justice in every circumstance and setting, without regard to social status, colour, ethnicity, gender, sexual orientation, creed, or any other individual or collective attribute; it is elastic, open, and inclusive and can accommodate the increasing social scale, urbanization, industrialization, social mobility, and modernization heralded by globalization.

9   Global Moral Social Order

The philosophers Thomas Hobbes and Simone Weil considered barbarism to be the permanent and universal characteristic of humankind. Critics of this appraisal object that it is unduly cynical about human nature. However, history affirms that human beings lack a natural inhibition against killing their own kind, and they will kill purely for vengeance. Hobbes reasoned that humankind needs restraint to rise above its primal nature; I propose that humankind needs a humane moral social order that will inspire us to transcendence, that is, to rise above the limitations and imperatives of our nature and realize our potential for humanity.

A Humane Moral Order

The growing void in consensual moral ethics in Western societies, incurred by the change to secular amoral-legal standards, is being filled by utility-rational ethics. In scholarly usage, 'rational' refers to a process of disciplined, logical reasoning from stated premises. When it is used to describe ethics, the term 'rational' confers a semblance of authenticity and legitimacy. However, any system of ethics can never be better than the authenticity and legitimacy of its premises, and ethics reasoned from defective premises, even if they are the product of the purest form of logical reasoning, can serve nefarious policies and actions. As a case in point, the U.S. elect body, reasoning from utility-rational premises, legitimated the indiscriminate killing of more than a million innocent and defenceless civilians in Hiroshima, Nagasaki, and Vietnam as doing the 'greater good/lesser evil.' Based on the same premises, it recently rationalized the killing of hundreds of thousands of Iraqi civilians, and currently it is writing off as 'collateral damage' many innocent Afghan and Pakistani children, women, and men killed by missiles fired from remote-controlled Predator drones in violation of international rules of law. This should give scholars pause when using the term 'rational' in connection with ethics The utility-rational premise that we must choose the option that offers the best proportion of 'good' over 'evil' begs an answer to the question: Who is mandated to determine what is 'good' or 'evil' in war? The victor or the victim?

We live in a world marked by profoundly distrustful and hostile relationships, presided over by greedy and ambitious national elect bodies bent on preserving or expanding their authority, and a growing number of these bodies have in their possession weapons of mass destruction. Any system of ethics reasoned from self-serving utility-rational premises threatens more and great crimes against humanity in future. To avert catastrophe, humankind needs a global moral order founded on ethics reasoned from the absolute principle within the social-relational concept of humane mutuality. Such a moral order can warrant liberty, social justice, human dignity, and humanity for all.

Below, I will elaborate and discuss such a humane global moral social order under the headings Moral Pluralism, Moral Ecumenicalism, and Implementation.

Moral Pluralism

Divided by racial, religious, and ethnic hostilities, humankind needs a global moral social order that can transcend national structures of authority and ethno-nationalism without threatening indigenous identities and loyalties. Those who advocate universal human rights insist on imposing a list of uniform domestic and international laws and regulations on all peoples, regardless of their social-cultural heritage. As noted before, this initiative to impose value-uniformity on culturally diverse societies has provoked antagonistic reactions and disputes over trespass of cultural and political self-determination; many non-Western societies regard it as an ethnocidal design and, for that reason, resist human-rights doctrine.

We can avoid such negative parochial reactions to the implementation of global moral order by endorsing moral pluralism, that is, acknowledging every society's autonomy to implement the absolute principle within the concept of humane mutuality in terms of duties and responsibilities that harmonize with its history, experience, resources, needs, and self-determined definition of human dignity and humanity. As described earlier, humane mutuality refers to a moral covenant of mutual duties and responsibilities based on the absolute principle and established by democratic discourse – a process very different from that supported by advocates of universal human rights. It gives all individuals the opportunity to participate as equals in the process of establishing the mutual duties and responsibilities of their social order. Just as culturally different societies satisfy the need for food and shelter in different ways, they can also satisfy the need and aspiration for human dignity and humanity differently. However, moral pluralism does not imply ethical relativism; moral autonomy must not compromise the integrity of the absolute principle and humane mutuality. Moral pluralism allows every society to translate the absolute principle into morality in harmony with its cultural uniqueness even as it brings them into a single integrated humane moral network of mutual understanding.

Moral pluralism can also meliorate intra-societal disputes over cultural self-determination. In some instances, diverse sub-societal world views may give rise to profound disagreements on specification of the absolute principle and the concept of humane mutuality in terms of mutual duties and responsibilities. Aboriginal peoples in Canada and the United States are examples of sub-societies which hold that their aspirations to human dignity and humanity are better met by a communal than an individualized system of duties and responsibilities. With rising migration in a world without borders, intra-societal diversity will increase, calling for tolerance of different cultural specifications of the absolute principle and the concept of humane mutuality. Moral pluralism will provide every society the autonomy and motivation for creative idealism in instituting the absolute principle within the concept of humane mutuality, thereby countering the economic-utilitarian-based doctrine and the regression from humanity portended by globalism. The resulting cultural diversity gives human communities the opportunity to adopt or adapt humanizing elements from each other's social-relational blueprints.

Moral Ecumenicalism

In September 1993 the Parliament of the World Religions meeting in Chicago, including leaders from Christian, Jewish, Muslim, Hindu, Buddhist, Confucian, Druid, Taoist, Theosophist, and other faiths, proclaimed a Declaration of a Global Ethic in which it advocated a 'global culture of human dignity, justice and peace.' This grand proclamation implies a commitment to an ecumenical code of humane social order. However, in the past, as well as since this Declaration was proclaimed, leaders from several of these religions have incited and mobilized their followers and citizens to wage war against those who hold beliefs different from their own.

Secular humanists, with good reason, are profoundly offended by the history of social injustice, genocide, ethnic cleansing, coerced flight, terrorism, and other crimes against humanity fostered by elect bodies in the name of sacred doctrines. This has motivated them to devise secular doctrines which express a commitment to a culture of human dignity, justice, and peace. But, like the religious individuals and groups whom they condemn, secular humanists frustrate the development of an ecumenical humane social order by creating dogmas that polarize people into antagonistic 'isms,' such as capitalism versus socialism and individualism versus collectivism; and they rally and mobilize their respective followers to violence and social injustice against those who hold beliefs different from their own.

Secularists cast the 'secular-sacred' dichotomy in terms of objectivity versus dogmatism; the religious cast it in terms of truth versus fallacy. This dichotomization polarizes people into antagonistic ideological camps and functions as an obstacle to achieving a consensus on a humanizing ethical system. By raising barriers between and within their respective camps, both secularists and the religious hinder progress towards an ecumenical humane social order. The absolute principle and the concept of humane mutuality stand above the spurious, divisive secular /sacred dichotomy and provide an ethical basis for reconciling the world views of religious people and secular humanists. As such, they hold promise for an ecumenical, global, humane, and moral social order.

Implementation

The implementation of a global humane moral social order will require the cooperation of national elect bodies. Historically, national elect bodies have a record of obstructing the quest for the Good Society by using their authority primarily to secure and enhance their status, wealth, and privilege. However, it is simplistic to imply that elect bodies necessarily constitute iniquitous entities. Generally, elect bodies do not exercise their authority with malicious intent, and, on occasion, enlightened members of elect bodies have been motivated to play a positive role in the quest for the Good Society. I propose that national elect bodies, in their configuration as the United Nations, are in a position to advance the quest for the Good Society by facilitating the implementation of the absolute principle and the concept of humane mutuality as basic standards of global moral social order.

The UN is fully mandated to carry out this mission. The First Article of the Declaration of Human Rights reads: 'All human beings are born free and equal in dignity.... They ... should act towards one another in a spirit of brotherhood.' However, in its misguided campaign to advance its human-rights agenda by prescribing domestic and international human-rights laws, the UN is alienating many non-Western states and impairing its efficacy in carrying out its other vital humanitarian efforts, such as peacekeeping, protecting and feeding refugees, fighting AIDs, halting nuclear proliferation, and promoting social development. Moreover, as we have seen, its endeavour to internationalize human rights through legal means has achieved its greatest prominence from widespread and ongoing disregard and violations of liberty, social justice, human dignity, and humanity by UN members themselves. Given the futility and counter-productive results of its human-rights initiative, the UN should reframe its charter and mission. To revitalize itself and restore a sense of purpose, it should undertake consultations with ordinary citizens in all societies on the drafting of a new humanitarian manifesto proclaiming the absolute principle as the highest-order principle and the concept of humane mutuality as the pre-eminent ethical standard for all domestic and international social relations.

The proposed manifesto would oblige all national governments to initiate a democratic discourse by their citizens regarding all existing indigenous traditions, customs, and institutional standards of their society with the objective of bringing all values and practices into conformity with the absolute principle and concept of humane mutuality. The manifesto and democratic discourse would serve to inspire and foster grass-roots movements to develop a humane moral social order in societies that are currently in thrall to perverse cultural values that condone slavery, child labour, sexism, homophobia, capital punishment, homelessness, and malnutrition in the midst of plenty. Moreover, establishing the absolute principle and the concept of humane mutuality in a UN-mandated international manifesto would arm citizens the world over with a universal ethical standard and moral justification to challenge violations of liberty, social justice, human dignity, and humanity by their state regimes.

An exemplary outcome of the manifesto and the discursive process would be the entrenchment of self-determined, indigenous moral covenants, based on the absolute principle and the concept of humane mutuality as the highest ideal, in domestic charters; and the requirement that all indigenous customs, norms, laws, regulations, and institutional practices conform to this ethical standard. Entrenching this requirement in nation-state charters as the paramount civic imperative will maximize every citizen's potential to call their respective governments to account when nation-state laws or corporate or religious policies and practices deny or violate liberty, social justice, human dignity, and humanity.

To ease parochial fears about a loss of cultural self-determination, the manifesto would be framed to mandate the citizens of each UN member state to implement the absolute principle and the moral covenant of humane mutuality in terms of duties and responsibilities that accord with their own world view, and in their own cultural idiom. Tolerance for diverse cultural conceptions of liberty, social justice, human dignity, and humanity will avert the distrust that currently inflames UN human-rights debates and facilitate acceptance of the absolute principle and the concept of humane mutuality as the ethical standard for a new moral social order in a diverse global society.

To oblige state-regime compliance with the ethical standard of the absolute principle and the concept of humane mutuality, the manifesto would embody articles authorizing and providing the UN with the means to monitor member-states' performance. To forestall state-regime resistance to UN monitoring of their performance, the manifesto would stipulate a procedure of enforcement that acknowledges the primacy of domestic jurisdiction. Citizens seeking remedy for violation of their liberty, social justice, human dignity, and humanity would first present their case before a domestic tribunal whose mandate, composition, and procedures would be established by democratic discourse. Rulings by the domestic tribunal would be subject to appeal to the UN; however, the UN panel hearing the appeal would be bound to adjudicate each case in accordance with the standards of the respective society's self-determined domestic moral covenant. By respecting domestic jurisdiction and sensibilities in this way, any ruling by the UN would be more readily supported by the international community of nations as legitimate and justified, and it would be broadly accepted by the citizens of offending state regimes.

Given the universal aspiration to liberty, social justice, human dignity, and humanity, it is reasonable to anticipate that a UN manifesto mandating a democratic discourse to establish social order based on the absolute principle and humane mutuality will be well received by nearly all citizens the world over. It would fall to domestic social institutions to undertake the major task of redefining, teaching, and promoting the new role expectations for all states consistent with their moral covenants. Over time, the humanizing mutual duties and responsibilities resulting from this process will progressively generate meaningful societal expectations for compliance and foster a self-understanding and identity that encourages individuals to view themselves and others as an integral part of a global community in which all human beings are equal in human dignity and humanity.

Moral and Amoral Authority

The history of liberty, social justice, human dignity, and humanity in diverse societies can be understood in terms of moral and amoral modes of social-order authority structures. As discussed in chapter 4, in the real world there is a valid function for both modes of authority, and in all societies social relations are governed by a mix of moral and amoral modes of social-order authority. I have delayed my discussion as to the appropriate mandate for each mode to this late point in the book because I wanted the reader to have a fuller understanding of the two modes of social-order authority. The subject of appropriate mandates for amoral and moral social order is a large and complex one; here, my comments are narrowly focused on the effectiveness of the two modes for the protection and enhancement of liberty, social justice, human dignity, and humanity.

When considering what constitutes the appropriate mandate for the respective modes of social order, it is important to keep in mind that individuals create liberty, social justice, human dignity, and humanity for each other by their social relationships. My earlier evaluation of moral social-order authority established that, when it is created by democratic discourse, it diffuses authority throughout the social body and gives rise to a sense of authenticity and ownership which translates into widespread societal expectation, support, and vigilance for individual compliance. This ethos is reinforced by the fact that violations of mutual duties and responsibilities, public and private, have the same moral meanings for victims and violators. Furthermore, the mutual duties and responsibilities of moral social order are internalized at a very young age and tend to be experienced as a 'natural' definition of right and good; affirmed by conscience, they function as an effective behavioural guide for practically all aspects of social relationships.

When the moral mode is based on authentic morality, social constraints are self-determined and harmonize with society's need for regulation of social relations; the individual is required to sacrifice only those freedoms deemed necessary by members for securing social justice, human dignity, and humanity, leaving untouched the citizen's residual social space and life. By contrast, the amoral mode, defined by a secular-legal order based on constitutional human rights, is a design for monopoly control by the elect body over citizen behaviour. Liberty is limited to narrowly specified rights, and the residual social space and life of citizens is regulated by a web of legal and administrative restrictions.

Earlier, I noted that traditional Polynesian culture distinguished between social transactions that fell in the category of 'human need' and those that fell in the broad class of 'economic exchange.' Transactions that occurred in the category of human need were performed as covenanted moral duties and responsibilities and judged by the criterion of mutuality, that is, symmetry between giving and the individual's human needs. Economic transactions were conducted according to the criterion of reciprocity, requiring equivalence of exchange. Reasoning from what we know about the properties of the two modes of social order, we can conclude that the moral mode based on authentic morality, and constituted as the absolute principle within the concept of humane mutuality, can better fulfil transactions that fall in the category of broadly held human needs and aspirations to liberty, social justice, human dignity, and humanity. The amoral mode constituted as state legal control can serve as an efficient system for administering transactions that fall in the broad class of 'economic exchange' and the mechanics of day-to-day citizen-government relations. I propose that its jurisdiction should generally be limited to civil issues relating to commerce, contract, property, trade, traffic, violations of physical person, and so on.

The appropriate lines of authority between moral and amoral spheres of social-order authority will not always be apparent and we can expect challenges regarding the respective mandates. When disputes occur, they should be arbitrated in accordance with criteria established by democratic discourse.

I want to emphasize that, by declaring liberty, social justice, human dignity, and humanity as the province of authentic moral rather than amoral-legal order, I do not exempt the state from responsibility to protect these principles. Yet, although the state should not legislate moral values or regulate moral social relationships, in real life it is frequently the chief violator of citizens' liberty, social justice, human dignity, and humanity. It is imperative, therefore, that all authority exercised by the state through its institutions and bureaucracies comply with the absolute principle and the moral covenant of humane mutuality. Its civic policies and programs must guarantee every citizen's opportunity for social and human self-validation by distributing social goods such as jobs, housing, health, nutrition, and education in a way that honours equally everyone's human dignity and humanity.

Summary

The deterministic forces of globalization are rapidly shrinking the world into a global 'village' filled with distrustful, fearful, and often hostile neighbours. To survive as human beings in this emerging world, we need a humane global social order. It is not possible to attain such an order by international law or by military force. It can be accomplished only by a voluntary moral consensus and mutual understanding that transcends all political, ethnic, and religious borders yet allows all societies to live their cultural differences. Unless we create such a moral social order, human beings will end up as slaves to the extra-human forces of global free-market capitalism and globalism.

To achieve a humane global moral order, we need a universal humane ethical principle. Historical and contemporary cross-cultural knowledge informs us that, in the context of functionally interdependent social relationships, all humankind uniformly and universally aspires to liberty, social justice, human dignity, and humanity. Reasoning from this social fact leads logically and persuasively to the idea of adopting the absolute principle as the highest-order principle and ethical foundation for our global moral social order. This principle is validated by human experience in living together; it is substantiated by social sensibilities in all cultures; it is corroborated by reason, intuition, inspiration, and revelation; and it is consistent with the highest ideals of all sacred and secular teachings.

My search for a social-relational system that can transcend all bordered parochialisms and accommodate the increasing social scale, urbanization, industrialization, social mobility, and other forces of modernization led to the concept of humane mutuality. Although I conceive of humane mutuality in terms of a functional moral covenant, my account of it has been intentionally abstract because my fundamental premise is that the absolute principle and moral covenant that define humane mutuality must be determined and specified by democratic discourse in culture-specific idioms.

There are, of course, some formidable social-cultural challenges to the creation of a humane global moral social order. As we have seen, in Western societies the moral mode of social order is regarded as the enemy of freedom, and moral knowledge and understanding has been eroded by human-rights doctrine. Furthermore, human-rights doctrine elevates the 'individual good' above the 'common good'; this has fostered narcissism and moral-ethical autism, which trap individuals within ego-boundaries and impairs their faculty for self-transcendence. Needless to say, reversing these social-cultural value trends, revitalizing the capacity to originate a new morality, restoring the moral mode of social-order authority, and rewriting national charters and constitutions to conform to the absolute principle and humane mutuality represent an awesome challenge. No less awesome are the social-cultural impediments in non-Western societies: many are trapped in ancient, firmly established repressive synthetic moral-religious belief systems which affirm, and sometimes render as sacred, pervasive violations of human dignity and humanity. In these societies, enlightenment and reformation are prerequisites for the creation of a humane global moral social order.

Moreover, we can anticipate vigorous resistance by all national elect bodies to rewriting their charters and constitutions to conform to a moral order founded on the absolute principle within the concept of humane mutuality. Their advantageous status, privilege, and property depend on the existing social-order authority and nation-state oligarchic authority structures, and they will oppose implementation of political and economic structures that diffuse their authority throughout the social body.

Given the social-cultural impediments and the opposition of powerful elect bodies, how can a humane global moral social order become generally accepted? A reason for optimism arises from humankind's universal aspiration to liberty, social justice, human dignity, and humanity, and the broad consensus that all human beings have a right to the same. Furthermore, as individuals we can realize this 'good' for ourselves only if others affirm our liberty, social justice, human dignity, and humanity. Elect bodies defraud themselves when they massively bias the distribution of wealth in their own favour: their status, privilege, and property may inflate their egos but not yield human dignity or enhance their humanity; like everyone else, they also need the humanizing social relations that a humane moral order can provide. These social facts provide a persuasive logic and personal motive for everyone to embrace the absolute principle and the concept of humane mutuality as a universal system of moral social order.

The UN can play a key role in implementing a humane global moral social order. To fulfil this role, it must abandon its divisive and futile endeavour to internationalize human rights through legal-political means. Instead, it should fully dedicate itself and its significant resources to the task of promoting an ethic of universal and equal human dignity and humanity as the basis for international relations and cooperation. The UN can provide moral leadership to humanize the world by creating a manifesto proclaiming the absolute principle as the highest-order principle and the concept of humane mutuality as the pre-eminent ethical standard for all domestic and international social relations. Such a manifesto, with implementing protocols, would serve as a template of a humane moral social order for all societies. It would pledge all member-states to allow their citizens to engage in a democratic discourse to realize the absolute principle and humane mutuality in terms of a self-determined covenant of moral duties and responsibilities. An ideal outcome would be the creation of domestic charters by all societies establishing the absolute principle and a moral covenant of humane mutuality as civic and social imperatives superior to any contrary laws.

The Reverend Martin Luther King, Jr gave expression to the absolute principle and the concept of humane mutuality in his vision of a world in which everyone's aspiration to human dignity and the fullness of humanity would be equally honoured. He referenced his vision to a God of love, and he publicly indicted white American religious leaders and churches who disregarded or opposed the civil rights movement's quest for equal dignity and humanity for all. His cause is usually identified as a human-rights movement and the record shows that he took full advantage of the social and political leverage that human-rights laws and the U.S. constitution carried in the United States in his time. However, he understood that laws alone would not ensure universal and equal human dignity and humanity; his vision of the Good Society was primarily a moral, not a legal, conception. His humane moral vision transcended identities of colour, class, creed, and ethnicity. His impressive accomplishment in a very brief lifespan against fierce opposition inspires optimism that the Millennial Generations can make great progress towards a humane global moral social order and the Good Society during their watch.

A humane global moral social order can transform a world of strangers who consider each other as means to self-serving ends, or who fear and hate each other, into friends who trust and value each other as human persons. It can inspire hostile neighbouring societies to engage each other in a dialogue that resolves conflicts in a way that honours each other's human dignity and humanity; even seemingly irreconcilable conflicts that are not amenable to political compromise, such as the hostile religious-racial-tribal claims by Israelis and Palestinians to the same territorial homeland, can be resolved without any loss of individual or collective moral and cultural identity by creating a multireligious, multicultural community living in peace, with mutual esteem for each other's human dignity and humanity.

A global moral social order founded on the absolute principle and the concept of humane mutuality embodies the universal aspiration of humankind, and the most important of humankind's purposes – that is, the fullest realization of everyone's potential for humanity. It transcends the barriers of languages, cultures, belief systems, political ideologies, and national interests that have caused wars and crimes against humanity; it will work against inequality, injustice, prejudice, discrimination, hatred, and oppression. By providing inspiration and guidance to the search for truth through philosophy, theology, science, and art, it can humanize the core of social thought and practice. Reinforced by education and social affirmation, its ethical discipline can be assimilated into the fabric of all world views, cultures, and institutions and be internalized by all individuals. Thus, all people will come to conceive of themselves and all others as equal in their claim to human dignity and humanity. To begin creating such a humane global moral social order is the noblest challenge and primary duty of the Millennial Generations.

PART FIVE

Myths of Reality

10   Scientific and Theological Myths of Reality

The term 'reality' here refers to our perceptions, beliefs, analyses, and constructs of the world and our experience of it. The wonders of life and the vastness of our world have excited a profound curiosity about reality and the forces that created it. Humankind, presented with ultimate mysteries that are beyond its comprehension, like the origin of the universe and life, has invented myths to explain reality.

The predominant myths of reality in our time have been developed by science and theology. Both offer engaging narratives of reality's essence, origin, and future. Science and theology both claim authenticity for their respective myths, but a fundamental feature of both narratives of reality is that they are conjectural. They are evolving parables based on subjective perceptions and beliefs about our world and being. This is necessarily the case because, as an integral part of reality, we lack an independent point of observation, a 'God's eye view,' from which to verify our understanding and representation of reality.

Although they present distinct conceptions of reality, the scientific and theological myths have some basic features in common: both hold that life and the universe came from nothing by some sort of First Cause; both hold the existence of a reality as self-evident; both hold that life and the universe are finite in space and time; both conceive of reality in terms of an ordered design. They differ in the way they endeavour to substantiate their respective myths: science cites 'objective facts' and reason; theology cites 'revealed truths' and faith. Also, they differ in the language they use to describe their respective realities: science employs a mathematical idiom; theology employs a numinous idiom. Although both hold that life and the universe came from nothing by some sort of First Cause, they differ profoundly in their respective understanding of the basic features of First Cause, that is, how life and the universe came into existence. Science attributes it to chance by natural agency; theology attributes it to design by divine agency.

Our conception of reality provides a frame of reference which we use to make sense of our lives; we know that it profoundly influences our self-understanding, aspirations, and collective destiny. It is appropriate, therefore, to conduct an assessment of the authenticity claimed for the scientific and theological myths of reality, and make an appraisal of their respective merits for realizing the Good Society.

The Scientific Myth

The Millennial Generations' enthrallment with the benefits yielded by science has engendered an uncritical faith in the scientific myth of reality. Given this standing, it is important that we place it under critical review. The scientific myth of reality is predicated on a number of fundamental principles. I will briefly consider two definitive principles of science which profoundly affect human self-understanding, aspirations, and destiny: one, that reality constitutes a natural phenomenon; and, two, that science must be value-neutral.

The Natural Universe

Science derives its myth of reality from studying the natural world. In recent years, scientific knowledge and understanding of the natural world has been dramatically enhanced by means of sophisticated technologies (e.g., electron microscopes, radio telescopes, etc.), and its conjectured properties of reality (e.g., time/space/motion) have been impressively elaborated by means of complex mathematical constructs. These developments are yielding increasingly complicated constructions of a naturalistic reality, and the principle of naturalism is firmly and securely established as a disciplinary doctrine and foundation of the scientific myth of reality. Some leading scientists aspire to a 'Theory of Everything' implying naturalistic determinism. They hold that all phenomena, animate and inanimate, can be explained by natural laws and are predictable by means of mathematical models.

The scientific myth holds that the universe came into existence by way of the 'Big Bang.' The Big Bang signifies the spontaneous release and transmutation of the absolute quantum of energy particles comprising the universe from an initial condition of nothingness, called 'cosmic singularity,' into an expanding multidimensional cosmic spherical geometry. Like Genesis, science imposes measured time and space on timelessness and spacelessness; the Big Bang marks the beginning of cosmic time and space.

To support its doctrine of naturalism and to establish theories of relative position, movement, and direction, science needs a finite universe, and in the scientific myth the farthest reaches of the expanding quantum of energy particles released by the Big Bang (that is, the outer edges of matter) mark the boundary of the universe: a cosmic version of the ancients' notion of the 'ends of the earth.' Common sense suggests the existence of a dimension beyond the boundary of the universe, but, because their instruments cannot tell us what lies beyond the boundaries of the natural world, scientists regard the extra-natural expanse beyond the expanding boundary of the finite universe as extraneous for an understanding of reality. For instance, the mathematical model that defines scientific reality assumes causal isolation; it disregards or precludes the possibility of reciprocal causality between the natural universe and the encompassing extra-natural dimension. The assumption and logic of causal isolation is not based on a scientific understanding of the causal connection between natural and extra-natural dimensions; the possibility of reciprocal causal implications is simply ignored.

The Law of Causality

Science claims objective authenticity for its myth of reality and bases its claim on 'laws of nature.' Laws of nature, also termed causal laws, are established by replicated observations of inevitable time-space sequentiality of natural phenomena and events. To establish causal law, science needs a theory of time-space sequentiality. Until recently, the theory of time-space sequentiality was based on the Newtonian assumption of a universe with absolute temporal-spatial borders. This theory was discredited by the discovery that the universe is expanding, and Einstein's common-sense observation that an expanding universe in a timeless and infinite world denies the logical possibility of absolute temporal-spatial borders. Consequently, science needed a new theory to establish causal law, and Einstein filled this need by originating a mathematical model of time-space sequentiality premised on the absolute speed of light and relative time-space position, movement, and direction.

Subsequent discoveries suggest that Einstein's causal-law paradigm entails some unresolved perplexities. Quantum physicists have reported findings that suggest Einstein's assumptions about origin, destination, and relative time-space sequentiality are inconsistent with observed subatomic particle behaviour. Using laboratory techniques, quantum physicists have noted a phenomenon which they have named 'teleportation.' Teleportation describes a process by which massless particles with no apparent physical connection pass messages among themselves which effect a change in their properties. These new findings indicate the possibility that all mass and energy may be linked in a 'relational whole,' so that any change in one particle inevitably changes every other particle instantaneously.

When applied to our understanding of light, the reported findings suggest the hypothesis that light may exist as an omnipresent relational whole comprising elementary particles of non-materiality, non-locality, and non-structure. The notion of a seamless relational whole implies the logical possibility that light does not 'travel'; rather, the animation of one light particle animates all light particles instantaneously, following all paths. This is consistent with the counter-intuitive phenomenon, described by Einstein, of the speed of light appearing exactly the same to every observer in every frame of reference. Given that the absolute speed of light is inferred from spaceless/timeless properties not found in nature, the theorized 'constant' may be a consistent fallacy of perception – an illusory property that exists only as a mathematical model. If 'cause-effect' is instantaneous, it renders the theory regarding relative time-space sequentiality on which the existing causal-law paradigm is based problematical. By even the most primitive standards of science, the inability to distinguish cause-effect disqualifies the claim of objective authenticity for the scientific myth of naturalistic reality.

Quantum physicists and cosmologists seeking to understand the subatomic and cosmic constituents of reality are unable to explain their observations in terms of natural phenomena. Apparently, both ends of the naturalistic spectrum, the infinitely small and the infinitely large, fade seamlessly into an extra-natural realm. In this extra-natural realm, sensory data and finite mathematical models are inadequate and inappropriate for an understanding of their observations. To cope with this dilemma, they invent naturalistic metaphors (e.g., 'subtle,' 'vague,' 'dark,' 'virtual,' or 'invisible' particles, matter, or energy) to describe what they can't observe. Empty spaces found inside the cosmos (termed 'dark matter,' 'missing matter,' 'cosmic voids,' and 'holes') are mapped and measured, and attributed to matter yet to be discovered. By attributing naturalistic properties to these extra-natural phenomena, science can fit their measurable effects into its finite mathematical models and laws.

The scientific myth is represented as originating from objectively authenticated observations, and science rationalizes the exclusion of extra-natural phenomena from its conception of reality by citing the absence of 'scientific evidence' for their existence. The spuriousness of this rationale is indicated by the methodology of science: as a discipline, science confines its research and discourse to measurable and reproducible sensory observations because that is all its methodology and mathematical models can comprehend; extra-natural phenomena cannot be observed and measured and, therefore, are not amenable to mathematical explanation. If our conception of reality is limited to natural phenomena, if we look only for natural phenomena, and if our 'falsification' tests are limited to natural phenomena, then it follows logically that under these specifications any repeated scientific observations and measurements will necessarily and invariably yield data limited to natural properties and affirm the myth that reality is a naturalistic phenomenon. In short, the scientific conception of reality is an artifact of its methods and subject of study: the natural world. Given this circumstance, it is disingenuous to cite the absence of 'scientific evidence' for the existence of extra-natural phenomena as proof for their non-existence.

Science, which proclaims a philosophy of free enquiry, originality, and imagination, routinely insists that all emergent facts must conform to its construct of natural reality: any observation, interpretation, and intellectual construct that contradict the essential assumption of naturalistic reality are deemed anomalous, arbitrary, or illusory; any gaps in knowledge are filled with conjectures that affirm science's naturalistic conception of reality. If a disaffirming observation, interpretation, or intellectual construct cannot be discredited, science compartmentalizes such a finding. Thus, by way of self-fulfilling methodology, tautological reasoning, metaphorical attribution, and decree, science precludes any results that contradict or disaffirm its myth of naturalistic reality. Although science readily acknowledges the incomplete and interim status of its understanding of reality, it resolutely insists that its naturalistic representation of reality is unarguable. Evidently, modern science does not end its journey of discovery with the myth of naturalistic reality; it begins its journey with this myth and looks only for confirming data.

The intransigent bias of science to limit its conception of reality exclusively to naturalistic phenomena is a relatively recent development. Pre-modern science integrated extra-natural assumptions, concepts, imagery, and language into its myth of reality. In this regard, an auspicious indication for reconciliation of the natural/extra-natural dichotomy in science's conception of reality can be inferred from recent reflections by the distinguished quantum physicist Frytof Capra in his book *The Tao of Physics*. Capra notes some striking parallels between the 'relational whole' models of subatomic physics and the extra-natural concepts, imagery, and language used by Buddhist, Hindu, and Taoist mystics in their accounts of reality. The mystics described reality as constituting natural and extra-natural phenomena in a seamless 'figure-background' pattern; that is, the extra-natural world existed mutually with the natural world. While Capra's reflections do not imply that scientists are ready to acknowledge causal connections between natural and extra-natural phenomena in their conception of reality, or even the existence of such phenomena, it suggests that quantum physicists, working at the frontier of their discipline, are opening up a discourse which may lead to the acknowledgment by science of a dimension of reality that involves extra-natural phenomena.

Einstein's cryptic remark that God 'does not throw dice' suggests a coded allegation about the unknown world that goes beyond merely an acknowledgment that time, space, and motion are illusory properties not found in nature; it implies extra-natural assumptions. And it is fair to say that Einstein devoted his life to unravelling the mystery of both natural and extra-natural phenomena revealed in the orderly design and laws of nature which he observed in the universe.

Value-Neutrality

In order to achieve its goal of 'objective' observations, science supports the principle of value-neutrality. This principle, which has attained the status of doctrine, requires that scientists cannot allow personal or collective moral-ethical values to influence the conduct of their research. It follows from this that the practitioners of science are deterred from making moral-ethical distinctions between research that potentially benefits or harms humankind. In its effect, value-neutrality creates an ethos of innocence and immunity from social responsibility for any negative consequences that result from scientific-research findings. This is the case even when research is conducted in full knowledge of premeditated harmful applications of the findings. Whenever scientists or the scientific enterprise come under critical public scrutiny for harmful applications or effects of their research, the scientific establishment hides behind the doctrine of value-neutrality and deflects social responsibility to the governmental and corporate sectors, the chief sources of funding for all scientific research.

Considering its significant influence and involvement in government and corporate policy decisions relating to scientific research, the scientific establishment's deflection of moral responsibility and social accountability to these sectors must be considered disingenuous. In its work for government, the scientific establishment insists on autonomy in every sphere of the scientific enterprise. It effectively exercises its monopoly over scientific knowledge and expertise to prescribe the government's research agenda and funding priorities. It also exploits its esteem and value in the public mind as political leverage to deter government restrictions on its research freedom. Its assignment of moral accountability and social responsibility to the corporate sector for negative applications of its research is equally spurious: the scientific establishment is fully aware of corporations' lack of moral conscience and social accountability in the application of its research findings and the potential for harm in selling its research knowledge and expertise to the corporate sector.

The doctrine of value-neutrality has opened the door for scientists to engage in research yielding the most destructive weaponry in history. One such example is the work done by scientists which led to the creation of the atomic bomb. After the near total destruction of Hiroshima and Nagasaki, influential members of the Western scientific community initially felt uneasy and some even expressed moral repugnance about science's role in this historic crime against humanity, raising expectations that in the future it would monitor its cooperation in the development of weapons capable of mass destruction. However, this expression of moral angst proved to be a transitory sentiment. Almost immediately after the bombs had been dropped, the scientific establishment joined with the government, military, and corporate sectors to develop technology for even more lethal weapons. This alliance continues today.

Currently, scientists, in the service of pharmaceutical corporations, are pursuing research into genetic 'distinctives' which may foreshadow new weapons of mass destruction. Without regard to the potential for harm to humankind, the scientific establishment is giving unqualified approval to a search for racial-ethnic gene-specific markers that possibly could be tailored to incapacitate or kill entire populations with a selected racial-ethnic genetic profile.

In the absence of personal or collective moral-ethical values to influence the conduct of research, the scientific enterprise will be highly susceptible to the imperatives of global free-market capitalism: the choice, purpose, and conduct of scientific research will be determined primarily by economic utility-rational calculations. This prospect poses a profound threat to the valuation of humanity. We can already see the contours of this peril in the current surge of scientific interest in eugenics. Working in a moral-ethical void and under immunity from social accountability, scientists in the service of the corporate complex and with the consent of government are engaging in a variety of eugenics-research endeavours.

Eugenics was given a deservedly repellent reputation by the barbaric experimentations perpetrated under Hitler's Nazi regime. It is important, however, to remember that as late as the mid-1930s the idea of eugenics was regarded with favour by Western elect bodies. In 1927 the esteemed American Supreme Court Justice Oliver Wendell Holmes wrote in the majority opinion on a landmark eugenics case: 'It is better for all the world, if, instead of waiting to execute degenerate offspring for crime, or to let them starve for their imbecility, society can prevent those who are manifestly unfit from continuing their kind.' In 1934, five years prior to the start of the war against Hitler's Nazis, the highly regarded *New England Journal of Medicine* approvingly wrote that 'Germany is perhaps the most progressive nation in restricting fecundity among the unfit.' As recently as the mid-1960s, court-directed sterilization of 'defectives,' a form of eugenics, was still being done in most Western democratic, human-rights regimes.

It is inconceivable that today's Western democratic, human-rights societies will endorse an explicit policy of eugenics which employs practices of coerced sterilization or outright extermination. However, there is an emergent scientific-philosophical view that eugenics has suffered unfairly from a bad reputation and that it is time to rehabilitate the idea as a non-authoritarian, humanitarian practice. This new attitude to eugenics can be inferred from John Rawls's widely acclaimed 1971 book, *A Theory of Justice*. Rawls contemplated that the parties to his proposed social contract will 'want to insure for their descendants the best genetic endowment' and this means that 'over time a society is to take steps at least to preserve the general level of natural abilities and to prevent the diffusion of serious defects.'

Currently, there are subtle indications in Western societies of an incipient ethos favourable to a non-authoritarian form of eugenics cloaked in the robes of human rights, free choice, and humanitarianism. Evidence for this assertion can be inferred from reaction to a study conducted by researchers from the University of Chicago. They reported that one effect of the right to abortion was a reduction in the offspring of poor, teenage, minority women and that this circumstance resulted in a measurable generational drop in U.S. crime rates. Without so much as a nod to the civility of political correctness, some media commentators speculated publicly and frankly about reducing future crime rates and relieving society of burdensome welfare costs by offering women of this segment of the population incentives to voluntarily exercise their human right to abortion.

Some leaders of the Black community denounced the idea as racial genocide; however, the absence of a popular outcry against the implication that human-rights doctrine might be exploited to rationalize and dignify a state policy designed to encourage the socially disadvantaged to abort their 'unfit' fetuses for reasons of crime reduction and cost containment does suggest a nascent ethos favourable to non-authoritarian eugenics. So does the growing social acceptance of voluntary post-conception screening and selection of human embryos for desired attributes such as preferred gender. Science has indirectly and inadvertently fostered public acceptance of eugenic policies and practices by 'elevating' the practice of eugenics from the personally intrusive, crude, and unacceptable methods of castration, sterilization, and euthanasia to the sophisticated impersonal methods of embryonic screening and selection.

Spurred by the virtual possibilities generated by recent progress in deciphering encrypted genetic information, the scientific establishment and the corporate sector, abetted by government, are engaging in a collaborative campaign to promote eugenics research as a humanitarian enterprise that saves lives by discovering cures for dreadful illnesses and diseases; the above-cited search for racial-ethnic gene-specific markers is an example of this. The new discoveries can save lives; however, the professed humanitarian motive is suspect. As quickly as life-saving discoveries are developed, if law permits, they are patented and monopolized by the corporate manufacturers and the benefits are withheld from those who cannot pay the fixed prices. This leaves millions of poor and disenfranchised people to suffer and die. For instance, in developing countries, AIDS patients have been dying in epidemic numbers with genocidal outcomes partly because corporate patents were exercised to prohibit the manufacture of affordable generic versions of life-saving AIDS medications.

The devaluation of humanity resulting from the philosophical convergence of value-neutral science and globalism is currently particularized by the harvesting of human embryonic stem cells for purposes of research. Human embryonic cells have the potential to be grown into human bones, muscles, brain cells, and other organs that can be utilized as replacements for those that are diseased or disordered. If this potential is fully realized, many people with debilitating and life-threatening diseases stand to be helped. Human embryonic-stem-cell research also holds out the prospect of an enormous monetary payoff. It is this prospect that is attracting private corporations to invest billions of dollars in a race to patent potentially lucrative discoveries from stem-cell research. Responding to pressure and inducements from the scientific-corporate establishment, a number of Western governments are devising official ethical positions, policies, laws, and economic incentives that are hospitable to the origination and sale of living human embryos for the purpose of stem-cell research; in effect, they are treated as 'biological property.' This initiative has resulted in the casual destruction of hundreds of thousands of living human embryos.

Stem cells can be gleaned from several sources that do not require the destruction of living human embryos (e.g., umbilical cords, placenta, and adult tissues such as bone marrow, blood, and body fat); in this regard, stem cells gleaned from a patient's own tissues provide a better genetic match than those taken from human embryos. But stem cells from living human embryos are cheaper, and, instead of aggressively pursuing promising alternative sources of stem cells, the scientific-corporate complex favours research strategies that give precedence to considerations of cost and convenience over concern for the valuation of nascent humanity. No regard is expressed for the erosion of the essential meaning of humanity implied by the origination and destruction of countless nascent human beings.

The scientific-corporate establishment adeptly distracts public attention from moral-ethical concerns about the negative consequences of this commoditization of human embryos by interpolating peripheral legal rationales such as 'informed consent' by the contributors of eggs and sperm; and it prominently features utilitarian considerations such as the potential 'cost benefit' of its inventions. It defends stem-cell research by citing dubious humanitarian 'means/ends' rationales although its patents will legally and financially restrict access by millions of persons to any benefits gained from human embryonic research.

Manifestly, when a society tolerates destruction of potential human beings for reasons of convenience, pecuniary, and 'mean/ends' calculations, without regard to the implied devaluation of the virtue of humanity, then humanity becomes vulnerable to any plausible utilitarian rationale. In effect, the living human embryo is the 'miner's canary' of humanity. Valuing humanity requires that the rules governing when one potential human being may be sacrificed for the benefit of another must be founded on the ethical principle of greatest enhancement or least derogation of the virtue of humanity.

Currently, science is originating knowledge to override and supersede the vagaries and 'defects' that attend natural selection and adaptation. Proceeding on the assumption that it can make a better human being than does natural selection, it is venturing into determinative eugenics and genetic engineering that may produce a 'fitter' human species but poses grave perils for the valuation of humanity. Some Western scientists are exploiting permissive government policies to explore genetic similarities between humans and animals with the purpose of creating part-human, part-animal hybrids, called 'chimeras.' The U.S. National Academy of Sciences (NAS) has expressed approval of such laboratory research and is advocating that the scientific establishment be mandated to regulate this research by means of rational rules and professional ethics. The co-chair of the relevant NAS subcommittee, Dr Richard O. Hynes, has acknowledged that this blurring of the distinction between humans and animals will cause some anxiety and that it will take some time for the public 'to get used to the idea.' To calm concerns over potentially deleterious consequences for humanity, he offered to ensure that chimerical entities will not be allowed to mate and added, bizarrely, that any entities that display 'human-like' behaviour will be killed after having served their purpose. The scientific-corporate complex is already lobbying government to pass patent laws that will protect its ownership of its eugenic creations.

The above critique of the two fundamental doctrines of science – naturalism and value-neutrality – are not intended to discredit the potential of science to aid our quest for the Good Society. As a body of knowledge and understanding of the natural world, science has great potential to serve this endeavour.

The first part of my critique is intended to demystify the claim that science's conception of reality represents objective actuality, and thereby dispel uncritical acceptance of scientific evidence for the myth that reality is purely a naturalistic phenomenon. Science assumes that, because it can explain selected natural phenomena with precision and certainty, this entitles it to acclaim itself as the exclusive and true arbiter of reality. Science can provide explanations for what it can observe, but reality encompasses more than the natural world. When science deliberately confines its knowledge and understanding of reality to the narrow band of sensory observation and omits the concept of humanity from its myth, it imprisons human self-understanding, imagination, and aspirations within the limitations of natural possibilities. When science insists that all thoughts, feelings, and aspirations are reducible to natural possibilities, it denies humankind's potential for humanity.

The second part of my critique seeks to draw attention to the threat posed to the future of humanity by value-neutral science. Science would have us believe that its work enhances humankind's potential for humanity, but, like the principle of naturalism, the principle of value-neutrality engenders an understanding of ourselves that derogates the virtue of humanity. Indentured to corporate capitalism, which is subject to the economic-utilitarian imperative of global free-market capitalism, value-neutral science is originating knowledge on weapons of mass destruction, biological engineering, human cloning, and the harvesting of human embryonic stem cells that portends an erosion of human self-consciousness and sensibility.

Scholars generally esteem science for its value-neutrality. A notable exception in this regard is the carefully reasoned and thoughtful analysis provided by Wendell Bell in his two-volume classic work *Foundations of Future Studies*. In volume 2, *Values, Objectivity and the Good Society*, Bell presents a cogent rationale for bringing 'justified, purposed, and tested' moral/ethical valuations, by which the consequences of science are judged, into scientific discourse and endeavours. Bell's analysis is addressed primarily to the social sciences but his rationale is equally applicable and valid for all branches of the sciences. Economic utility-rational ethics and self-regulation by the scientific establishment cannot protect humanity from the 'Mad Science' foreshadowed by the philosophical convergence of value-free science and globalism. A moral conscience is needed to restrain the greed of corporate capitalism, and science needs to critically assess its role and the effect its principle of moral value-neutrality has upon the valuation of humanity.

The Theological Myth

The search for understanding of reality has yielded the Judeo-Christian-Islamic theological myth which proclaims God as the First Cause of all things, the divine ruler with absolute authority. For thousands of years, mainstream theologians of these religions accepted the literal Genesis account of the creation of the world as immutable truth. Because it is more problematical to acknowledge and correct errors of immutable truth than errors of fact, theology has been lagging science in adjusting its myth to accommodate new knowledge and understanding. In this regard, the secular revolutions of the Enlightenment and scientific discoveries have discredited the literal Genesis account of creation and rendered the long-standing theological myth of reality vulnerable to charges of anti-intellectualism, ignorance, irrationality, and superstition.

To counter widespread and growing scepticism of their myth, many theologians have been adopting a metaphorical interpretation of the events related in Genesis, and some are moving towards 'theistic evolution' (that is, the idea that God used natural selection to accomplish his creative work) while still holding that First Cause occurred by divine agency. Furthermore, they have begun to integrate selected scientific-naturalistic assumptions and explanations into their myth of reality which their forebears, who pitted a literal Genesis against science, repudiated as sacrilege.

The Judeo-Christian-Islamic theological myth of reality allegedly characterizes God as a spiritual being; however, it resorts to ambiguity on this point. Theologians have transmuted the spiritual experience of seeing God in nature into seeing nature in God. On the one hand, theologians hold that, as a spiritual being, God is not a phenomenon based on evidence in the physical sense that can be substantiated by scientific methods; and they insist that God is an unknowable deity who can be apprehended only by faith. On the other hand, to render God closer to human understanding and psychologically more accessible for a personal relationship, they have made God into man; they represent God as a father figure with natural sensibilities of love, anger, and revenge and possessing the human attributes of intelligence, memory, knowledge, and wisdom as well as a full array of sensory capacities.

By representing God as an anthropomorphized being with absolute authority, the theological myth readily lends itself to exploitation by elect bodies. Throughout history, elect bodies, posing as God's agents, have arrogated and manipulated God's authority to justify their control of people.

The arrogation of God's authority by elect bodies is generally identified with theocratic regimes; however, secular Western democracies, which proclaim the principle of separation of church and state, have never taken God's authority out of politics. For instance, U.S. elect bodies exploited God's authority during the Revolution, the Civil War, and the fight against Communism. They continue to do so today: U.S. President George W. Bush, in his capacity as chief of state and commander-in-chief of U.S. military forces, was quoted by the BBC as saying that he was 'driven with a mission from God' to invade Iraq; he asserted that God told him, 'George, go and end the tyranny in Iraq.' He mobilized American citizens to support the invasion not only by appealing to their patriotism but by implying that those who were with him were with God, and by characterizing the war in religious terms, as a 'crusade against terrorism' – in other words, a 'holy war.' Like the Imam Ayatollah Khomeini of Iran, who branded the United States the 'Great Satan,' President Bush framed the invasion in terms of good versus evil and used the language of religion to brand Iraq, Iran, and North Korea the 'Axis of Evil.' With few exceptions, Americans remained silent or approved of this melding of religion and state. In part, this was because of the politicization of religion, especially the fundamentalist variety, which seeks to influence legislators on issues such as abortion and homosexual marriage by playing the partisan political card. In effect, each uses the other to advance its ambitions.

The exploitation of the theological myth through religion by elect bodies is writ large and tragically in the history of wars among Jews, Christians, and Muslims. These were not wars in the name of different Gods; all the religions involved are monotheistic ones whose theologies and respective pre-eminent exemplars and prophets, Moses, Jesus, and Muhammad, proclaim the same God of Abraham. But, even as they worship and profess a sacred commitment to the same Abrahamic God, the elect bodies of these religions are deliberately promoting divisive parochial identities and fanning the flames of sectarian hatred, one against the other. Respectively, they self-righteously invoke God as a confederate who sanctifies their killing of the others' children, women, and men. They have corrupted their God into a partisan benefactor who aids and abets their basest ambitions, motives, desires, and actions.

Those who reject the theological myth of reality tender a variety of reasons beside the iniquities perpetrated by elect bodies in the name of God. Some consider God to be a fiction of the mind and cite the lack of physical evidence for the existence of God; some discredit the myth because of religious literalism relating to the Genesis account of creation; some spurn the myth because they reject the idea of being judged and condemned according to what they consider to be alien moral-ethical standards; some reject the myth because they regard the idea of God as a matter of faith and belief, which they consider a forfeit of reason; some oppose it because they conceptualize God in terms of predestination and an infringement on the principle of self-determination; some reject it because they assume that God involves homage, obeisance, and fear; and even believers sometimes doubt the myth because they cannot reconcile the idea of an omniscient, compassionate creator with a world of violence, misery, and suffering.

It is noteworthy that all of the above-listed rationales for rejecting the theological myth of reality are referenced to the particular conception of God described by the theological myth. This assertion is demonstrated in the writings of self-styled atheists such as Richard Dawkins and Christopher Hitchens. They seem blissfully unaware that their atheistic enterprise is in a symbiotic relationship with the theology they censure and that they are deeply indebted for their atheistic celebrity to theologians who have given them a myth they can readily caricature and discredit. Their discussion is always referenced to the God of the theological myth.

Dawkins and Hitchens equate God with religion and discredit God with banal lectures about scriptural literalisms and by chronicling the great harm that organized religion has perpetrated in the name of God. The concept of God is generally equated or confused with religion; however, it is conceptually distinct from religion. Freud described religion as the 'universal obsession of humanity.' I propose that the universal obsession observed by Freud is best understood as a pervasive aspiration by human beings to escape the limitations of their nature and realize the full expression of their humanity; they see God as the means to this end. Through the ages, religion has presented itself as the sole gateway to God – hence, the 'universal obsession' with religion.

A reasoned acceptance or rejection of the theological myth of reality necessarily implies a particular conception of God. In this regard, we are not limited to any existing conception of God; representations of God have varied over time and across civilizations, from polytheistic to monotheistic, from localized to omnipresent, from physical to spiritual, from particular to universal. As a disciplinary endeavour, theology, like science, has the potential to help our quest for the Good Society. But before this can happen, theology must abandon its myth and doctrinal assertion of a quasi-natural God with absolute authority over the natural world as the ultimate reality. As we have seen, this myth allows elect bodies to assume the role of God's agents and gives rise to sectarian doctrines and religions that divide people into hostile camps. To help realize the Good Society, theology must conceive a myth that represents God as a spiritual presence and ideal (without any religious or political subtext), characterized by an unconditional, transcending love open to everyone, as the ultimate reality. Such a myth has the potential to inspire a consciousness that enhances individual and collective humanity by honouring everyone's dignity. It can be embraced as a common good by secular humanists, the religious, and peoples of all cultures and nations.

Scientism and Theologism

On the fringes of the disciplines of science and theology we find advocates of scientism and theologism. These terms refer not to disciplinary fields of endeavour but to closed belief systems about how the universe and humankind originated.

The champions of scientism transform Darwin's empirical theory of multigenerational diversification (speciation) of life forms through natural selection into a doctrine of the origin of life; and they invoke it as indisputable authentication and authority for their belief about the natural origin of life. The champions of theologism transform the literal Genesis account of the six days of creation into a doctrine of the origin of life; and they invoke it as indisputable authentication and authority for their belief about the divine origin of life.

Obsessed with their respective dogmas, believers in scientism and theologism are engaged in a rancorous debate about First Cause. Both sides clamorously and gratuitously disparage and discredit each other's belief system, oblivious to the fact that First

Cause is a mystical concept and that any attempt at authentication is beset with logical problems of self-creation and infinite regression. Fixated on speculating how we came to be, instead of what we might become, their tiresome squabbling distracts and encumbers our quest for the Good Society.

11 A Humane Myth of Reality

To realize the fullest expression of our potential for humanity, we need a myth of reality that will liberate us from the limitations of our nature and inspire a self-understanding and universal consciousness of transcendent humanity. Our discussion of such a humane myth requires that we distinguish between the concepts of 'human commonality' and 'transcendent humanity.'

The idea of human commonality is expressed in various religious doctrines. Judaism, Christianity, and Islam acknowledge all of humankind as God's creation; however, all of these religions have been known to self-servingly parse the idea of human commonality in ways that exalt the human worth of their own members above that of others. For instance, the Puritan colonists, who piously proclaimed all of humankind to be God's creation, justified the seizure of lands inhabited by American Indians from time immemorial by declaring that God created the earth for 'his obedient children.' In the current conflicts in the Middle East, the idea of human commonality by virtue of God's creation is parsed to mean religious-tribal kinships. Grievous violations of others' dignity and humanity, including genocide, ethnic cleansing, and slavery, have been perpetrated and rationalized by all of the major religions that acknowledge the idea of human commonality in their ethical systems.

Secularists acknowledge human commonality in their intellectual and philosophical perspectives, on the premise of shared human genetic identity. This notion of human commonality was recently given scientific significance when the Human Genome Project reported that, as a species, humankind is 99.9 per cent genetically identical. (Incidentally, basing human commonality on genetic criteria may inadvertently provide a scientific rationale for racist state policies if future research finds ethno-race-based genetic distinctives.) Humanity, however, is more than the sum of genes, and recognition of a shared human genetic identity does not constitute an acknowledgment of everyone's equal dignity and humanity. This is indicated by Western human-rights charters which condone flagrant violations of equal human worth by letting many go hungry and homelessness in the midst of inordinate wealth and wasteful consumption. It is noteworthy that, in a world where most societies accept the religious and/or secularist ideas of human commonality, all blatantly foster a parochial self-consciousness and identity that exalts the human worth of their own kind above that of others.

Transcendent humanity signifies a different standard than religious and secularist notions of human commonality. It rises above the social bonds of ancestry, tribalism nationality, culture, language, religion, and any other form of fraternity and consanguinity. It includes not only contemporary peoples; it regards future generations as an unbro-ken chain of humanity and has a profound regard for their well-being. Transcendent humanity expands individual self-consciousness in a way that eliminates all social boundaries and bordered identities that are contrary to the recognition of every person's equal human worth; it acknowledges and honours every individual's intrinsic potential for and aspiration to equal dignity and humanity; it generates in every individual a conscious sense of being part of all others' humanity. Transcendent humanity implies more than an endorsement of toler-ance and blindness to differences; it defines 'the other' as 'the self' and conceives the humanity of others as one's own. This means that any violation of another's dignity and humanity constitutes a violation of one's own dignity and humanity. A belief that the ideal of transcendent humanity is present in the minds of others can create trust that bonds even strangers in a culturally and politically diverse global world.

The philosopher Karl Jaspers gave expression to the idea of tran-scendent humanity when he addressed the issue of guilt over the Holocaust as follows: 'There exists a solidarity among men as human beings that makes each responsible for every wrong and every injus-tice in the world.' The Reverend Martin Luther King, Jr was inspired by the idea of transcendent humanity when he wrote from Birmingham Jail: 'We are caught in an inescapable network of mutuality, tied in a single garment of destiny. Whatever affects one directly affects all indirectly.'

Jesus of Nazareth

There are a huge number of books, documentaries, movies, and theological theses and articles devoted to the person of Jesus. Most focus on history, biography, Old Testament prophecies, the psychic need for a saviour, and the veracity of literal accounts of his conception, divinity, miracles, death, resurrection, ascension, and pending return. A crucial deficiency of most of these accounts is that they disregard, obscure, or gloss over Jesus' essential message of God as unconditional, transcending love and the inspiration for transcendent humanity.

Virtually from the beginning, Jesus' message was obfuscated by conflicts of authority among his disciples and disagreements within the fledgling church over secondary, often trivial, theological differences. Moreover, he has become identified with denominational Christianity and sectarian religious doctrines that have raised obstacles to the acceptance of his message and have rendered it divisive and objectionable to many. But, stripped of all extraneous theological baggage and stereotyping, his essential message is a simple, straightforward, and clear call for transcendent humanity articulated as universal and equal dignity of all humankind.

Religiously, culturally, and ancestrally, Jesus was a Jew; he was a rabbi who venerated the Torah and the Prophets. The New Testament records that he generalized the ethical standard of transcendent humanity implied in the injunction by Leviticus in the Hebrew Bible to 'Love your neighbor as yourself' from a parochial moral order to a universal moral imperative; he ordained that treating all others with equal dignity is a primary and universal moral obligation. He gave eloquent expression to the idea of transcendent humanity as social action in his parable of the Good Samaritan and in the Sermon on the Mount, emphasizing peace, social justice, forgiveness, compassion, and generosity in all social relationships.

If the nations that call themselves 'Christian' lived Jesus' message, they would not make war on defenceless civilians and the Holocaust would not have happened. As symbols of transcendent humanity, the words 'Christian' and 'Christianity' have been so completely discredited by the actions of so many who lay claim to them that they are beyond rehabilitation and are best abandoned. Jesus' message of God as unconditional, transcending love needs a new inauguration without the taint of 'religion.'

Humankind comes to its fullest consciousness of transcendent humanity through relationships of love. Love, like power, is a social-relational concept; it finds expression and meaning in interaction between and among individuals. The capacity, need, and desire to be loved are universal. In contemporary popular usage, the connotations of the word 'love' refer mainly to familial, romantic, sexual, friendship, and other personal attachments. These forms of love are universal but they are generally conditional and limited to unique relationships between individuals; they do not involve a consciousness of transcendent humanity. Transcendent humanity implies a love that is unconditional and that transcends all ego and social borders; it takes us beyond the deontological Golden Rule, which links individuals by having them regard each other from the perspective of reciprocity. Such a love is extra-natural, that is, it rises above nature and biology; it defies reason based on natural assumptions; it relies on extra-natural explanations.

To establish the possibility of unconditional, transcendent love and transcendent humanity, we need to refute naturalism. Those who believe in the idea of a purely naturalistic reality consider the absence of physical evidence for extra-natural reality as evidence for its non-existence. However, to quote Carl Sagan, 'absence of evidence is not evidence of absence.' Earlier, we invalidated the axiom of naturalism by establishing the possibility of extra-natural phenomena; that is, not everything in the natural world has a physical explanation. Given the difficulty science has distinguishing cause and effect in its observations of natural phenomena, science is limited to making provisional statements about nature. It follows that, from a scientific perspective, the existence of extra-natural reality is indeterminate; scientific methods cannot provide evidence to refute or affirm extra-natural explanations. While this fact does not prove the existence of extra-natural phenomena, it allows for the possibility of their existence.

In the absence of physical evidence, how can we discern the reality of an extra-natural phenomenon like unconditional, transcending love? Although it is not discernible by the methods of science, such love is more than a conception of the mind. It has a verifiable reality as a social-relational fact and as a causal force in human space and time – that is, where we live and relate to each other. It is ascertainable through the process of rational thought and empirical evidence. Rational confirmation for the existence of unconditional, transcending love is indicated by acts of sacrificial compassion and altruism between strangers; and it is manifest in acts of forgiveness between enemies. The natural brain can elevate us to reciprocal compassion and altruism, but not to acts of sacrificial compassion, altruism, and forgiveness of enemies. Empirical confirmation for the existence of unconditional, transcending love as a causal force is evident in the transformational effect that sacrificial compassion and altruism, given and received, has on social relationships; it changes conscious reality. These transformational effects meet the standard of 'scientific evidence' inasmuch as they are measurable and can be affirmed by replicated observation.

In short, the reality of extra-natural unconditional, transcending love lies in acts of sacrificial compassion and altruism and their causal force in social relations. When we acknowledge acts of unconditional, transcending love and their transformational causal impact in our social-relational experience, then, in effect, we acknowledge that humankind can rise above nature and we admit to the existence of extra-natural reality: the two are one and the same.

, A myth of reality founded on the ideal of unconditional, transcending love does not ensure a political-economic-social utopia. However, it can inspire a moral ethic and code of human behaviour that has limitless humanizing potential. It embodies a moral truth that can free humankind from the narrow bounds of naturalism; move us away from ego; eliminate social barriers; heal divisions among diverse and often hostile societies and social groups; and inspire a global moral social order that warrants liberty, social justice, universal, and equal dignity. In a world divided by cultural and political hatred and hostilities, a myth of reality founded on the ideal of unconditional, transcending love as the ultimate reality can facilitate a convergence of humane values that can heal these divisions and foster relationships of transcendent humanity.

Summary

Our myth of reality is a significant issue in our quest for the Good Society. It influences our self-understanding, aspirations, and destiny. In effect, we invent our myth of reality and it in turn defines us. It is the most vital legacy we the Millennial Generations will bequeath to future generations. Therefore, our primary concern should be to get it as right as we possibly can. I have reviewed and critiqued the two pre-eminent myths of the Millennial Generations. Both science and theology aspire to serve as the primary arbiter of reality. They have devised and evolved their respective myths of reality in separate, virtually closed, and generally adverse intellectual discourses. The result is two alien categories of knowledge and understanding and divergent, virtually opposing, conceptions of reality.

Science and theology each proclaims authenticity for its myth of reality, but, inasmuch as the creators of the myths are an integral part of the reality they perceive, the two myths must be considered as unprovable conjectures. Both myths are reasoned from a mystical First Cause and both posit provisional subjective observations and assumptions which are subject to ongoing revision, to accommodate newly discovered facts and revealed truths. However, both science and theology adamantly and vigorously insist on the fundamental authenticity of their myth.

My review and critique gave more attention to the scientific myth than the theological myth because the Millennial Generations live in awe of what science has learned about the natural world. Its practical accomplishments and promises for the future have induced a significant shift in popular trust from the theological to the scientific myth. This fact is particularly evident in the world view, lifestyles, government policies, and value systems of Western societies, where the scientific conception of reality significantly defines individual and collective images of present and future possibilities. Moreover, popular belief in the scientific myth is fortified by the fact that the universe and life have a natural form, and by the circumstance that, as physical beings, we are subject to the forces of nature and experience life as a natural phenomenon.

Although scientists readily acknowledge that they cannot give a natural account of all aspects of reality, they dogmatically insist that everything about reality has a natural explanation. Their myth, however, has some crucial shortcomings. Even as it liberates humankind from the oppression of superstition, it stifles the fulfillment of its potential for humanity by imprisoning self-understanding, imagination, and aspirations within the parameters of natural possibilities. Another shortcoming of the myth lies in its doctrine of value-neutrality. Value-neutrality in scientific research is generally praised in scholarly literature as a mark of enlightenment; however, it desensitizes scientists to any consequent devaluation of humanity that may result from their work. Thoughtful analysis suggests good reasons for introducing moral-ethical values into the scientific enterprise.

The theological myth of reality, like the scientific myth, has some crucial shortcomings. Its conception of God traps individuals and entire cultures in adverse sectarian belief systems that engender divisive identities, spawn distrust and prejudice, and serve as a breeding ground for extremism that perpetrates violence and genocide. The theological myth of reality has fostered organized religions which are content to confine the ideal of universal human dignity and humanity to rhetoric, and to obscure it with liturgy, ritual, and customs. It needs to be said that this critique of the theological myth is not a general indictment of individual religious believers or churches: when a believer or a church expresses the essence of God as unconditional and transcending love by honouring the human dignity and humanity of all others in daily relationships, they foster transcendent humanity; and when theology and religion affirm ultimate reality as unconditional, transcending love and integrate it as a guiding moral principle in behaviour and action, they can play a significant role in advancing transcendent humanity.

I have stated that it is not possible to objectively authenticate our conception of reality. This fact, however, does not diminish the importance of our myth of reality in our quest for the Good Society. As ways of knowing and understanding the mysteries of reality, the disciplines of science and theology can facilitate our quest for the Good Society by working collaboratively to create a new myth of reality that will inspire all of the world's societies to a sense of transcendent humanity. For this to happen, however, scientists and theologians, respectively, need to liberate themselves from the deeply embedded disciplinary convictions and limitations which trap imagination and aspirations within the finitude of naturalism or the false self-consciousness of sectarianism; they need to work cooperatively to create humanizing knowledge and understanding. Given the subjective and provisional assumptions on which the scientific and theological myths are based, there are no insuperable barriers to such cooperation. The most formidable barriers are personal career ambitions and professional reputations derived from the existing disciplinary structures.

To realize the Good Society, we need a myth that will animate a universal consciousness of transcendent humanity defined as selfless acknowledgment of one another's dignity and humanity. I have proposed that we need a myth of reality founded on the ideal of unconditional, transcending love. Some will regard this idea as a forfeit of objectivity because it incorporates an extra-natural assumption into our conception of reality. In fact, any conception of reality is necessarily based on evolving subjective perceptions and beliefs about our world and being, and the extra-natural phenomenon of unconditional, transcending love can be as much a part of our reality as a natural phenomenon.

The myth of reality based on unconditional, transcending love provides a humane moral-ethical foundation for global social-relational interdependence. It validates and reinforces the absolute principle and moral covenants of humane mutuality; and it can bring self-determined definitions of human dignity and humanity by diverse autonomous societies into an integrated humane global moral network, fostering a pervasive sense of transcendent humanity.

Reason affirms that only good can come from a myth of reality and a moral social order based on the ideal of unconditional, transcending love. Those who give or receive such love in their relationships with others are transformed by its humanizing effect. When we witness the good such love can do, we are enthralled by it. When it is taught as mutual duties and responsibilities, it will gradually become part of our self-understanding and daily relationship with each other, thus encouraging the fullest realization of our potential for transcendent humanity.

Epilogue

Collectively and individually, we, the Millennial Generations, stand at a juncture in history where the decisions we make will determine human destiny. The Good Society will not materialize by divine intervention nor will it evolve by a process of natural selection. We need to become conscious of our pivotal position in humankind's journey and acknowledge that achieving the Good Society is a matter of human volition: the volition to create a global moral social order that honours everyone's aspiration to dignity and fosters transcendent humanity.

Biologists have categorized three broad forms of volition: 'tendency' (as in plants); 'instinct' (as in insects); and 'cognition' (as in animals). A particular life form may evidence one or more of these faculties of volition, all of which express the intentionality of naturalistic survival and well-being. Tendency and instinct express this intentionality in a pattern (more or less) of stimulus-response to naturalistic imperatives. The volitional faculty of cognition expresses intentionality in a (more or less) deliberate pattern; that is, correlative with its neural complexity, it can mediate its response to naturalistic imperatives, subject to the constraints of naturalistic necessity.

Science conceives of human volition as a brain function: an exclusively natural aptitude and process, ancillary to biological evolution as it was observed and understood by Charles Darwin. This implies that the distinction between the volition of humankind and that of other animal species can be explained by differences in neurological complexity and cognitive functioning, such as intelligence, which can be plotted on a continuum of linear genealogical evolution. Based on the assumption that the capability of the human brain is subject to the constraints of nature, some scientists reason that, if all relevant natural variables were known and fully understood, it would be possible to predict human volitional choices on the basis of purely natural internal and external causal necessity – that is, a deterministic system. Indeed, if we accept that human volition is exclusively a naturalistic phenomenon, then we must accept the logic of behavioural determinism as self-evident.

We know, however, that humankind has the ability to transcend natural imperatives. By what means and process? I propose that human agency is a function of volitional dualism. Humankind is endowed with two distinct volitional faculties: cognition and will. Cognition exists and functions as a natural faculty; it exercises a biologically determined volition, involving decision making, planning, goal setting, and means-ends thinking, which enables humankind to make deliberate responses to the imperatives of nature in order to survive as a biological genus. Will exists and functions as an extra-natural faculty; it has the capacity to transcend natural imperatives and provide the humane ethical-moral directionality that allows humankind to rise above nature and realize its potential for humanity. The idea of dual volitional faculties involves two orders of self-consciousness and sensibility: the faculty of cognition exhibits the natural self-consciousness and sensibility of a *species* being; the faculty of will exhibits the extra-natural self-consciousness and sensibility of a *human* being. Significations of cognitive capabilities have been discerned in animal species; it is the faculty of will that makes humankind unique among all species beings.

Unlike the natural faculty of cognition, which affects its volition by neurological mechanics that can be mapped and understood in terms of molecular and environmental processes and functions of the various parts of the brain, the extra-natural faculty of will affects its volition by means that are not susceptible to sensory observation. However, the absence of physical evidence for its existence does not mean that the faculty of will lacks evidential credibility. Distinct from abstract concepts such as 'soul' and 'natural rights of man,' which must be accepted on faith or as self-evident, the faculty of will has a functional life-force that can be inferred from compelling evidence of our capacity to rise above our naturalistic and utilitarian predispositions and imperatives and elevate ourselves to transcendent humanity. This capacity is not a function of natural intelligence; it is the extra-natural essence of will that enables us to make a conscious personal commitment and a deliberate decision to strive to realize the ethical ideals of universal and equal dignity and transcendent humanity in our daily relationships with others.

I posit the concept of *mind*, without a biological location, as the locus and nexus of volitional dualism: the two distinct and disparate faculties – natural cognition and extra-natural will – are joined by reciprocal ties to constitute the mind; they activate each other, interact continuously, and work co-dependently in the mind's exercise of human agency. Cognition, the seat of natural consciousness and intelligence, has the competence to think, reason, and create knowledge and understanding; the faculty of will has the capability to determine to what purpose the competence of cognition will be applied in the mind's exercise of human agency. This conception of the mind implies the potentiality for functional discord between the two volitional faculties with regard to intentionality and behaviour. Coherence in purpose between the two distinct faculties is achieved through a bridging principle that vests will with volitional ascendancy over cognition as arbiter in the mind's exercise of human agency.

The capability of the mind to rise above natural consciousness and sensibility in its exercise of human agency is a function of humane ethical-moral knowledge and understanding. By reason of its volitional ascendancy over cognition, will is able to give ethical-moral guidance to cognition in the creation of humane knowledge and understanding. This humane knowledge and understanding enables the mind to elevate self-realization from that of a species being to a human being and frees human agency from naturalistic causal necessity. Under the bridging principle, it follows that, unless the volitional ascendancy of will is exercised to give humane ethical-moral directionality to cognition in the creation of knowledge and understanding, the mind will be a prisoner of natural and utilitarian predispositions and imperatives unable to rise above natural consciousness and sensibility in its exercise of human agency.

The idea of human agency as comprising dual volitional faculties implies two distinct, albeit interrelated, patterns and forms of evolutionary progression in humankind. Fossil records reveal that the volition of cognition advances in correlation with naturalistic selection and adaptation. The volition of will is not imprinted in fossil records and does not fall on the continuum of natural selection and adaptation, instead advancing in correlation with the creation of ethical-moral knowledge and understanding. It follows that the ranking of neurological complexity on a linear genealogical continuum, which describes the volitional progression of cognition, does not describe the volitional progression of will and, therefore, does not provide a full and correct understanding of human evolution. Distinct from *biological* evolution, *human* evolution, that is, the development of our humanity, requires humane ethical-moral knowledge and understanding. In circumstances of deteriorating humanizing knowledge and understanding, the mind becomes increasingly subject to naturalistic cognitive volition, entailing an evolutionary retreat from the status of human being to that of species being. The implication is that we are the masters of our own evolution as human beings; our being, our becoming, and our destiny as human beings, distinct from species beings, lie in the volition of will to 'cause' the cognitive origination of humanizing knowledge and understanding that gives meaning to an existence which rises above nature.

Some scholars point to what they loosely call 'civilization' (implying a higher order of knowledge and understanding) as evidence of human evolution. In the past millennium, the complexity of our knowledge and understanding has increased exponentially, and cultures have become vastly more sophisticated; however, history shows that human evolution has been ambiguous at best. The scale of our barbarities has increased from personal hostilities in ancient times to the horrific crimes against humanity of our time, unprecedented in scale and impersonality. In the past century, humankind has perpetrated the Holocaust; mass executions in the USSR, China, and Cambodia; the nuclear bombings of Hiroshima and Nagasaki; genocidal wars in Darfur, Rwanda, Bosnia, and Congo; and ongoing atrocities in various regions of the world. To this horrific record can be added innumerable assaults against humanity through wilful neglect of the world's hungry, sick, and homeless, even though remedies for such afflictions are available to us. And the gravest of these crimes and assaults against humanity have been perpetrated by the most 'civilized' societies. The elect bodies of these highly civilized societies have created the nuclear bomb and the means to deliver it to human targets; and they stand in a constant state of distrust, if not enmity, prepared to annihilate one another. Clearly, 'civilized' does not mean 'humane.' If human evolution is to take its meaning from 'civilization' as demonstrated by these societies, then we have reason to be profoundly alarmed.

Our volitional faculties give us the agency to advance human evolution by creating ethical-moral knowledge and understanding that will free us from the limitations of our natural being and foster humane self-consciousness, sensibility, and the fullest realization of our potential for humanity. In the past, we have focused our resources and energies primarily on creating knowledge and understanding to advance our biological survival and well-being. If we continue neglecting to exercise our agency to create humanizing knowledge and understanding, human evolution will suffer a setback; globalism will place our species on a trajectory of incremental erosion of humane self-consciousness and sensibility, causing a retreat from humanity.

Globalism portends a Hobbesian society of 'smart animals' in serfdom to an autonomous extra-human tyranny. To avert this catastrophic future and make progress towards the Good Society, we need to establish a global moral social order that encompasses the duties and responsibilities essential to securing the common good of universal and equal human dignity and humanity and to accommodating the increasing social scale, urbanization, industrialization, social mobility, and modernization heralded by globalization. My search for such a humane paradigm led to social order in the moral mode, authenticated by democratic discourse and founded on the absolute principle within the concept of humane mutuality. I envision these ideas as basic elements of a humane moral social order that can override nationalistic and sectarian interests and place humankind on a course of intergenerational progress towards the global Good Society.

Our progress towards the global Good Society depends upon how we cope with the deterministic force of globalization. Most international conflicts, past and present, can be understood as dysfunctional responses to these forces: elect bodies have sought to thwart the deterministic force of globalization by perpetrating wars, genocides, ethnic cleansings, and forced population transfers, and by retreating behind destructive ideologies such as imperialism, nationalism, and religious fundamentalism.

I have stated that any initiative to manage the forces of globalization by implementing a humane global moral social order threatens the existing oligarchic authority structures which secure the property, status, and privilege of national elect bodies. It is bound to provoke resistance. There are, however, several circumstances that may motivate elect bodies to consider engaging in a meaningful international discourse to develop a constructive response to the forces of globalization. Significant in this regard is the fact that, in the current phase of globalization, the traditional nation-state and the authority of the elect bodies that govern them are unable to cope with a growing number of deteriorating international circumstances. One of these circumstances is the proliferation of biological, chemical, and nuclear weaponry in the hands of corrupt regimes, which poses the omnipresent threat of stateless biological, chemical, and nuclear terrorism. The old Cold War formula of mutually assured destruction is ineffective to counter these scourges. Military stratagems, even 'victories,' do not bring peace or security; they breed and feed terrorism.

Other circumstances that may motivate national elect bodies to consider a constructive response to the deterministic forces of globalization are the accelerating depletion of essential resources, the alarming depredation of planetary life-support systems resulting from pollution, ecological devastation and global climate change, and the appearance of new global deadly pandemics. While these negative realities, of themselves, will not inspire a shared sense of humanity, they will awaken a worldwide shared sense of impending cataclysm that will raise awareness and a sense of urgency for the need to make fundamental social-political changes. From a utility-rational perspective, diplomatic initiatives are preferable to a global cataclysm. This may induce national elect bodies to abandon their self-serving ambitions and, for their own survival, engage in a meaningful international discourse that fosters mutual trust and leads to the development of a humane global moral social order.

Also, as we have seen, there are some major social-cultural impediments to achieving a humane global moral social order. Western societies, under human-rights regimes, have repudiated the moral mode of social-order authority as the enemy of individual freedom, and the enforcement of moral values has been outlawed as an infringement on constitutional human rights, thereby practically eliminating the authority of moral social order. Many non-Western societies are trapped in ancient, sometimes sacred, firmly established repressive synthetic moral-religious belief systems which reject the idea of universal, equal human dignity and humanity.

On the other hand, there are some serviceable human sensibilities which have a potential to motivate humankind to strive for a humane global moral social order. In this regard, we can draw encouragement from the fact that, in times of great human tragedy and distress, such as instances of natural disaster, serious disease epidemics, and extreme privation, people have shown themselves capable of relating to each other in the spirit of the absolute principle and humane mutuality. All of humankind has a personal understanding and inherent aspiration to human dignity and humanity; and all societies demonstrate a historically rooted and broadly based ethical consensus acknowledging universal and equal human dignity and humanity as the common good. Achieving a humane global moral social order will be facilitated by waning political and economic borders, by the exponential growth in social communications, and by allowing cultural pluralism in the determination of mutual duties and responsibilities.

Humankind has always aspired to the Good Society and has created myths of reality to help it attain this goal. The philosophers of the Enlightenment sought to achieve the Good Society by transforming social order from a moral to an amoral endeavour and establishing the myth of a social contract embodying the principles of natural rights and rule by representation. They idealistically envisioned that these principles would yield a social order that diffuses authority and thereby secures liberty, social justice, and equal human dignity and humanity for all. Their vision, however, has been betrayed; the shift to an amoral mode of social order has not liberated Western societies from oligarchic structures and authority. It has merely changed the legitimating rationale for such authority from a sacred to a primarily secular premise.

The most influential myths of reality of our time are provided by science and theology. Both give us insights into the nature of our world and being. However, both have serious flaws that disqualify them as myths for the Good Society. The scientific myth is disqualified because its naturalistic precept immures human imagination and volition in a prison of naturalism, and its doctrine of value-neutrality is effecting a devaluation of humanity. Under the economic-utilitarian imperative of the global free-market system, science is originating knowledge and technology that portends an incremental erosion of human self-consciousness and sensibility and a regression in the evolution of our humanity. The theological myth is disqualified because it enables elect bodies to arrogate and exploit 'divine authority' to further their nefarious ambitions; and because it gives rise to religions that create a false self-consciousness which lends itself to manipulation by elect bodies to incite sectarian distrust, bigotry, hate, violations of human dignity, and crimes against humanity.

In an infinite and eternal universe of billions of galaxies, humankind is cosmically insignificant. If we became extinct, the universe would go on as it did billions of years before we existed. Individually and collectively, we draw our significance from the meaning and purpose we give to our existence. If we neglect to create knowledge and understanding that gives humane meaning and purpose to our existence, then, in the words of Stephen Hawking, we are no more than 'an advanced breed of monkeys on a minor planet of a very, very average star.' Who we are and what we will become is profoundly influenced by our myth of reality. The authenticity of our myth will not be determined by scientific facts and/or theological truths, but by its promise for fostering a self-understanding and aspiration to the fullest realization of humankind's potential for humanity.

The Good Society needs a myth of reality that promotes universal and equal human dignity and transcendent humanity. To create such a myth, we need an ideal that transcends and transforms natural reality. This requires that we imagine and acknowledge the existence of forces outside our natural world. I have advanced a myth of reality based on the ideal of unconditional, transcending love. When this ideal defines ultimate reality and our vision of the Good Society, when it forms the basis of global moral social order and is taught in all societies, it will free human beings from their ego, social, and religious ghettos; it will inspire universal and equal human dignity and transcendent humanity. Human self-consciousness will rise above natural limitations, and human agency will be elevated to the highest level for the fullest development of our potential for humanity.

Realizing the Good Society involves a synergy between the collectivity and the individual. On the one hand, creating a global moral social order based on the absolute principle and humane mutuality implies a collective endeavour. On the other hand, the implication of my premise of human agency is that realization of the Good Society comes down to the individual striving to honour the idea of transcendent humanity by treating all others with human dignity in all social relationships and under every circumstance. Thus, 'minorities of one' can build the Good Society by living the ideal of unconditional and transcending love in their daily relationships.

The Millennial Generations have had in their cohort celebrated exemplars like Mohandas K. Gandhi, Martin Luther King, Jr, Nelson Mandela, Mother Teresa, Daniel Ellsberg, and citizen Jimmy Carter, who have articulated and exemplified the idea of transcendent humanity in their lives. Also, we have in our midst many ordinary people who honour the idea of transcendent humanity by treating all others with human dignity in their daily relationships. As more and more individuals are inspired to commit to the ideals of the humane myth of reality, they will engender expanding social networks of transcendent humanity; and, as its benefits become personally evident to more and more people, popular endorsement and support for a humane global moral social order will gain momentum and become a force that can change the human world.

The Millennial Generations are aware that they have an obligation to their descendants; and, provided they don't bomb it into nothingness, they will pass on an impressive heritage of real estate, infrastructure, and technological and intellectual property. The current prevailing sentiment is that our gravest offence against future generations is a legacy of massive debt, overpopulation, ecological degradation, global climate change, and depletion of natural resources. Grim as this legacy is, the ultimate offence the Millennial Generations can commit against future generations is to break the intergenerational chain of human evolution by conceding their future to globalism. This portends a fate where the only hope rests in the beguiling illusions offered up by naturalistic, value-neutral science; expressed more starkly, if we continue on our present course, we place humanity on a trajectory into oblivion and diminish humankind to a species being.

The world will not right itself; if we do not actively participate in originating a humane global moral social order, we doom humankind to servitude under a faceless extra-human ruler. Our species may survive, but future generations will be denied their birthright to realize their inherent potential for humanity. For this crime of *humanicide,* our memory will deservedly be cursed by our descendants. But, if we give our descendants the moral means to nurture each other's human dignity and humanity, they will find a way, if not to solve, at least to cope with the legacy of adversities and survive as *human* beings.

We do not stand helpless before the deterministic forces of globalization; we can reactivate and trust the inspiration of the Enlightenment *philosophes* that the future of humanity is in our hands. By virtue of our faculties of cognition and will, we have a choice: we can apply our agency to originate knowledge and understanding based on the absolute principle and humane mutuality, and, inspired by the ideal of unconditional transcending love, we can place humankind on the path to the Good Society; or, by default, we can concede human destiny to the extra-human agency of global free-market capitalism and the dehumanizing affect of globalism.

This does not involve a struggle between Good and Evil or a return to Eden. However, we, the Millennial Generations, need to renounce the prevailing ethos of indifference and fecklessness, and eschew cynicism, fatalism, and defeatism. Building the Good Society requires a will to apply practical idealism to the task of creating a myth of reality and establishing a global moral social order that nurtures everyone's human dignity and humanity, bringing all peoples together in a relationship of transcendent humanity. The Good Society is a visionary alternative to an unfolding dystopian future. There are many obstacles on the path, but not to start on this journey will mean the end of humanity. The society that takes the lead in this journey will flourish in our time and be honoured by those who come after.

Bibliography

Abelson, R., and M.L. Frequenon. 1975. *Ethics for Modern Life*. New York: St Martin's Press.

Ackelsberg, M. 1988. 'Communities, Resistance and Women's Activism.' In A. Bookman and S. Morgan, eds., *Women and the Politics of Empowerment*. Philadelphia: Temple University Press.

Airalesinen, T. 1988. *Ethics of Coercion and Authority: A Philosophical Study of Social Life*. Pittsburgh: University of Pittsburgh Press.

Anderson, C. 1990. *Pragmatic Liberalism*. Chicago: University of Chicago Press.

Andrews, J. 1987. *Key Guide to Information Sources on the International Protection of Human Rights*. New York: Facts on File Publications.

Angell, R. 1958. *Free Society and Moral Crisis*. Ann Arbor: University of Michigan Press.

An-Naim, A., and F. Deng. 1990. Editors' preface. In *Human Rights in Africa: Cross-Cultural Perspectives*. Washington, D.C.: Brookings Institute.

Archer, M. 1990. 'Theory Culture and Post-Industrial Society.' In M. Featherstone, ed., *Global Culture: Nationalism, Globalization and Modernity*. London: Sage Publications.

Arensberg, C., and S. Kimball. 1965. *Culture and Community*. New York: Harcourt Brace and World.

Aristotle. [1996]. *Politics and the Constitution of Athens*. S. Everson, ed. New York: Cambridge University Press.

Arrington, R. 1989. *Rationalism, Realism and Relativism: Perspectives in Contemporary Moral Epistemology*. Ithaca, N.Y.: Cornell University Press.

Arthur, J. 1977. 'Rights and the Duty to Bring Aid.' In W. Aiken and H. La Follette, eds., *World Hunger and Moral Obligation*. Englewood Cliffs, N.J.: Prentice Hall.

Baizell, E., ed. 1968. *The Search for Community in North America*. New York: Harper and Row.

Barr, O. 1969. *The Christian New Morality: A Biblical Study of Situation Ethics*. New York: Oxford University Press.

Barry, B. 1989. 'Justice v. Humanity.' In *Theories of Justice*. Berkeley: University of California Press.

Baumeister, R. 1991. *Meaning of Life*. New York: Guilford Press.

Beauchamp, T., ed. 1980. *Matters of Life and Death*. Philadelphia: Temple University Press.

– 1975. *Ethics and Public Policy*. Englewood Cliffs, N.J.: Prentice Hall.

Becker, H. 1957. 'Current Sacred-Secular Theory and Its Development.' In H. Becker and A. Baskoff, eds., *Modern Sociological Theory*. New York: Holt, Rinehart and Winston.

Becker, L. 1986. *Reciprocity*. Chicago: University of Chicago Press.

Bell, D. 1962. *The End of Ideology: On the Exhaustion of Political Ideas in the Fifties*. Glencoe, Ill.: Free Press.

Bell, W. 2000. 'New Futures and the Eternal Struggle between Good and Evil.' *Journal of Future Studies*, 5, no. 2.

– 1997. *Foundations of Future Studies. Volume 1: History, Purpose and Knowledge; Volume 2: Values, Objectivity and the Good Society*. New Brunswick, N.J.: Transaction Publishers.

– 1996. 'World Order, Human Values and the Future.' *Futures Research Quarterly*, 12, no. 1.

– 1994. 'Using Religion to Judge Preferable Futures.' *Futures Research Quarterly*, 10, no. 3.

– 1994. 'The World as a Moral Community.' *Society*, 81, no. 5.

– 1993. 'Bringing the Good Book Back In: 'Values, Objectivity and the Future.' *International Social Science Journal*, 137.

– 1993. 'Why Should We Care about Future Generations?' In H.F. Disbury, Jr, ed., *The Years Ahead*. Bethesda, Md.: World Future.

Bellah, R. 1975. *The Broken Covenant*. New York: Seabury Press.

Bellah, R., R. Madsen, W. Sullivan, A. Swidler, and S. Tipton. 1985. *Habits of the Heart: Individualism and Commitment in American Life*. Berkeley: University of California Press.

Bentham, J. 1961. *The Utilitarians: An Introduction to the Principles of Morals and Legislation*. Garden City N.Y.: Doubleday.

Berger, P. 1977. 'Are Human Rights Universal?' *Commentary*, 64 (September).

Berlin, I. 1969. 'Two Concepts of Political Liberty.' Inaugural lectures at Oxford, reprinted in *Four Essays on Liberty*. Oxford: Oxford University Press.

Berman, M. 1970. *The Politics of Authenticity: Radical Individualism and the Emergence of Modern Society.* New York: Atheneum.

Berry, D. 1985. *Mutuality: The Vision of Martin Buber.* Albany, N.Y.: State University of New York Press.

Betsworth, R. 1990. *Social Ethics: An Examination of American Moral Traditions.* Louisville, Ky.: Westminster/John Knox Press.

Boldt, M. 1993, 1994, 1995. *Surviving as Indians: The Challenge of Self-Government.* Toronto: University of Toronto Press.

– 1987. 'Defining Suicide: Implications for Suicide Behavior and for Suicide Prevention.' *Crisis: Journal of the International Association of Suicide Prevention,* 8, no. 1.

– 1982. 'Normative Evaluations of Suicide and Death: A Cross-Generational Study.' *Omega: Journal of Death and Dying,* 13, no. 1.

Boldt, M., and A. Long, eds. 1988, 1992, 1996. *The Quest for Justice: Aboriginal Peoples and Aboriginal Rights.* Toronto: University of Toronto Press.

– 1984. 'Tribal Philosophies and the Canadian Charter of Rights and Freedoms.' *Racial and Ethnic Studies,* 4, no. 4.

Boli-Bennett, J. 1981. 'Human Rights or State Expansion: Cross-National Definitions of Constitutional Rights, 1870–1970.' In V.P. Nanda, ed., *Global Human Rights.* Boulder, Col.: Westview Press.

Borovoy, A. 1988. *When Rights Collide.* Toronto: Lester and Orpen Dennys.

Bourke, V. 1964. *The Will in Western Thought.* New York: Sheed.

Brandt, R. 1954. *Hopi Ethics: A Theoretical Analysis.* Chicago: University of Chicago Press.

Braum, R.C. 1981. *The Holocaust and the German Elite: Genocide and National Suicide in Germany, 1871/1945.* Totowa, N.J.: Rowman and Littlefield.

Brown, S. 1993. *The Politics of Individualism: Liberalism, Liberal Feminism and Anarchism.* Montreal: Black Rose Books.

Brunner, E. 1937. *The Divine Imperative: A Study in Christian Ethics.* O. Wyon, trans. London: Lutterworth.

Cajete, G. 2000. *Native Science: Natural Laws of Interdependence.* Santa Fe, N.M.: Clear Light Publishers.

Campbell, T.O. 1971. *Adam Smith's Science of Morals.* University of Glasgow Social and Economic Studies. Totowa, N.J.: Rowman and Littlefield.

Capra, F. 1982. *The Turning Point: Science, Society and the Rising Culture.* New York: Simon and Schuster.

– 1975, 1981. *The Tao of Physics: An Exploration of the Parallels between Modern Physics and Eastern Mysticism.* London: Wildwood House.

Card, C., ed. 1991. *Feminist Ethics.* Lawrence: University Press of Kansas.

Carrithers, M. 1993. *Why Humans Have Cultures: Explaining Anthropology and Social Diversity.* Toronto: Oxford University Press.

Carroll, J., ed. 1972. *Language, Thought and Reality: Selected Writings of Benjamin Lee Whorf.* Cambridge, Mass.: MIT Press.

Cassirer, E. 1953. *Substance and Function; and Einstein's Theory of Relativity.* New York: Dover.

Cattell, R. 1972. *New Morality from Science: Beyondism.* New York: Pergamon Press.

Chalmers, D. 1996. *The Conscious Mind: In Search of a Fundamental Theory.* Oxford: Oxford University Press.

Clarke, T., and M. Barlow. 1995. *MAI: The Multinational Agreement on Investment and the Threat to Canadian Sovereignty.* Toronto: Stoddart.

Cohen, A. 1966. *Deviance and Control.* Englewood Cliffs, N.J.: Prentice Hall.

Cohen, R. 1989–91. 'Human Rights and Cultural Relativism: The Need for a New Approach.' *American Anthropologist,* 91, no. 4.

Cohn, N. 1966. *Noah's Flood: The Genesis Story in Western Thought.* New Haven, Conn.: Yale University Press.

Conetti, E. 1962. *Crowds and Power.* C. Stewart, trans. New York: Viking Press.

Cragg, W., ed. 1987. *Contemporary Moral Issues.* Toronto: McGraw-Hill Ryerson.

Cranston, M. 1973. *What Are Human Rights?* New York: Taplinger.

Cunningham, R. 1970. *Situationism and the New Morality.* New York: Appleton-Century-Crofts.

Dahrendorf, R. 1968. *Essays in the Theory of Society.* Stanford, Calif.: Stanford University Press.

Daly, M. 1978. *Gyn/ecology, the Metaethics of Radical Feminism.* Boston, Mass.: Beacon Press.

Dawkins, R. 2006. *The God Delusion.* Boston: Houghton Mifflin.

Dearden, R. 1972. *Education and the Development of Reason.* London: Routledge and Kegan Paul; New York: Humanities Press.

Degler, C. 1991. *In Search of Human Nature: The Decline and Revival of Darwinism in American Social Thought.* New York: Oxford University Press.

Dennett, D. 1996. *Kinds of Minds: Toward an Understanding of Consciousness.* New York: Basic Books.

– 1995. *Darwin's Dangerous Idea: Evolution and the Meaning of Life.* New York: Simon and Schuster.

– 1991. *Consciousness Explained.* Toronto: Little, Brown.

– 1984. *Elbow Room: The Varieties of Free Will Worth Wanting.* Cambridge, Mass.: MIT Press.

– 1969. *Content and Consciousness.* London: Routledge and Kegan Paul; New York: Humanities Press.

Dewdney, C. 1988. *Last Flesh: Life in the Transhuman Era.* Toronto: Harper Collins.

Dewey, J. 1930. *Individualism, Old and New.* New York: Milton Balch.

Dionne, Jr., E. 1991. *Why Americans Hate Politics.* New York: Simon and Schuster.

Donnelley, J. 1989. *Universal Human Rights in Theory and Practice.* Ithaca, N.Y.: Cornell University Press.

– 1984. 'Cultural Relativism and Universal Human Rights.' *Human Rights Quarterly,* 6.

– 1982. 'Human Rights and Human Dignity: An Analytic Critique of Non-Western Conceptions of Human Rights.' *American Political Science Review,* 76, no. 2.

Douglas, J. 1971. *American Social Order: Social Rules in a Pluralistic Society.* New York: Free Press.

Drews, E., and L. Lipson. 1971. *Values and Humanity.* New York: St Martin's Press.

Dreyfus, H., and P. Rabinoro, eds. 1983. *Michel Foucault: Beyond Structuralism and Hermeneutics. Chicago:* University of Chicago Press.

Dumont, L. 1986. *English Essays on Individualism: Modern Ideology in Anthropological Perspective.* Chicago: University of Chicago Press.

Dworkin, R. 1977. *Taking Rights Seriously.* London: Duckworth.

Edel, A. 1969. 'Humanist Ethics and the Meaning of Human Dignity.' In P. Kurtz, ed., *Moral Problems in Contemporary Society.* Englewood Cliffs, N.J.: Prentice Hall.

– 1960–1. 'Science and Value: Some Reflections on Pepper's "The Sources of Values."' *Review of Metaphysics,* 14, no. 1.

Elshtain, J. 1981. *Public Man, Private Women: Women in Social and Political Thought.* Princeton, N.J.: Princeton University Press.

Emmet, D. 1979. *The Moral Prison.* New York: St Martin's Press.

– 1966. *Rules, Roles and Relations.* London: Macmillan.

Etzioni, A. 1991. 'Too Many Rights, Too Few Responsibilities.' *Social Science and Modern Society,* 28, no. 2.

Evans, J., ed. 1987, 1988. *Moral Philosophy and Contemporary Problems.* Cambridge: Cambridge University Press.

Fainberg, J. 1980. 'The Nature and Value of Rights.' In *Rights, Justice and the Bounds of Liberty: Essays in Social Philosophy.* Princeton, N.J.: Princeton University Press.

Featherstone, M. 1995. *Undoing Culture: Globalization, Postmodernism and Identity.* Thousand Oaks, Calif.: Sage Publications.

– 1991. *Consumer Culture and Post-Modernism.* London: Sage Publications.

– 1990. *Global Culture: Nationalism, Globalization and Modernity.* London: Sage Publications.

Featherstone, M., S. Lash, and R. Robertson, eds. 1995. *Global Modernities.* Thousand Oaks, Calif.: Sage Publications.

Fineberg, J. 1973. *Social Philosophy.* Englewood Cliffs, N.J.: Prentice Hall.

Finkelkraut, A. 1995. *The Defeat of the Mind.* J. Friedlander, trans. New York: Columbia University Press.

Finnis, J. 1980. *Natural Law and Natural Rights.* Oxford: Clarendon Press.

Firth, C. 1951. 'Ethical Absolutism and the Ideal Observer.' *Philosophy and Phenomenological Research,* 14.

Fisk, M. 1980. *Ethics and Society: A Marxist Interpretation of Value.* Brighton, U.K.: Harvester Press.

Foucault, M. 1980. *Power/Knowledge: Selected Interviews and Other Writings, 1972–1977.* C. Gordon, ed. New York: Pantheon Books.

– 1979. *Discipline and Punishment.* New York: Random House.

Frankl, V. 1997. *Man's Search for Ultimate Meaning.* New York: Insight Books.

Fraser, N. 1985. 'Is Michel Foucault a Young Conservative?' *Ethics,* 96.

– 1983. 'Foucault's Body Language: A Post-Humanist Political Rhetoric.' *Salmagundi,* 61.

Friedman, J. 1994. *Cultural Identity and Global Process.* Thousand Oaks, Calif.: Sage Publications.

Friedman, J., and M. Sherman. 1985. *Human Rights: An International and Comparative Law.* Westport, Conn.: Greenwood Press.

Friedrich, C. 1958. *The Philosophy of Law in Historical Perspective.* Chicago: University of Chicago Press.

Fromm, E. 1965. *Escape from Freedom.* New York: Avon Books.

Fuich, J. 1976. 'Symposium on Psychology and Religion' (3d: 1973 Fuller Theological Seminary). *The Nature of Man: A Social-Psychological Perspective.* Springfield, Ill.: Thomas.

Fukiyama, F. 1992. *The End of History and the Last Man.* New York: Free Press.

Gans, H. 1988. *Middle American Individualism: The Future of Liberal Democracy.* New York: Free Press.

Gauthier, D. 1986. *Morals by Agreement.* Oxford: Clarendon Press.

Gerth, H., and C. Mills, eds., 1946. *From Max Weber: Essays in Sociology.* New York: Oxford University Press.

Gidden, A. 1991. *Modernity and Self-Identity: Self and Society in the Late Modern Age.* Stanford, Calif.: Stanford University Press.

Gilbert, A. 1990. *Democratic Individuality.* New York: Cambridge University Press.

Glendon, M. 1991. *Rights Talk: The Impoverishment of Political Discourse.* New York: Free Press.

Goldman, A. 1972. 'Toward a Theory of Social Power.' *Philosophical Studies,* 23.

Gordon, C., ed. 1980. *Michel Foucault: Power and Knowledge: Selected Interviews and Other Writings, 1972–1977.* Brighton, U.K.: Harvester Press.

Gotesky, R., and E. Laszlo, eds. 1970. *Human Dignity.* New York: Gordon and Breach.

Gough, J. 1956. *John Locke's Political Philosophy.* Oxford: Clarendon Press.

Grassian, V. 1981. *Moral Reasoning: Ethical Theory and Some Contemporary Moral Problems,* 2nd ed. Englewood Cliffs, N.J.: Prentice Hall.

Greeley, A. 1968. *The Crucible of Chance.* New York: Sheed and Ward.

Gross, B. 1970. 'Friendly Fascism.' *Social Policy,* 1, no. 4.

Gusfield, J. 1975. *Community: A Critical Response.* New York: Harper and Row.

Haan, N. 1983. 'An Interactional Morality of Everyday Life.' In N. Haan, R. Bellah, P. Rabinow, and W. Sullivan, eds., *Social Science as Moral Inquiry.* New York: Columbia University Press.

Hallin E. 1995. 'The Modern Error.' In M. Featherstone, S. Lash, and R. Robertson, eds., *Global Modernities.* London: Sage Publications.

Hansen, O. 1990. *Aesthetic Individualism and Practical Intellect: American Allegory in Emerson, Thoreau, Adams and James.* Princeton, N.J.: Princeton University Press.

Hare, R. 1972. *Applications of Moral Philosophy.* London: Macmillan.

Harken, T. 1979. 'Human Rights and Foreign Aid: Forging an Unbreakable Link.' In P. Brown and D. MacLean, eds., *Human Rights and U.S. Foreign Policy: Principles and Applications.* Lexington, Mass.: Lexington Books.

Harris, J. 1985. *The Value of Life.* London: Routledge and Kegan Paul.

Hart, H. 1955. 'Are There Any Natural Rights?' *Philosophical Review,* 64, no. 2.

Heinemann, F. 1958. *Existentialism and the Modern Predicament.* New York: Harper Torchbooks.

Helvey, T. 1971. *The Age of Information: An Interdisciplinary Survey of Cybernetics.* Englewood Cliffs, N.J.: Educational Technology Publications.

Hermann, C., and H. Lasswell. 1976. 'A Global Monitoring System: Appraising the Effects of Government in Human Dignity.' *International Studies Quarterly,* 20, no. 2.

Himmelfarb, G. 1995. *The De-Moralization of Society: From Victorian Virtues to Modern Values.* New York: Alfred A. Knopf.

Hitchens, C. 2007. *God Is Not Great: How Religion Poisons Everything.* Sydney: Allen and Unwin.

Hobbes, T. 1841. *The Questions concerning Liberty, Necessity and Chance in the English Works of Thomas Hobbes.* W. Molesworth, ed. London: John Bohn.

Hobhouse, L. 1922. *The Elements of Social Justice.* London: G. Allen and Unwin.

Hofstadter, D., and D. Dennett, eds. 1981. *The Mind's I: Fantasies and Reflections on Self and Soul.* New York: Basic Books.

Hollenbach, D. 1982. 'Human Rights and Religious Faith in the Middle East: Reflections of a Christian Theologian.' *Human Rights Quarterly*, 4.

Hoover, H. 1973. *The Challenge to Liberty*. New York: Da Capo Press.

Horton, J. 1964. 'The Dehumanization of Anomie and Alienation.' *British Journal of Sociology*, 15 (December).

Howard, R. 1992. 'Dignity, Community and Human Rights.' In *Human Rights in Crosscultural Perspective: A Quest for Consensus*. Philadelphia: University of Pennsylvania Press.

– 1986. *Human Rights in Commonwealth Africa*. Totowa, N.J.: Rowman and Littlefield.

Humann, C. 1992. *World Human Rights Guide*. New York: Oxford University Press.

Hume, D. 1739 [1964]. *A Treatise of Human Nature*. L. Selly-Bigge, ed. Oxford: Clarendon Press.

– 1751 [1983]. *An Enquiry concerning the Principles of Morals*. J. Schneewind, ed. Indianapolis, Ind.: Hackett Publishing.

Huxley, A. 1958. *Brave New World Revisited*. New York: Harper and Row.

– 1932. *Brave New World*. New York: Harper and Brothers.

Ignatieff, M. 2001. With commentary by A.K. Anthony Appiah; Amy Gutmann, ed. *Human Rights as Politics and Idolatry*. Princeton, N.J.: Princeton University Press.

– 1986, 1984. *The Needs of Strangers*. New York: Penguin Books.

Ingram, R. 1978. *What's Wrong with Human Rights?* Houston: St Thomas Press.

Ishaque, K. 1974. 'Human Rights in Islamic law.' *Review of the International Commission of Jurists*, 12 (June).

Jacobs, J. 1992. *Systems of Survival: A Dialogue on the Moral Foundations of Commerce and Politics*. New York: Random House.

James, W. 1921. 'The Dilemma of Determinism.' In W. James. *The Will to Believe*. New York: Longmans, Green.

Johnes, S. 1995. *Cybersociety: Computer-Mediated Communications and Community*. Thousand Oaks, Calif.: Sage Publications.

Jordan, B. 1989. *The Common Good: Citizenship Morality and Self-Interest*. Oxford: Oxford University Press.

de Jouvenal, B. 1949. *On Power: Its Nature and History of Growth*. New York: Viking Press.

Kahn, J. 1995. *Culture, Multiculture and Postculture*. Thousand Oaks, Calif.: Sage Publications.

Kalenda, K., ed. 1988. *Organizations and Ethical Individualism*. New York: Praeger.

Kane, R. 1985. *Free Will and Values*. Albany: State University of New York Press.

Kant, E. 1785 [1959]. *Foundations of the Metaphysics of Morals*. New York: Liberal Arts Press.

– 1781 [1982]. *The Critique of Pure Reason: Concise Text*. Aalen, Germany: Scientia Verlag.

Kenichi, O. 1995. *The End of the Nation State*. Tokyo: Kadansha.

Khushalani, Y. 1983. 'Human Rights in Asia and Africa.' *Human Rights Law Journal*, 4.

Kierkegaard, S. 1846 [1978]. *Two Ages: The Age of Revolutions: The Present Age: A Literary Review*. H. Hong and E. Hong, eds. and trans. Princeton, N.J.: Princeton University Press.

King, Jr, M. 1964. *Why We Can't Wait*. New York: Harper and Row.

Kingwell, M. 2000. *The World We Want: Virtue, Vice, and the Good Citizen*. Toronto: Penguin Books.

Kleinig, J. 1991. *Valuing Life*. Princeton, N.J.: Princeton University Press.

Knopff, R. 1989. *Human Rights and Social Technology: The New War on Discrimination*. Ottawa: Carleton University Press.

Konig, R. 1968. *The Community*. E. Fitzgerald, trans. London: Routledge and Kegan Paul.

Kroes, R. 1989. 'The Human Rights Tradition in the United States.' In J. Berting et al., eds., *Human Rights in a Pluralist World: Individuals and Collectivities*. Westport, Conn.: Meckler.

Kuhn, T. 1993. 'Afterwords.' In P. Horvich. *World Changes: Thomas Kuhn and the Nature of Science*. Cambridge, Mass.: MIT Press.

Kupers, L., and M. Smith, eds. 1969. *Pluralism in Africa*. Berkeley: University of California Press.

Kurtz, P. 1969. 'What Is Humanism?' In *Moral Problems in Contemporary Society: Essays in Humanistic Ethics*. Englewood Cliffs, N.J.: Prentice Hall.

Lasch, C. 1991. *The True and Only Heaven: Progress and Its Critics*. New York: W.W. Norton.

Lasswell, H. 1971. *A Preview of Policy Sciences*. New York: Elsevier.

– 1965. 'The World Revolution of Our Time: A Framework for Basic Policy Research.' In H. Lasswell and D. Lerner, eds., *World Revolutionary Elites*. Cambridge, Mass.: MIT Press.

Laszlo, E. 1971. 'Human Dignity and the Promise of Technology.' *Philosophy Forum*, 9, nos. 1/2.

Lazreg, M. 1979. 'Human Rights, State and Ideology: An Historical Perspective.' In A. Pollis and P. Schwab, eds., *Human Rights: Cultural and Ideological Perspectives*. New York: Praeger.

Lee, K. 1985. *A New Basis for Moral Philosophy*. London: Routledge and Kegan Paul.

Legesse, A. 1980. 'Human Rights in African Political Culture.' In E. Thompson, ed., *The Moral Imperatives of Human Rights: A World Survey*. Washington, D.C.: University Press of America.

Lewin, R. 1993. *Human Evolution: An Illustrated Introduction*. Malden, Mass.: Blackwell Scientific Publications.

Lewis, C. 1965. *The Abolition of Man*. New York: Macmillan.

Lickma, T., ed. 1976. *Moral Development and Behavior: Theory, Research, Social Issues*. New York: Holt, Rinehart and Winston.

Locke, J. 1794. *Essay concerning Human Understanding*. Boston, Mass.: Manning and Loring.

Lukes, S. 1978. 'Power and Authority.' In T. Bottomore and R. Nisbet, eds., *A History of Sociological Analysis*. New York: Basic Books.

– 1974. *Power: A Radical View*. London: Macmillan.

Lycan, W. 1987. *Consciousness*. Cambridge, Mass.: MIT Press.

Machan, T. 1989. *Individuals and Their Rights*. La Salle, Ill.: Open Court.

MacIntyre, A. 1981. *After Virtue: A Study of Moral Theory*. Notre Dame, Ind.: University of Notre Dame Press.

Manetti, G. 1966. *Two Views of Man: Pope Innocent III on the Misery of Man, Giannozzo Manetti on the Excellency and Dignity of Man*. New York: F. Ungar.

Manfred, S. 1978. *The Technological Conscience: Survival and Dignity in an Age of Expertise*. New York: Free Press.

Martindale, D. 1968. *Institutions, Organizations and Mass Society*. Boston, Mass.: Houghton Mifflin.

Maruyama, M. 1971. 'The Second Cybernetics: Deviation Amplifying Mutual Causal Process.' In F. Katz, ed., *Contemporary Sociological Theory*. New York: Random House.

Marx, K. [1977]. 'On the Jewish Question.' In D. McLellan, ed., *Karl Marx: Selected Writings*. Oxford: Oxford University Press.

Maslow, A. 1968. *Toward a Psychology of Being*, 2nd ed. New York: Von Norstrand.

Mauss, M. 1967. *The Gift: Forms and Functions of Exchange in Archaic Societies*. I. Cunnison, trans. New York: W.W. Norton.

May, L. 1987. *The Morality of Groups: Collective Responsibility, Group-Based Harm, and Corporate Rights*. Notre Dame, Ind.: University of Notre Dame Press.

Mazzini, G. 1966. *The Duties of Man and Other Essays*. London: J.M. Dent.

McClenahan, B. 1946. 'The Community: The Urban Substitute for the Traditional Community.' *Sociology and Social Research*, 30 (March–April).

McDougal, M., H. Lasswell, and L. Chen. 1980. *Human Rights and the World Public Order: The Basic Policies of an International Law of Human Dignity.* New Haven, Conn.: Yale University Press.

McGinn, C. 1991. *The Problems of Consciousness: Essays toward a Resolution.* Oxford: Blackwell.

McKnight, J. 1995. *The Careless Society: Community and Its Counterfeits.* New York: Basic Books.

McLuhan, M. 1994. *Understanding Media: The Extension of Man.* Cambridge, Mass.: MIT Press.

McLuhan, M., and Q. Fiore. 1967. *The Medium Is the Message.* New York: Bantam.

Means, R. 1969. *The Ethical Imperative: The Crisis in American Values.* Garden City, N.Y.: Doubleday.

Megill, A. 1985. *Prophets of Extremity.* Berkeley: University of California Press.

Merland, J., and M. Krausz, eds. 1982. *Relativism, Cognitive and Moral.* Notre Dame, Ind.: University of Notre Dame Press.

Mill, J. [1965]. *Mills Ethical Writings.* J. Schneewind, ed. New York: Collin Books.

Milnar, D., and S. Greer. 1969. *The Concept of Community.* Chicago: Aldine.

Mociner, R. 1971. *Community: A Sociological Study.* New York: Benjamin Blom.

Montesquieu, C. de S. [1977]. *The Spirit of Laws: A Compendium of the First English Edition.* D. Carrithers, ed. Berkeley: University of California Press.

Montgomery, J. 1986. *Human Rights and Human Dignity.* Grand Rapids, Mich.: Zandervan.

Moore, C., and A. Morris, eds. 1968. East-West Philosophers Conference (4d1:1964 University of Hawaii). *The Status of the Individual in East and West.* Honolulu: University of Hawaii Press.

Morrow, L. 1995. 'The Museum of Slavery?' *Time Magazine* (14 August).

Moser, S. 1968. *Absolutism and Relativism in Ethics.* Springfield, Ill.: Thomas.

Miligram, S. 1974. *Obedience to Authority.* New York: Harper and Row.

Narveson, J. 1967. *Morality and Utility.* Baltimore: Johns Hopkins University Press.

Nickel, J., and L. Hasse. 1981. 'Review of Shue's Basic Rights.' *California Law Review,* 69.

Niebuhr, R. 1968. *Faith and Politics: A Commentary on Religious, Social and Political Thought in a Technological Age.* R. Stone, ed. New York: G. Brazilla.

– 1952. *The Irony of American History.* New York: Scribner.

– 1932. *Moral Man and Immoral Society: A Study in Ethics and Politics.* New York: Scribner.

Nietzsche, F. [1995]. *Human, All Too Human*. G. Handwerk, trans. Stanford, Calif.: Stanford University Press.
– 1887 [1967]. *On the Genealogy of Morals*. W. Kaufmann and R. Hollingdale, trans. New York: Vintage.
Nisbet, R. 1962. *Community and Power*. London: Oxford University Press.
– 1953. *The Quest for Community: A Study in the Ethics of Order and Freedom*. New York: Oxford University Press.
Norman, C. 1981. *The God That Limps: Science and Technology in the Eighties*. London: W.W. Norton.
Northrop, F. 1959. *The Logic of the Sciences and the Humanities*. New York: Meridian Books.
Norton, D. 1976. *Personal Destinies: A Philosophy of Ethical Individualism*. Princeton, N.J.: Princeton University Press.
Nozick, R. 1974. *Anarchy, State and Utopia*. New York: Basic Books.
Oldenquist. A. 1986. *The Non-Suicidal Society*. Bloomington: Indiana University Press.
Orwell, G. 1966. *Nineteen Eighty-Four*. London: Secker and Warburg.
Osbert, R. 1970. *Humanism and Moral Theory: A Psychological and Social Inquiry*, 2nd ed. London: Pemberton.
Otto, R. 1967. *The Idea of the Holy*. New York: Oxford University Press.
Oye, K., D. Rothchild, and R. Lieber, eds. 1979. *Eagle Entangled*. New York: Longman.
Paine, T. [1999]. *The Rights of Man*. Donald Herder, ed. Mineola, N.Y.: Dover Thrift Edition.
Palumbo, M. 1982. *Human Rights: Meaning and History*. Malabar, Fla.: Robert E. Krieger.
Pennoch, J. 1981. 'Rights, Natural Rights and Human Rights: A General View.' *NOMOS*, 23. New York University.
Polanyi, M. 1966. *The Tacit Dimension*. Garden City, N.Y.: Doubleday.
– 1959. *The Study of Man*. Chicago: University of Chicago Press.
– 1958. *Knowledge: Toward a Post-Critical Philosophy*. Chicago: University of Chicago Press.
Poplin, D. 1972. *Communities*. New York: Macmillan.
Power, J. 1981. *Amnesty International: The Human Rights Story*. New York: McGraw-Hill.
Prezel, B., H. Lasswell, and J. McHale, eds. 1977. *World Priorities*. New Brunswick, N.J.: Transaction Books.
Rabinon, P., ed. 1984. *The Foucault Reader*. New York: Pantheon.
Rasmussen, D., ed. 1990. *Universalism vs. Communitarianism*. Cambridge, Mass.: MIT Press.

Rawls, J. 1971. *A Theory of Justice*. Cambridge, Mass.: Harvard University Press.

Regan, T., and D. Van De Veer. 1982. *And Justice for All: Introductory Essays in Ethics and Public Policy*. Totowa, N.J.: Rowman and Littlefield.

Reich, C. 1970. *The Greening of America: How the Youth Revolution Is Trying to Make America Livable*. New York: Random House.

Reich, R. 1991. *The Work of Nations: Preparing Ourselves for 21st Century Capitalism*. New York: A.A. Knopf.

Reisman, D. 1954. *Individualism Reconsidered*. Glencoe, Ill.: Free Press.

Reisman, D., N. Glazer, and R. Denney. 1950. *The Lonely Crowd: A Study of the Changing American Character*. New Haven, Conn.: Yale University Press.

Renteln, A. 1990. 'International Human Rights: Universalism v. Relativism.' *Frontiers of Anthropology*, Vol. 6. Newbury Park, Calif.: Sage Publications.

Rescher, N. 1975. *Unselfishness: The Role of the Vicarious Affects in Moral Philosophy and Social Theory*. Pittsburgh: University of Pittsburgh Press.

Ricour, P. 1966. *Freedom and Nature: The Voluntary and the Involuntary*. E. Koliak, trans. Evanston, Ill.: Northwestern University Press.

Robertson, A. 1982. *Human Rights in the World: An Introduction to the Study of International Protection of Human Rights*. 2nd ed. New York: St Martin's Press.

Rorty, R. 1985. 'Postmodernist Bourgeois Liberalism.' In R. Hollinger, ed., *Hermeneutics and Praxis*. Notre Dame, Ind.: University of Notre Dame Press.

Roszak, T. 1968. *The Making of a Counter Culture: Reflections on the Technocratic Society and Its Youthful Opposition*. Garden City, N.Y.: Doubleday.

Russell, B. 1962. *Human Society in Ethics and Politics*. New York: New American Library.

Ryan, C. 1980. 'The Normative Concepts of Coercion.' *Mind*, 89.

Ryle, G. 1949. *The Concept of Mind*. London: Hutchinson's University Library.

Said, Abdul Aziz ed. 1978. *Human Rights and World Order*. New York: Praeger.

– 1975. *The New Sovereigns: Multinational Corporations as World Powers*. Englewood Cliffs, N.J.: Prentice Hall.

Said, E. 1979. 'Human Rights in Islamic Perspective.' In A. Pollis and P. Schwab, eds., *Human Rights: Cultural and Ideological Perspectives*. New York: Praeger.

– 1974. *Culture and Imperialism*. New York: Knopf.

Said, E., and L. Simmons, eds. 2000. *The New Sovereigns: Multinational Corporations as World Powers*. Englewood Cliffs, N.J.: Prentice Hall.

Sandel, M. 1996. *Democracy's Discontent: America in Search of a Public Policy*. Cambridge, Mass.: Belknap Press of Harvard University.

Sartorius, R. 1975. *Individual Conduct and Social Norms: A Utilitarian Account. Ethics*, 82, no. 3.

Sartre, J. 1986. *The Age of Reason.* E. Sutton, trans. London: Penguin Books.

– 1956. 'Being and Doing: Freedom.' In *Being and Nothingness.* H. Barnes, trans. New York: Philosophical Library.

Saul, J. 1995. *The Unconscious Civilization.* Concord, Ont.: Anansi.

– 1992. *Voltaire's Bastards: The Dictatorship of Reason in the West.* New York: Viking.

Sayre, K. 1976. *Cybernetics and the Philosophy of Mind.* London: Routledge and Kegan Paul.

Scaff, L. 1989. *Fleeing the Iron Cage: Culture, Politics, and Modernity in the Thought of Max Weber.* Berkeley: University of California Press.

Scherer, J. 1972. *Contemporary Community: Sociological Illusion or Reality?* London: Tavistock Publications.

Schneewind, J. 1996. *Giving: Western Ideas of Philanthropy.* Bloomington: Indiana University Press.

Scott, A., ed. 1964. *Democracy and Social Ethics.* Cambridge, Mass.: Belknap Press of Harvard University.

Scott, J. 1990. *Domination and the Arts of Resistance: Hidden Transcripts.* New Haven, Conn.: Yale University Press.

Scribner, S., and M. Cole. 1973. 'Cognitive Consequences of Formal and Informal Education.' *Science,* 182 (9 November).

Seattle, T. 1976. *In Search of a Third Way: Is a Morally Principled Political Economy Possible?* Toronto: McClelland and Stewart.

Sennett, R. 1978. *The Fall of Public Man: On the Social Psychology of Capitalism.* New York: Vintage Books.

Shim, R. 1992. *Forced Options: Social Decisions for the 21st century.* San Francisco, Calif.: Harper and Row.

Shue, H. 1980. *Basic Rights.* Princeton, N.J.: Princeton University Press.

Siegal, F. 1991. 'Individualism, Statism and the A.C.L.U.' *Social Science and Modern Society,* 28, no. 2.

Sikora, R., and B. Barry. 1978. *Obligations to Future Generations.* Philadelphia: Temple University Press.

Simons, H., and M. Billig, eds. 1994. *After Postmodernism: Reconstructing Ideology Critique.* Thousand Oaks, Calif.: Sage Publications.

Singer, P. 1979. *Practical Ethics.* Cambridge: Cambridge University Press.

Skinner, B. 1971. *Beyond Freedom and Dignity.* New York: Knopf.

– 1953. *Science and Human Behavior.* New York: Macmillan.

Smith, A. 1976. *The Theory of Moral Sentiments.* Indianapolis, Ind.: Liberty Classics.

Smith, M., and L. Guarnizo. 1998. 'Transnationalism from Below.' *Comparative Urban and Community Research*. New Brunswick, N.J.: Transaction Publishers.

Snyder, R., C. Hermann, and H. Lasswell. 1976. 'A Global Monitoring System: Appraising the Effects of Government on Human Dignity.' *International Studies Quarterly*, 20, no. 2.

Spencer, H. 1936. *Government and Politics Abroad*. New York: Holt.

Spiegelberg, H. 1971. 'Human Dignity: A Challenge to Contemporary Philosophy.' *Philosophy Forum*, 9, nos. 1/2.

Spurrier, W. 1974. *Natural Law and the Ethics of Love: A New Synthesis*. Philadelphia: Westminster Press.

Stackhouse, M. 1984. *Creeds, Society and Human Rights: A Study in Three Cultures*. Grand Rapids, Mich.: W.B. Eerdman.

Stanley, M. 1978. *The Technological Conscience: Survival and Dignity in an Age of Expertise*. New York: Free Press.

'Statement on Human Rights.' 1984. *American Anthropologist*, 49.

Storer, M., ed. 1980. *Humanist Ethics, Dialogue on Basics*. Buffalo, N.Y.: Prometheus Books.

Strauss, L. 1953. *Natural Rights and History*. Chicago: University of Chicago Press.

Sultanhussein, T. 1970. *A Muslim Commentary on the Universal Declaration of Human Rights*. London: T. Goulding.

Summer, L. 1984. 'Rights Denaturalized.' In R. Frey, ed., *Utility and Rights*. St. Paul: University of Minnesota Press.

Summer, W. 1966. *What Social Classes Owe to Each Other*. Caldwell, Ind.: Caxton Printers.

Sydney, O. 1969. *The Christian New Morality: A Biblical Study of Situation Ethics*. New York: Oxford University Press.

Taylor, C. 1979. *Hegel and Modern Society*. Cambridge: Cambridge University Press.

Teeple, G. 1995. *Globalization and the Decline of Social Reform*. Atlantic Highlands, N.J.: Humanities Press International.

Thurman, H. 1971. *The Search for Common Ground: An Inquiry into the Basis of Man's Experience of Community*. New York: Harper and Row.

Tinder, G. 1981. *Against Fate: An Essay on Personal Dignity*. Notre Dame, Ind.: University of Notre Dame Press.

– 1980. *Community: Reflections on a Tragic Ideal*. Baton Rouge: Louisiana State University Press.

Tipton, S. 1982. *Getting Saved from the Sixties: Moral Meaning in Conversion and Cultural Change*. Berkeley: University of California Press.

Tocqueville, A. [1969]. *Democracy in America.* J. Mayer, ed., G. Lawrence, trans. Garden City, N.Y.: Anchor Books.

Toffler, A. 1970. *Future Shock.* New York: Bantam Books.

Tönnies, F. 1957. *Gemeinschaft and gesellschaft (Community and Society).* C. Loomis, trans. East Lansing: Michigan State University Press.

Turiel, E. 1983. *The Development of Social Knowledge: Morality and Convention.* New York: Cambridge University Press.

Turner, B. 1993. 'Outline of a Theory of Human Rights.' *Sociology,* 27, no. 3.

The U.N. Charter. Article 2[7]. General Assembly Resolution 2131.

The Universal Declaration. Articles 55 and 56.

U.S. State Department. Country Reports on Human Rights Practices.

Vattimo, G. 1988. *The End of History.* Oxford: Polity.

Vesey, G., ed. 1978. *Human Values.* Hassocks, U.K.: Harvester Press.

Villaneuva, E., ed. 1991. *Consciousness:* Atascadero, Calif.: Ridgeview Publishing.

Warrander, H. 1983. *Thomas Hobbes, 1588–1679. De cive.* English version entitled, in the first edition, *Philosophical Rudiments concerning Government and Society.* Oxford: Clarendon Press.

– 1957. *The Political Philosophy of Hobbes, His Theory of Obligation.* Oxford: Clarendon Press.

Weber, M. 1978. *Economy and Society: An Outline of Interpretive Sociology.* Berkeley: University of California Press.

Weil, S. 1952. *The Need for Roots: Prelude to a Declaration of Duties towards Mankind.* New York: Putnam.

West, R. 1972. *Conscience and Society: A Study of the Psychological Prerequisites of Law and Order.* Westport, Conn.: Greenwood Press.

Westermarck, E. 1970. *Ethical Relativity.* Westport, Conn.: Greenwood Press.

Whalen, L. 1989. *Human Rights: A Reference Handbook.* Santa Barbara, Calif.: ABC- CLIO.

White, A. 1984. *Rights.* Oxford: Clarendon Press.

White, S. 1988. *The Recent Works of Jurgen Habermas: Reason, Justice and Modernity.* Cambridge: Cambridge University Press.

Wiebe, R. 1967. *The Search for Order, 1877–1920.* New York: Hill and Wang.

Wiener, N. 1954. *The Human Use of Human Beings.* Garden City, N.Y.: Doubleday.

Williams, B. 1985. *Ethics and the Limits of Philosophy.* London: Fontana.

– 1981. *Moral Luck.* Cambridge: Cambridge University Press.

– 1973. *Problems of the Self.* Cambridge: Cambridge University Press.

Wilson, E. 1978. *On Human Nature.* Cambridge, Mass.: Harvard University Press.

Winter, G. 1966. *Elements for a Social Ethic: Scientific and Ethical Perspectives on Social Process*. New York: Macmillan.

Wiseberg, L., and H. Scable. 1978. 'Human Rights as an International League.' In E. Said, ed., *Human Rights and World Order*. New York: Praeger.

Wolf, C. 1969. *Garrison Community*. Westport, Conn.: Greenwood.

Wolf, S. 1981. 'The Importance of Free Will.' *Mind*, 190.

Wong, D. 1984. *Moral Relativity*. Berkeley, Calif.: University of California Press.

Wordsworth, W. [1989]. *Oxford English Dictionary*. Oxford: Clarendon Press.

Wrong, D. 1994. *The Problem of Order: What Unites and Divides Society*. New York: Free Press.

– 1979. *Power: Its Forms, Bases and Uses*. Oxford: Basic Blackwell.

– 1961. 'The Oversocialized Conception of Man in Modern Society.' *ASR*, 26, no. 2.

Wuthnow, R. 1987. *Meaning and Moral Order: Explorations in Cultural Analysis*. Berkeley: University of California Press.

Index

system, 125–6; the media as, 126–9; organized religion, 129–30; and social order, 125. *See also* social order

social justice, 109–11, 162–3

social liberty, 105

social networking, 168–9

social order: and absolute principle, 166–7; defined, 77; and the Enlightenment, 137; humane mutuality, 167–71; humanity, 4; moral and amoral authority, 178–80; originators of, 153–4, 156; purpose of, 151; social-order authority, 12. *See also* authority; globalism; global moral social order; social institutions

social relationships: and community, 168; and death, 116; and human dignity, 164–6; and humanity, 4; and power, 10–11

social welfare, 170

society (basic character of), 10

sovereignty: decline of, 156; and European Union (EU), 66–7; and human rights, 143–4; international agreements, 54; and the Universal Declaration of Human Rights, 140. *See also* authority; the nation-state

Soviet Union, 14, 15–16

special-interest groups, 109–10

Spencer, Herbert, 82–3

sports metaphors, 93

Starr, Kenneth, 124

stem cells, 196–7

strategic alliances, 47, 48, 66

strategic hegemony: future of, 66–7; and military stratagems, 43–4. *See also* hegemony

subcontracting, 96–7, 99

subprime-mortgage crisis, 40–1

Sudan, 145

synthetic democracy. *See* Western democracy

synthetic moral order, 78, 80

Taoism, 192

The Tao of Physics (Capra), 192

technology, 154–5

teleportation, 190

territorial hegemony, 43

terrorism: American patriotism, 56; anti-American sentiment, 50–3; and humanity, 121; and law, 107–9; and nuclear weapons, 44, 45; proliferation of, 218; and torture, 147–8

Thailand, 18, 150

Thatcher, Margaret, 122

theistic evolution, 199

theology: ethical principles, 166; First Cause, 199, 202–3; theological changes, 129–30; theological myth, 199–202, 210, 219. *See also* religion

Theory of Everything, 188

A Theory of Justice (Rawls), 195

time-space sequentiality, 189–90

Tocqueville, Alexis de, 10

Tokyo, 59

Tönnies, Ferdinand, 83

torture, 147–8

totalizing discourse: defined, 88; of human rights, 88, 106–7, 141–2; of Western democracies, 88, 94

trade: American trade deficits, 34, 35, 37, 39; the global free-market system, 21–4; and human rights, 149–50; U.S.–China trade relationship, 38–9; World Trade